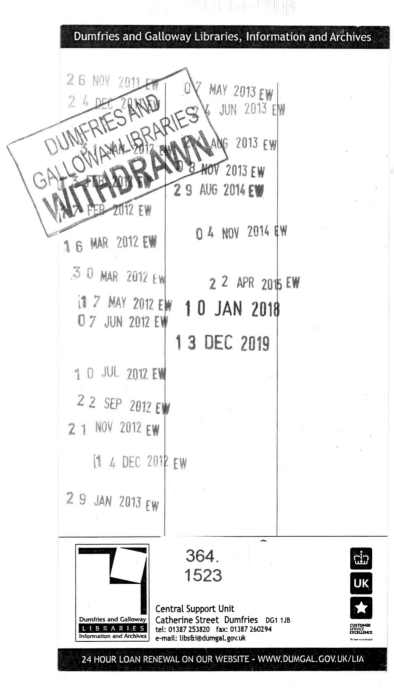

Dead Men Walking

True Stories of the Most
Evil Men and Women on Death Row

Dead Men Walking

Christopher Berry-Dee
and Tony Brown

JOHN BLAKE

Published by John Blake Publishing Ltd,
3 Bramber Court, 2 Bramber Road,
London W14 9PB, England

www.blake.co.uk

First published in hardback in 2008

ISBN: 978 1 84454 592 6

British Library Cataloguing-in-Publication Data:

A catalogue record for this book is available from the British Library.

Design by www.envydesign.co.uk

Printed in the UK by CPI William Clowes Beccles NR34 7TL

1 3 5 7 9 10 8 6 4 2

Papers used by John Blake Publishing are natural, recyclable products made
from wood grown in sustainable forests. The manufacturing processes conform to
the environmental regulations of the country of origin.

In memory of Louis 'Buddy' Musso, 1939–98

Contents

Prologue

When two authors collaborate on a joint project it is perhaps inevitable, indeed healthy, that they do not always share the same views. For this book my co-writer Tony Brown has written the Introduction and it falls to me to write a short Prologue, in which I refer to four hard facts:

1: The cowardly killers featured throughout the following pages have committed the most heinous crimes against defenceless men, vulnerable women, children and the elderly. Shooting, stabbing, cutting, filleting and dismemberment, beating, bludgeoning, hammering, setting on fire, running over with a vehicle, dropping from a height, drowning, strangling, throttling, suffocating, poisoning and burning to death with caustic agents, prolonged sexual assault, vaginal and anal rape: these were terrible acts perpetrated on living and dead bodies, all crimes of such sado-sexual ferocity against fellow men and women that they would make a Nazi sado-surgeon green with envy, for, take it from me, these monsters are in a league of their own.

2: All of these offenders were certified sane at the time they committed their crimes and were certified mentally competent to stand trial. And so overwhelming is the evidence against each offender that their fate is sealed; all of them will die in prison, from either natural causes or execution. Some may prove some form of mitigation for their crime and have their sentence commuted to life without parole, while others – here substitute 'bullshit' for 'mitigation' – will inevitably fail. They can only be released from their confinement wearing a pine suit.

3: All of these killers have been found guilty of their crimes by a jury of their peers in a court of law. Some of them have since been executed, others are still running through the appeal process and a few have had their death sentence affirmed. And it may well be that most of these brutal murderers will outlive the investigating police officers, the attorneys, the judge and the jury.

4: Each offender knew that, when they committed their capital crimes, they were doing so in a jurisdiction whose statute books permitted the death penalty. So it was the offender who made the decision to step outside the law, to commit a horrific crime, and that person knew all too well the dread consequences.

For my part, the moral rights or wrongs of the application of the death penalty do not concern me in this book. Nor does any mitigation an offender may offer up in his defence. I am content to allow the barbarous facts of the crime to be reported and for readers to then form their own judgement on the punishment.

I am often asked, 'What are your opinions on the death penalty?' These sentiments I keep to myself. Everyone is entitled to their own point of view, and I respect those who support capital punishment (69 per cent of Americans polled, Gallup, 2007), as well as those who are against, for good, solid arguments are held by either side.

However, what I will say is that the pro-death penalty lobby runs on the 'an-eye-for-an-eye' ticket, completely ignoring the fact that its application has not only proven to be a costly financial disaster, but to be no deterrent against capital murder at all.

For its part, the anti-death-penalty lobby relies on the basic moral stance that all life is sacrosanct and in today's enlightened world 'an eye for an eye' is completely unacceptable.

Perhaps the way out of this impasse is to refer back to the offender who committed the crime. It is that person who made the irreversible decision to take a human life in cold blood. And they made that decision in full knowledge of the outcome should they be caught, tried and found guilty.

Most Death Row inmates appeal their sentences, and, while complaining about their own self-perceived injustices, they receive lengthy and costly due process, and expect compassion, fairness and humanity, right up to the US Supreme Court, a State Governor or, in federal and military cases, the President himself.

Therefore, we are obliged to ask these killers: What compassion, fairness, humanity and dignity did you offer to your victims while you selfishly stole away their lives? Did these innocent victims enjoy an impartial appeal process against their own death sentences? Of course not!

Sadly, we live in times when more compassion is offered to the violent criminal fraternity than to the victims and their close relatives, whose lives are left shattered.

Today we live in a world where many clearly dysfunctional

people fall in love and feel the compulsion to marry monsters who are locked away on Death Row across the USA. In doing so, these lonely souls demean human decency; these desperately pathetic individuals, in becoming pen pals of the damned, insult the precious lives and fond memories already destroyed by their would-be spouses.

Bear all of this in mind as you meet the Dead Men Walking.

Introduction

'It's easy to kill a monster. It's hard to kill
a human being.'

Sister Helen Prejean, author of the novel *Dead Man Walking*

All over the world, in cities and major towns can be found districts where the homes are symbols of opulence and the addresses are exclusive. These are the places where only a small fraction of the population, the extremely wealthy, can afford to live. However, there is another, even smaller fraction of the population who live in places where no amount of wealth can buy you a home. Such places, where money doesn't talk so loudly, and yet where the inhabitants seldom work, their clothes being laundered for them and their meals prepared and served to them by others, are often occupied by some of the poorest people on the planet. These exclusive homes are the condemned cells of Death Row. The price that has been paid to obtain a place here is the highest, that of a human life, and the people who live on Death Row are the killers who took those lives, convicted murderers every one of them.

For them there is only one way out, and that is the door leading to their place of execution when they walk the short distance that takes them to their death. By that time, in the eyes of many, they are to all intents and purposes already dead. In prison they are known as 'Dead Men Walking'. This term is not a badge of distinction to be borne with pride. To be known in a prison as a Dead Man Walking is to be stigmatised, an outcast, a leper.

And what is it like to be a Dead Man Walking? This condition of supreme wretchedness is described at first hand in a book written by Robert Wayne Murray, a 39-year-old condemned man who was convicted of the killing in 1991 of Dean Morrison, 65, and Jacki Applehans, 60, during a robbery in Arizona. In his book *Life on Death Row*, Murray provides an insider's view of life in a condemned cell:

'It's a long time never to see a blade of grass or feel sunshine on your face, or to actually see a tree, or hear a bird, or feel the wind across your cheek. Think of a thousand days without a face-to-face conversation, or ever touching another person. Think of a thousand days, every day, seven days a week, sitting in a concrete box with nothing to stare at but a concrete wall 10 feet away… Think of it in terms of an average bathroom. Eighty square feet is not much. Hang out there for a thousand days and it gets smaller. Somewhere there is a library, hospital, cafeteria, laundry and other support services. Death Row inmates never visit such places… Many spend years in here without ever going more than 50 feet from their cells.'

He recounts how, one day in September 1999, he was taken from his cell to the Governor's office, where he was informed that a date had been set for his execution. The State Supreme Court had issued an execution warrant and his life, he was told, was to be ended in 38 days' time, on 3 November.

'My mind raced through the past, searching for something to hold on to. I tried to keep my composure... In addition to all of the mockery they were making of my feelings they were carrying on easily with light banter as cheerful as any I could recall.'

The execution was stayed and Murray is still on Death Row, but the shock of that moment has remained with him and will doubtless be every bit as intense when a date for his execution is again set and the moment is re-enacted.

The ritual that accompanies capital punishment rises to a crescendo during the month leading up to the execution, described by the writer Dennis Wagner as 'a choreographed dance among guards, the condemned and other inmates'.

Murray depicts the suicide-watch nature of the procedures: 'One is no longer trusted to shave himself. Instead, he's handcuffed behind the back while officers do it with an electric shaver... The only thing left in life is the humiliation, the destruction of self-esteem and the utter helplessness for the events to come. At a time when a person most needs to have supportive communication and privacy, the State puts him in total isolation and watches him every second of the day.'

Perhaps because there is no mention in his book of the suffering inflicted on the victims of this killer, it is difficult not to feel some sympathy for the man himself as he waits his turn to be processed in the killing machine that has been provided by the State.

Chris Berry-Dee has interviewed many of the most notorious serial killers on Death Row and the experience of walking among them left him with indelible memories:

'I have walked many a Death Row, where the smell is always the same smell: disinfectant, cooking fat, urine, faeces and human sweat permeate every metre and brick of the Green Mile.

'The inmates tasked with cleaning that most dread part of every penitentiary move silently; not a word passing between themselves or with the guards whose orders are curt and to the point. No first-name terms here. And when a visitor passes, the cleaners drop their mops and stand to attention with their noses pressed against the wall – no eye contact at all.

'When a condemned man is brought before you for an interview, parts of the prison are locked down, and this can mean a lot of prison. He is shackled with restraints, the ankle chains permitting him only to shuffle. And he'll be flanked by four close-custody officers; burly men, immaculately dressed to impress the media, one on either side holding each arm, a guard behind, and a senior officer in front, calling out, "Dead man walking" as each security door hisses open and clangs shut.'

It is true that most murders are hot-blooded affairs and that most murderers commit only one such crime. Nevertheless, for a moment, in some existential nightmare, they have lost control of their actions to an extent of which few of us are capable and in doing so they have taken the life of another. These men and women are on Death Row to pay for their crimes with their own lives and it is fair to say that, in many cases and to varying degrees, they are themselves victims, and as such are deserving of sympathy.

The British criminologist Colin Wilson relates the story of George Hayward, who in 1927, having been dismissed from work, bludgeoned to death the landlady of the New Inn, near Manchester, and stole about £40 from her. He was easily caught and was hanged for his crime. The most pathetic aspect of this case was that Hayward, a married man, had immediately used some of the money to pay two instalments of hire purchase on his furniture. Not an evil man, he had been rendered desperate by the loss of his job and in his panic was seeking only security and peace of mind when his actions momentarily ran out of control. And £40 was the value placed on the two lives.

All too easily justice can become a casualty when the voice of the people is at its loudest. In December 1984, Bernhard Goetz shot four black youths on a New York subway train. He emptied his gun at point-blank range, shooting two of them in the back. His actions were deliberate. One of the teenagers, Darrell Cabey, was shot twice. He subsequently lapsed into a coma and was left brain-damaged and paralysed for the remainder of his life. Three of the boys were sitting down at the time and, although Goetz had been approached with a request for money, he had not been threatened.

On the face of it, this was attempted murder. However, the case attracted enormous, widespread attention and generated much rabble-rousing comment. Bernhard Goetz was white and his victims were black. The youths were unfairly demonised and it degenerated into an issue of 'good guy' versus 'bad guys'. The nastiest elements of public opinion came to the surface with the result that Goetz was widely viewed with sympathy, perceived to be almost the victim, while the true victims were viewed as violent muggers who had received their just deserts at the hands of a vigilante in the style of Charles Bronson's character in the film *Death Wish*. In the period before the gunman's identity became known, Goetz was widely referred to as the 'Subway Vigilante', a title that is still occasionally attached to his name more than 20 years after the event.

All of this loud background noise distorted the judicial process and heavily influenced the outcome. Goetz had confessed to the crime and no evidence had been presented to the jury that any of the victims had tried to rob him. The only weapon at the scene of the crime had been the gun that Goetz discharged into his victims. He had the upper hand and could easily have walked away without shooting. Despite all this, Goetz was acquitted of attempted murder. He was found guilty of only one relatively minor charge of illegal possession of a weapon.

Even if one of the boys had died from his wounds, it is doubtful that a charge of murder would ever have been successfully prosecuted in those circumstances. On the other hand, it is easy to see that, had the victims been white and Goetz a black man, this would have put an entirely different complexion on the case in the eyes of the jury and the public, with the result almost certainly a conviction. In that event, the gunman might well have been dubbed the 'Subway Monster'. This is the danger when popular opinion, reflecting the socio-political concerns of the time, is allowed to govern justice and dictate a verdict.

Today Bernhard Goetz lives as he has done for more than 20 years since he walked from court a free man. On another day, in other circumstances and for the same crime, Goetz could just as easily have made his way into history as a convicted killer, seeing out his days in a condemned cell, a Dead Man Walking. There are some who say that the victims of Bernhard Goetz were lucky. Paralysed and brain-damaged as he still is, 'lucky' is most certainly no way to describe Darrell Cabey. This book tells the stories of some of those whose victims weren't lucky, convicted killers who joined the ranks of the damned to become Dead Men Walking.

Suzanne Margaret Basso

They say that the female is more deadly than the male and, to set a sado-homicidal benchmark for the degree of destruction that follows in this book, one need look no further than the dreadful torture and murder of Louis 'Buddy' Musso. The depth of depravity of this act, committed by Suzanne Basso and five twisted sycophants, almost exceeds human comprehension. If anyone deserves execution, it is Basso.

Louis Musso's body was found on Wednesday, 12 August 1998. According to court documents from Harris County, Texas, Mical Renz was jogging on Main Street in Galena Park, a city east of Houston, at around 6.15am, when he saw what he took to be someone lying on the embankment at the side of the road. Renz didn't investigate the matter any further and continued on his way. However, after finishing his morning run and preparing for work, he went back to the place where he had seen the recumbent figure.

By then it was a few minutes before 8am, and when he got close to the figure he discovered that it was the body of a dead man. He phoned the police.

Within minutes Officer Kevin Cates of the Galena Park PD arrived at the scene. Cates observed that the dead man was dressed in clean clothes despite the fact that his body was bloody and very badly bruised. This macabre state of affairs led the officer to conclude that the body was that of a murder victim who had been moved to that location and dumped, rather than having been killed there.

Shortly afterwards, Assistant Chief Robert Pruett arrived, and arranged for a police dispatcher to check neighbouring cities for reports on missing persons. Information from Jacinto City, which borders Galena Park, indicated that a woman by the name of Suzanne Basso had recently filed a missing-persons report. On receiving this information, Robert Pruett headed out to Basso's address, hoping for a lead on the as yet unidentified victim.

Forty-four-year-old Suzanne Basso lived in an apartment in Jacinto City with her son, James O'Malley. When Pruett arrived there she was not at home; she had gone to the police department to give officers an identification card belonging to the missing man, Louis Musso.

Pruett waited, and within a few minutes Basso returned. From the initial conversation he learned that Musso lived there along with Basso and her son. Basso invited the policeman into her home, where he was introduced to O'Malley, and where he was surprised to see some bloodstained clothing and a sheet near a temporary bed in the living room.

In response to Pruett's questions about the bloodstained articles, Basso said that Musso slept in the living room and that the clothing was his. Pruett then asked Basso and O'Malley to accompany him to where the body was, to determine whether they could identify it, which they did without expressing any surprise or other emotion. The identification completed, Pruett asked Basso and O'Malley to accompany him to the police station to give written statements.

There O'Malley broke down and very soon confessed to involvement in the murder. He gave oral and written statements which outlined the events surrounding the killing and named all the other persons involved.

What emerged from that initial confession and the subsequent murder investigation was an horrific story in which a mentally retarded man had been subjected to an appalling catalogue of torture and violence at the hands of six people. Moreover, the monster who was the instigator, orchestrator and driving force behind the murderous episode was none other than O'Malley's mother, Suzanne Margaret Basso.

According to the records of the Texas Department of Corrections, inmate # 999329 Suzanne Margaret Basso is five feet two inches in height with grey hair and blue eyes. She lists her previous occupations as office clerk, seamstress and labourer, and at the time of her arrest she had no previous criminal convictions.

It isn't easy to piece together a reliable personal history of this woman, for much of what she would have the world believe about her has been discredited and exposed as downright lies. What is true, however, is that she was born on Sunday, 15 May 1954 in Albany, New York State, and has two adult children, both alive, one of whom is James O'Malley.

What is also beyond dispute is that this middle-aged woman, waiting her turn on Death Row, is one of the most evil killers of modern times and is as deserving of the death penalty as any man, but, whatever she did in the 44 years before she was arrested for murder, it is certain, as it has been attested to in court, that Basso frequently demonstrated a penchant for cruelty and deviant behaviour. Her 23-year-old son James professed to be terrified of her, and her daughter, Christianna Hardy, said that their mother had abused both her and her brother emotionally and sexually.

In fact, there can be no more vivid indictment of this evil woman than that which was provided by Christianna, who said jubilantly when the jury voted in favour of the death sentence, 'It's wonderful. Justice has finally been served. She is off the streets. She can't hurt anybody any more.' She went on to say, 'Let the inmates kill her, I don't care. She didn't feel any sadness for Buddy. She didn't feel any sadness for anybody else that she's hurt. Why should we give her sympathy?'

The first recorded reference to Basso's earlier life comes from the *Houston Press* in an article concerning the circumstances surrounding the death of her husband, Carmine Basso. Carmine's body was found on 27 May 1997, in Suite 215 of an office building at 6633 Hillcroft, in south-west Houston. It also appears that she had placed a wedding announcement in the *Houston Chronicle* of Sunday, 22 October 1995. The grandiosely worded and wildly inaccurate announcement said that 'Suzanne Margaret Anne Cassandra Lynne Theresa Maria Veronica Sue Burns-Standlinslowski' and Carmen Basso had tied the knot. The newly wed Mrs Basso, as well as having nine forenames, claimed to have 11 brothers and to be the heiress to 'the Oil Dynasty in Halifax, Nova Scotia'.

As if this were not enough, this heiress to an empire in 'black

4

gold' claimed to have been educated in England, at no less a seat of learning than St Anne's Institute in Yorkshire, where she obtained a degree in Home Economics and Trade Sewing. A model of all the virtues, she rounded off her education by entering a convent and becoming a nun, known as Sister Mary Teresa.

Perhaps her role model was Mother Teresa of Calcutta, although she in no way resembled the saintly winner of the Nobel Peace Prize. Standing only five feet two inches tall and weighing in at a massive 365 pounds, the porcine Basso was built for the world of gridiron football rather than a convent and very clearly had never followed a regime of fasting and abstinence. In any event, the convent's officials soon disabused the Houston press of any notions that this may have been true, stating they had never heard of the woman.

What is more, this may not have been all that was untrue in this woman's curriculum vitae, richly embroidered as it was with merit and distinction. According to Arlene Basso, Carmine Basso's stepmother, Suzanne's new in-laws were far from sure that Carmine and she were even married at all. Arlene Basso is quoted as saying, 'Believe me when I tell you, *she* is off the wall.'

Arlene also says that newly wed Suzanne had claimed to have twin daughters. She sent a photo of the twins to the Basso family, who could see that the picture was very obviously one girl looking into a mirror.

Nor did Suzanne neglect her new husband's pedigree when she devised the pretentious quarter-page advert, for she stated that her spouse was a holder of the Congressional Medal of Honor. He was not. However, her assertion that he was the owner of Latin Security and Investigation proved to be true. The company's office was registered at Suite 215, 6633 Hillcroft, Houston, which is precisely where Officer J.R. Martinez found Carmine Basso's corpse.

Although the autopsy showed no apparent trauma to the body, the subsequent murder of Louis Musso has caused the Houston Police to take a fresh look at Carmine Basso's death and the circumstances surrounding it. According to the medical report, it seemed that Suzanne Basso was the last person to speak to her husband, and that was on 20 May 1997 at 11am. She had phoned him from New Jersey, where, she claimed, she had been visiting her mother. The report also says that, although there were no restrooms or hygiene facilities in the office suite, the couple had been apparently living there for several months and the results were not pleasant. It goes on to state that 'there were several trash cans with faeces and urine in them'. In truth, the office was so dirty that the cleaners would not go near it because of the horrendous smell coming from inside. And Carmine Basso's slowly decomposing corpse cannot have helped matters either.

The post-mortem examination was carried out by Harris County Chief Medical Examiner Joye Carter, who ruled that Carmine Basso had died of natural causes. She concluded that his death was the result of erosive oesophagitis (inflammation of the lower oesophagus from the regurgitation of gastric acid contents). In Carmine's case this erosion had extended to the trachea and a portion of the cervical spine area. The only other major abnormality noted was 'a strong ammonia smell in the body'.

In short, it seemed that Carmine Basso died, at the age of 47, from a fatal case of acid indigestion and nothing more. Nevertheless, Dr Carter was prompted to say two years later, 'When Mr Basso was found dead, it did not appear to be foul play, but it did appear to be a little strange. In the light of the Musso case, I think it may warrant a second look.'

While the debate over whether to exhume Carmine Basso is unresolved at the time of writing, there is no doubt that there was nothing natural in the cause of the next death in which Suzanne Basso was involved. Louis 'Buddy' Musso had most certainly been murdered.

Fifty-nine-year-old Musso had learning difficulties, and was described by those who knew him as a trusting soul but with the mental capacity of a child of eight.

'Buddy' was born and raised in the 'Garden State', New Jersey. He was a regular churchgoer, and it was at church that he met Mimi Averill, about 20 years before his death. Mimi, who has a mentally retarded grandson herself, had warmed to Buddy and he became something of an adopted member of the Averill family.

Eventually, however, in 1998, Buddy came into contact with Suzanne Basso and her son James, himself mildly retarded. Somehow, Basso persuaded Buddy that it would be a good idea if they married, and in the June of that same year, without any word to the Averills, Buddy left New Jersey and headed for Texas to live with Basso and her son in Houston. At Basso's trial, Mimi Averill told the court, 'I made a promise to Buddy that I would always take care of him, and I hurt, and I will always carry that guilt.'

The trio lived in Basso's apartment in Jacinto City, and immediately the bride-to-be took control of Buddy's life, beginning with his finances. She tried to get his Social Security cheques sent directly to her and wrote cheques to herself from his bank account. Within a month of his arrival his intended spouse made out a will in Buddy's name, which he signed, naming her as the sole beneficiary of his estate. This nefarious scheme was devised so that Basso might collect on Buddy's life insurance policy. Under the terms of this policy, the insurance company would pay $56,000 if Buddy were to meet a violent death, which is exactly what the murderous Basso intended to happen.

During the time between his arrival in Houston and his death, approximately two months later, Buddy was allowed to speak to his friends, the Averills, just once. During the telephone call he wept and told them that he missed them, so no further calls were allowed him. Basso herself phoned the Averills, but despite their requests they were not permitted to speak with Buddy.

Basso and her son were friendly with Bernice Ahrens, who lived in a nearby apartment with her adult children, Craig and Hope, and Hope's boyfriend, Terence Singleton.

On Saturday, 22 August 1998, in response to a phone call, Houston PD sent Officer Jeffery Butcher to a reported assault in progress. When he arrived at the scene he was met by the complainant, Jeffery Jones. Also present were Buddy Musso, James O'Malley and Craig Ahrens. Jones told the officer that O'Malley and Ahrens had been forcing Buddy to run on the spot. The officer noticed that Buddy had severely blackened eyes and various signs of violence about his body. He noticed also that Buddy was mentally retarded and seemed to be suffering from exhaustion.

When questioned, Buddy explained that he had been beaten up by some Mexicans, and denied that O'Malley and Ahrens were responsible for his injuries. With nothing else to go on, the officer drove Buddy to the apartment of Bernice Ahrens, where he met Suzanne Basso. She explained that she was Buddy's guardian and added that Buddy had been abused when he was living in New

Jersey. The self-styled 'Angel of Mercy' went on to say that she had sent O'Malley and Ahrens to take Buddy running, as he was always wanting to run in the apartment. At this point Buddy apparently went up to Basso and put his head on her shoulder in an affectionate manner.

Convinced by this that Buddy was now in safe hands, Officer Butcher went away, leaving Buddy in Basso's care. It was a clever deception by the evil woman and a fatal misjudgement by the lawman, as, from the moment the officer left Bernice Ahrens's apartment, Buddy was subjected to a regime of inhumanly cruel torment and violence which would end only when he died, some three days later.

The extent of the brutality which Buddy was forced to undergo, and his misery during those final days of his life is graphically documented in the court records of Harris County. For the next few days, Buddy, Basso and O'Malley stayed at the Ahrens's apartment and during that time all the occupants, egged on by the evil and avaricious Basso, subjected this trusting soul to beatings and abuse.

Buddy was forced to sit in what is described as a 'hurricane position' with his knees on a mat and his hands on the back of his head. Any time the hapless man failed to hold this position, he would be punished. This chastisement involved such treatment as Singleton kicking Buddy 'in the tail' with force and Basso hitting him about the head with a shoe and a metal part from a vacuum cleaner, which caused the first of 17 gashes to his head. At one point Craig Ahrens suggested that they take Buddy to hospital and have his head stitched, but the idea was not taken seriously and the beatings continued.

Throughout the entire period until he died, Buddy was denied food of any sort and, as time progressed, the beatings and abuse intensified, with baseball bats, a belt and steel-tipped boots being used. At the trial one of the defendants also admitted that they had bathed him with cleaning fluids and bleach and then scrubbed him with a wire brush.

At some point an argument erupted over whether Suzanne Basso had told Buddy that she wanted to have sex with him. Craig Ahrens, O'Malley and Singleton confronted Buddy about this and began to beat him. Singleton used the baseball bat to hit him while O'Malley, wearing steel-tipped boots, kicked him in the head and chest and stomped on his arms. According to testimony from Bernice Ahrens, Buddy was pleading for relief from the constant beatings and asking to be taken to hospital because he wasn't 'feeling well'.

On the Tuesday evening, before dinner, O'Malley and Singleton took Buddy to the bathroom to give him a bath. He slipped in the tub and hit his head. At this, O'Malley jumped in the tub and stamped on his head and chest, causing him to bleed from a deep cut on his head. Hope Ahrens then entered the room and the three together punched and kicked the retarded Buddy, which made his ear swell and his head bleed even more. They then dragged him out of the bath and left him on the floor while they went into another room to eat dinner.

During the meal Basso went to the bathroom and hit Buddy on the head, leaving an x-shaped cut. Singleton joined her and, as Buddy was by this time barely responsive, they put him back in the tub and savagely poured surgical spirit and peroxide on his cuts before returning to their food.

Shortly after dinner it was discovered that Buddy, who viewed life as would an eight-year-old child, had given up the struggle and had mercifully died.

To distance herself from the death, and with the insurance payout in mind, Basso arranged that they clean up Buddy's corpse, dress him in clean clothes, put him in the boot of Bernice Ahrens's car and drive to a location where his body could be dumped. They left him on Main Street, Galena Park, where he was found the next morning.

Following the discovery of the body and the arrest of Basso and O'Malley, the police went to the Ahrens's apartment. They recovered copious evidence of the orgy of savage violence which had resulted in Buddy Musso's horrific death. Among the items found were handcuffs and two baseball bats, both of which were stained with the dead man's blood. There was blood too on the carpet and in Bernice's car. All of it was Buddy Musso's.

Among the many injuries that the medical examiner, Dr Shrode, detailed at the trial were fractured ribs, a broken nose, a skull fracture, cigarette burns, chemical burns and bruises extending from the bottom of his feet to his upper torso, including his genitals, eyes and ears. Blood was discovered in the oral cavity and windpipe. The autopsy revealed that the immediate cause of death was 'skull fracture from multiple blunt impact trauma', but the injuries to the genital area were so serious that they themselves could have resulted in death. Testimony was also presented that the tragic victim had lost up to 30 pounds in weight during the few weeks that he had spent with the sadistic Basso.

Although all the participants were found guilty, the death penalty was not sought for Basso's five co-defendants. Only she was singled out for the ultimate sentence as she had masterminded the entire plot to gain the insurance payout. The prosecution painted an accurate picture of an evil and unscrupulous confidence trickster who used several aliases, and the police discovered that Buddy was not the only one whose death would be of benefit to Basso: she had taken out life insurance policies on several people, including an eight-year-old child who didn't exist.

Perhaps the final word on the matter should go to Basso's daughter, Christianna, who plans to celebrate when her mother's death sentence is carried out. She said, 'I might just sit at home and pop a bottle of champagne when the lethal injection is given. I have no remorse for her.'

This murderous and manipulative freak of nature even attempted to extract misplaced sympathy from the jury by appearing in a wheelchair at her trial after having shed an enormous 200 pounds in an attempt to look frail. Her ploy failed, and on Wednesday, 1 September 1999 Suzanne Margaret Basso was sentenced to be executed by lethal injection.

Willie Seth
Crain Jr

After Willie Seth Crain Jr was found guilty by a jury of 12 people of average intelligence and promptly sentenced to death by a crusty judge, one might have thought that some day the judicial train would finally haul itself into the right station and Crain would be executed for murder most foul. So it is remarkable that this barely literate condemned man seems to be doing very well for himself as he manipulates his way through an appeals process that may one day end in his freedom.

'I want the world to know I'm innocent,' proclaimed 55-year-old Crain from the pages of Florida's *St Petersburg Times*. 'They railroaded me in the media,' he whines. 'I'm coming back on appeal and beating it because *I am* innocent.'

In a badly spelled letter to the authors, Crain argued, 'First I am not gilty of this crimb of first degree murder and Kidnapping of Amanda Brown. The mudia and TV and Roido stations cape

Telling the people all over the World Abought my past charge of Sexual Battery on back in 1985.

'And the two Attorney they gave me sold me down the river buy not calling people to testifive on my be hafe my attorney wounte me to be found guilty in trail.'

Nevertheless, despite his adamant assertions, it seems that Crain faces something of an uphill struggle in his quest to get himself off the hook.

The appellant, a crab fisherman by calling, was convicted for the kidnapping and murder of seven-year-old Amanda Victoria Brown in 1998. It appears that he had established a relationship with Amanda's mother. However, the true motive behind this was his unhealthy attraction to her daughter. In due course, an opportunity presented itself and one night when he was drunk he snatched the girl from her bed while her mother slept in an adjoining room. He later disposed of the child's body in one of his crab traps and her remains have never been found.

During the media frenzy that followed Amanda's disappearance, Crain's picture appeared on TV. Two women came forward saying that they recognised him as the man who had raped them when they were children. One of the women said that Crain had raped her in 1970, when she was ten. The other woman alleged that Crain had raped her repeatedly during the 1960s, and this had started when she was just eight.

Nor is it the case that slick Willie Crain was of 'previous good character', for he had been convicted of raping three women during the 1980s, again while they were children. It was this evidence and their testimony that helped the jury in its deliberations during the death-penalty phase of the trial.

In view of the conviction and death sentence for the Amanda Brown murder, Florida decided not to press the two rape charges, deeming them to be an unnecessary waste of taxpayers' money. Curiously, however, Crain sees this as something of a vindication. Probably the least of his problems is that during proceedings he was also charged and convicted of possession of marijuana.

Five feet nine inches tall, with brown hair and blue eyes, and sporting a tattoo of a naked lady on his right arm, inmate # A096344 Willie Seth Crain Jr (aged 61 at the time of writing) is still on Death Row in Florida.

After nine years Amanda's father's pain is as raw as the cold winter wind blowing across Tampa Bay. Roy Brown still visits the Courtney Campbell Causeway boat launch to visit the only grave his daughter may ever have. 'I work across the bridge, so I come by here every day. I'll stop by here from time to time,' he explained to a reporter from *ABC Action News* as he gazed out over the water. 'I just really believe she's right there.'

Kenneth Lee Boyd

'Not everyone comes home from the war
wounded, but the bottom line is nobody comes
home unchanged.'

Paul Rieckhoff, former Marine and founder of Iraq and
Afghanistan Veterans for America

At 2am on Friday, 2 December 2005, Kenneth Lee Boyd
became the thousandth person to be executed since the
United States Supreme Court lifted the ban on capital punishment
in 1976. This unenviable honour was one that the condemned man
would dearly have foregone, having said that he didn't want that
infamous distinction. 'I'd hate to be remembered as that, I don't
like the idea of being picked as a number,' Boyd told the Associated
Press in a prison interview.

'He would love to live and he would love to have the Governor and the courts step in, but he's also facing the possibility that won't happen,' said Boyd's lawyer, Thomas Maher.

But Boyd's hope of a reprieve was not to be and, at North Carolina Central Prison in Raleigh, he was put to death by lethal injection.

'Brutal murder just doesn't happen in Stoneville,' claims proud Chief of Police Gary L. Walker, head of just five law-enforcement officers dedicated 'To Protect and Serve' the town's one thousand or so residents.

Stoneville, formerly called Mayo, was renamed in 1877 after its Bible-thumping mayor, Reverend Francis L. Stone. The town is considered a 'treasure' by its citizens, who regard themselves as 'the salt of the earth'. As Martha Smith, a local resident, says, 'We do church. We do barbeques, and we mind our own business and we don't pay no mind to others minding ours. We are a real community and God-fearing people at that.'

And that is how it was until Kenneth Lee Boyd arrived in town.

Born on Wednesday, 14 January 1948, Boyd had led an unexceptional life until, at the age of 18, he joined the Army and was sent to serve in West Germany. He later volunteered to go to Vietnam and while he was serving there as a bulldozer operator he was daily shot at by snipers. The insufferable pressure from the constant fear of being an easy, slow-moving target as he drove the lumbering vehicle preyed on him and he began to suffer blackouts. The condition became severe enough to cause his honourable discharge from the Army in 1969. He returned home to North Carolina but it was obvious to those who had known him all his life that he was not the same man.

Like so many other Vietnam veterans, Kenneth Boyd had been irreparably damaged by what had happened to him during his military service and it was damage that would have far-reaching repercussions. He continued to suffer blackouts and flashbacks and he turned increasingly to drink.

Nowadays Boyd's condition would be diagnosed as post-traumatic stress disorder, often referred to as 'shell shock', but at that time no such medical condition was officially deemed to exist. There was certainly no recognised treatment or organised help.

Boyd began drinking and almost inevitably his first marriage failed. Then he met another girl, Julie Curry, whom he married. Although the couple had three children, their relationship was not happy. Boyd now had a serious drinking problem and often hit Julie. They had split up on a few occasions and in 1987 Julie left him for good, moving to Stoneville, where she and their three sons settled down to live with her father, Thomas Dillard Curry. But she was by no means safe, as events were to prove.

On Friday, 4 March 1988, Kenneth Boyd drove to his father-in-law's house and collected his three children: Christopher, 13, Jamie, 12, and Daniel, 10, saying he was going to take them for pizza. But pizza was not on the menu. A few days earlier Boyd had bought a .357-calibre Magnum pistol and it was on the seat of his car, between him and his boys. Fearful, Christopher hid the gun under the seat in the hope that his father wouldn't be able to reach it, but he did so in vain.

Boyd drove around the neighbourhood a few times before returning to the Curry home, where he pulled up in front of the house, and it is chilling to imagine the position that Boyd's three young sons found themselves in, with their father, drunk, armed and in a rage, no longer open to reason. They could smell the drink and certainly Christopher was old enough to appreciate the seriousness of their terrifying predicament. Their father was not playing games.

For the next ten minutes he was no longer their father: he became instead a deranged monster on the loose and they were to witness the entire nightmare. He yelled at Christopher to give him the pistol but the frightened boy ran into the house to warn his grandfather that Boyd was carrying a gun.

Tragically, it was all too late. Boyd went round to the back of the house and fired through the doorway, his bullet killing Thomas Curry. Then he entered the property and found his wife, Julie, standing in the doorway of her bedroom. She held out her arms in a futile attempt to protect herself from the madman. He emptied the remaining bullets into her, then ran outside and reloaded his gun.

Somehow in the midst of the slaughter, Christopher had become pinned under his mother's body as Boyd unloaded the .357 into her. Miraculously the boy was not himself killed and he succeeded in edging his way under a bed to escape the shooting. Another son grabbed the pistol while Boyd tried to reload but he was powerless. The deranged veteran then re-entered the house and began firing again at Julie. At autopsy, her body was found to have been hit eight times.

Craig Curry, Boyd's brother-in-law, had meanwhile armed himself and was moving his wife and his own children to nearby woods for safety. Boyd saw Craig and fired three or four times at him. However, the bullets all missed the fugitive Craig, who continued to move to the safety of the trees. His rage apparently sated, Boyd then returned to the house and called 911, informing the operator that he had just killed his wife and father-in-law and telling them to come and get him. When the police arrived he surrendered peacefully. The monster within him had subsided.

Boyd later made the following statement to the police:

'I walked to the back door [of Dillard Curry's house] and opened it. It was unlocked. As I walked in, I saw a silhouette that I believe was Dillard. It was just like I was in Vietnam. I pulled the gun out and started shooting. I think I shot Dillard one time and he fell. Then I walked past him and into the kitchen and living room area. The whole time I was pointing and shooting. Then I saw another silhouette that I believed was Julie come out of the bedroom. I shot again, probably several times. Then I reloaded my gun. I dropped the empty shell casings on to the floor. As I reloaded, I heard someone groan, Julie I guess. I turned and aimed, shooting again. My only thoughts were to shoot my way out of the house. I kept pointing and shooting at anything that moved. I went back out the same door that I came in, and I saw a big guy pointing a gun at me. I think this was Craig Curry, Julie's brother. I shot at him three or four times as I was running towards the woods.'

At his trial, two experts in forensic psychology, Dr Patricio Lara and Dr John Warren, testified for Boyd. Dr Lara stated that at the time of the offences the defendant suffered from an adjustment disorder with psychotic emotional features, alcohol abuse and a personality disorder with predominant compulsive dependent features. Further, Dr Lara opined that Boyd's emotional condition was impaired and that he suffered from some level of alcoholic intoxication at the time of the offences. Likewise, Dr Warren testified that at the time of the offences the defendant suffered from chronic depression, alcohol abuse disorder, dependent personality disorder and a reading disability.

On Thursday, 14 July 1994, at Rockingham County Superior Court, despite the doctors' testimony, the jury decided that Boyd's condition was not sufficient to mitigate a sentence of death for each murder.

While on Death Row, Boyd stated that he was sorry for the pain he had caused and hoped that Julie's mother, Hilda Curry, would forgive him someday for all he had taken from her. He also reflected on the damage his actions had caused to his sons, one of whom was sent to prison for two years for his involvement in a convenience-store robbery.

Before going to his death, Kenneth Boyd enjoyed a last meal of New York strip steak, a baked potato with sour cream, a salad with ranch dressing and cola. He had attracted support from many quarters and a larger than usual crowd had gathered outside the State Prison to maintain a vigil leading up to his execution. His attorneys had sought clemency from Democratic Governor Mike Easley, but there was little hope of success given that in his five years in office he had granted clemency only twice, while during that time 22 inmates had been executed.

'He made one mistake and now it's costing him his life,' said Boyd's son Kenneth Smith, 35, who visited with his wife and two children. 'A lot of people get a second chance. I think he deserves a second chance.' That second chance never came and, after 17 years on Death Row, at 2am on Friday, 2 December 2005, the lethal injection was administered. At 2.15am Kenneth Lee Boyd was pronounced dead.

Today there is increasing concern in the USA about the way that those who have served in the military during war have been affected. The suicide rate among veterans has been estimated to be as high as 23 per cent and on any given night there are almost 200,000 veterans among the ranks of the homeless.

Daniel Akaka, the chairman of the Senate Veterans' Affairs Committee, said, 'For too many veterans, returning home from battle does not bring an end to conflict. There is no question that action is needed.'

For Kenneth Lee Boyd, and many others like him, this concern was expressed far too late.

Dennis Wayne Bagwell

Under Texas law, murdering more than one person during the same criminal transaction is a capital offence. In the case of Dennis Wayne Bagwell, that provision was purely academic. On Thursday, 7 November 1996, Bagwell was sentenced to death for the murder of his 47-year-old mother Leona Boone (née McBee), his half-sister Libby Best, 24, her four-year-old daughter Reba Best and 14-year-old Tassy Boone, granddaughter of Ronald Boone, Leona's husband. The killings had taken place on Thursday, 20 September 1995 at Bagwell's mother's mobile home, near San Antonio, Texas. But that was not all, for just weeks before the multiple killing he had kicked to death 63-year-old George Barry, a janitor from Seguin. For this crime he was sentenced to life imprisonment.

Bagwell had a history of parole violations. He also had a lengthy history of threats of violence, disciplinary violations and refusals to accept psychiatric treatment while in prison. In fact, he had to wear leg restraints during his trial for capital murder because of numerous threats he had made to law-enforcement personnel. He was a frequent abuser of cocaine.

At the time of the 1995 killings, Bagwell was on parole after having served only eight years of an 18-year prison sentence imposed on Monday, 27 September 1982, his nineteenth birthday, for the attempted murder of an illegal immigrant whom he had robbed. He had slit the man's throat. Even when put as baldly as that, the enormity of Dennis Bagwell's actions is staggering, but when those actions are examined in more detail they assume nightmarish proportions.

Often it is unpleasant work to pick one's way through the research material attached to a murder. As each item is uncovered, one's opinion of the killer is pushed in one direction or another so that sometimes, in the final analysis, it is possible to feel a degree of sympathy. But Bagwell evokes no such feelings. Moreover, it isn't stretching the truth to say that one of the very few facts to emerge about this very unpleasant man that wasn't connected in some way to an anecdote of violent excess was that the former meat salesman was born in Denver and grew up in the Rio Grande Valley and the Dallas area, which is about as good as his story gets.

To summarise the events of Thursday, 20 September 1995, Bagwell and his girlfriend, Victoria Wolford, lived north of Stockdale, near San Antonio, in a small travel trailer which Bagwell had parked on property belonging to his mother, Leona McBee, and stepfather, Ron Boone, who themselves lived on the same property in a mobile home.

About two weeks before the killings, McBee asked Bagwell and Wolford to stop living on the property. Bagwell and Wolford moved out and went to stay with friends in San Antonio. According to Wolford's testimony at the trial, she and Bagwell had returned to his mother's house to borrow money. Present in the house at the time, as well as McBee, were Libby Best, Reba Best and Tassy Boone. Wolford had had a headache and had gone to sit in the travel trailer while Bagwell spoke with his mother. A short time later, Bagwell walked over to the trailer and told Wolford that his mother would only give him $20, which was not enough.

Bagwell had then gone back into Mrs McBee's house. Wolford had stood outside the trailer and, through the window of the house, she saw Bagwell strike his mother. She heard screams and what she described as two popping noises. She heard Tassy shouting, 'No, no,' and heard Reba Best scream. Then, for a moment or two, everything went quiet until she heard McBee yell at her dogs and a sound as though she was gasping for air. Through the window Wolford saw Bagwell strike his mother with a long-handled gun.

Shortly afterwards, Bagwell emerged from the house and wetted some towels with a garden hose. He wiped down a hammer and said that he was going to go back inside the house to wipe off any fingerprints that he may have left behind him. He told Wolford that he was trying to make the crime look as though it had been a robbery and rape of Tassy Boone.

When Ronald Boone came home from work that afternoon, he discovered a ghastly scene of gruesome violence. His wife, Leona McBee, had been beaten and strangled so violently that her neck was broken, and there were several cuts and abrasions about her body.

Libby Best had been shot twice in the head.

Tassy Boone had been beaten, strangled and sexually assaulted. The teenager's neck was broken, such had been the violence of her strangulation.

Little Reba Best had been beaten, and her skull crushed with a hammer and an exercise bar.

At trial the State of Texas offered several witnesses, including Victoria Wolford, who testified that she was with Bagwell when he committed the murders, and that she had led the police to various locations along the getaway route where Bagwell had discarded incriminating evidence.

Law-enforcement officers testified that, on the basis of information provided by Wolford, they recovered numerous items taken from the Boone residence, including a pair of tennis shoes and a pair of shorts.

Scientific experts linked significant physical evidence from the murders to Bagwell. An expert witness testified that the imprint of one of the tennis shoes matched a bloody shoe print found at the crime scene under the body of Tassy Boone. Other witnesses testified that the tennis shoes in question belonged to Bagwell. Furthermore, a firearms expert testified that the bullet fragments removed from Libby Best's cranium had been fired from a shattered rifle that the law-enforcement officers had recovered.

For his part, Bagwell denied having been to his mother's home on the day of the killings and, in an outrageous attempt to cast the blame elsewhere, he accused Tassy's mother, Monica Boone, of being the killer, claiming that she and her daughter had had a difficult relationship. Monica Boone, however, was able to offer proof that she had been in California at the time. Given the physical strength that would have been required to carry out the four murders, the notion that she had committed them is bizarre.

A jury convicted Dennis Bagwell of capital murder in November 1996 and sentenced him to death. The Texas Court of Criminal Appeals affirmed the conviction and sentence in March 1999. All of his subsequent appeals in state and federal courts were denied.

Prosecutors described Bagwell at his trial as a 'natural-born killer', yet his attorney has been accused of failing to adequately investigate and present mitigating evidence to the jury; evidence such as Bagwell's traumatic childhood, which began on Friday, 27 December 1963. This omission denied the jury the opportunity to hear that, as it is claimed, Bagwell was often left unsupervised as a child and was beaten by his alcoholic stepfather. Reportedly, Bagwell was made to sleep in the same room as his mother while she engaged in sexual activity. His stepfather frequently forced Bagwell and his sister to stare at a blank television screen for hours at a time.

When this issue was raised on appeal, the US District Court responded to the trial attorney's failure to find and present this evidence by asserting that the State does not require a counsel to exercise 'clairvoyance'. Quite apart from that, it would take considerably more to be put on the table to mitigate the monstrously savage nature of Bagwell's *modus operandi*.

Then there is the question of the murder of George Barry. It almost escapes notice in the shadow of the brutal quadruple slaying, but it is no less heinous, no less capable of shocking and no less savage when viewed in the spotlight on its own.

According to the records of the 25th Judicial District Court, Guadalupe County, on Tuesday, 5 September 1995, at Seguin, near San Antonio, 15 days before the killings at Stockdale, a delivery man discovered the body of George Barry, 63, in the stockroom of Jim's Place, a bar where Barry worked as a night stocker. During the investigation Bagwell became a suspect and was eventually charged with the killing. At trial, the most damning evidence was given, once more, by Victoria Wolford. It has to be said that Vicki Wolford had been provided with immunity from prosecution in return for her testimony.

Wolford testified that, on the evening of 4 September, she and Bagwell met Donnie Halm, the owner of Jim's Place, at a rest stop on Highway 123. There, Bagwell sold Halm a television, a stereo system and a VCR, all of which belonged to a local rent-to-own store, for $200. Bagwell and Wolford took the money from this sale and went to the home of Anthony Jackson, where they bought some rocks of crack cocaine for $150. The pair took the cocaine to the trailer they shared and smoked it, then Wolford prepared for bed. At this point, Bagwell decided that he wanted to return to Seguin for more drugs, this time marijuana. Wolford dressed and they drove to Jim's Place. Bagwell drove around the bar a couple of times, telling Wolford he was looking for an employee, Robin Whitman, who he thought would sell him some marijuana.

Bagwell was a familiar face at Jim's Place. He had been there several times, had sold or tried to sell items to employees there and knew all the staff by name. When he didn't see Robin Whitman, he stopped the car and went into the bar to look for him. He came back shortly and asked Wolford for a quarter as he had not found Robin and wanted to call his home. At that point he told Wolford that he planned to rob and kill George Barry, who was in the restaurant, stocking beer for the next day. It is important to mention that it was also Barry's job to make the night deposit for the bar and it was the bar takings that Bagwell intended to steal.

Bagwell went back into the restaurant and Wolford remained in the car. She testified that while Bagwell was in the bar she could hear pounding and thumping noises. Bagwell returned some 20 minutes later with three money bags and an injured finger. The two drove out of Seguin, before stopping to transfer the money from the bags to Bagwell's pockets. Then they headed for Jackson's, where they purchased more crack. On the drive from Jackson's to their trailer, Bagwell told Wolford that he had killed Barry by crushing his throat with his foot. Wolford testified that Bagwell was wearing black heavy boots on the night of the murder. The next morning, the pair left Seguin for San Antonio.

Supplementing Vicki Wolford's testimony, Bagwell's fingerprints and one of his palm prints were found on the filing cabinet near Barry's body, where the deposit money was kept.

Finally, several witnesses testified that Bagwell had provided inconsistent stories about how he had hurt his hand, saying at times that he had hit a black man, that he had hit a black man and robbed him or that he had smashed his hand down on the roof of an automobile.

The defence presented no witnesses.

The jury found that Dennis Wayne Bagwell had killed George Barry during the course of a robbery by stamping on his face and neck. The State of Texas waived the death penalty and the jury sentenced Bagwell to life imprisonment.

In an examination of material recording the criminal career of Dennis Bagwell, nothing emerges to contradict the perception that he was an evil monster of a man who was capable of inflicting the worst excesses of murderous violence on other human beings. Yet he was out of prison on parole at the time that he stamped George Barry to death and, two weeks later, savagely slaughtered his mother and three female relatives.

The records show that he had been paroled in October 1989 but had been returned to prison in 1992 for a parole violation involving violence. A few months later, in January 1993, solely in order to meet the strict prison population caps imposed on Texas by US District Judge William Wayne Justice, this extremely dangerous man was granted parole once more. In assessing that Dennis Bagwell was fit to be returned into society on parole despite his having refused psychiatric treatment while in prison, someone is guilty of a grave error of judgement, the consequences of which were five very brutal murders, and that assessment calls into question the system that allowed these deaths to happen. In short, once inside prison, Dennis Bagwell should never have emerged.

In any event, on Saturday, 17 February 2005, at Huntsville, Texas, Dennis Wayne Bagwell took his last walk from his cell on Death Row and at 6.19am was pronounced dead after having been executed by lethal injection. In going to his death, he expressed no remorse for his actions, saying only to those he had invited to witness his death, 'I love you all.'

Dennis Wayne Bagwell will be remembered as a monster guilty of five savage slayings and one throat slitting. But he also leaves behind him another, less sanguinary monument. There are those aficionados whose interest is in the details of the last meal to be eaten by the killers who face imminent execution and in this respect Bagwell's last meal will not disappoint. Staggering in its sheer size, it is, without doubt, a meal fit for a monster: beef steak, medium rare with A1 Sauce, three fried chicken breasts, three fried chicken thighs, BBQ ribs, a large order of French fries, a large order of onion rings, a pound of fried bacon, a dozen scrambled eggs with onions, fried potatoes with onions, sliced tomatoes, a salad with ranch dressing, two hamburgers 'with everything', ketchup, salt and pepper, peach pie, milk and coffee and iced tea with real sugar.

Joe Elton Nixon

In the *New York Law Journal* of 17 November 2004, Thomas Adcock wrote:

'The horrific life of Joe Elton Nixon, briefly referenced last week during a narrow procedural hearing before the US Supreme Court, is at the heart of a capital murder case that Eric M. Freedman predicts will be studied in law schools for years to come.

'Freedman, part of a team of New York attorneys in the cause of winning Nixon a new trial in Florida, is a professor of constitutional law at Hofstra University School of Law [Long Island]. The Nixon case, he said, "illustrates all the elements that typify death penalty cases, and the people who wind up getting sentenced to death. Race, lousy counsel – all the fundamental problems".'

A mentally retarded black man, Joe Elton Nixon did indeed suffer an horrific life, growing up as a victim of poverty, incestual rape, sexual humiliation, forced labour in tobacco fields and almost daily beatings at home, on the job or in juvenile institutions. And the reason why he was the subject of Adcock's article was the controversy surrounding the conduct of his trial and the resultant sentence. Joe Nixon was under sentence of death, having been tried and convicted of a murder of the most gruesome nature.

On Monday, 13 August 1984, near Tallahassee, in Leon County, Florida, a passing motorist was horrified to discover the charred remains of a woman. Thirty-eight-year-old Jeanne Bickner had been tied to a tree and set on fire while still alive. Her left leg and arm and most of her hair and skin had been burned away. The next day the police found her car, abandoned and on fire.

Court records show that the police arrested 23-year-old Joe Elton Nixon later that morning after his brother informed the sheriff's office that he had confessed to the murder.

Questioned by the police, Nixon described in graphic detail how he had kidnapped his victim and killed her. He recounted that he had approached Bickner, a stranger, in a mall, and asked her to help him jump-start his car. Bickner offered Nixon a ride home in her 1973 MG sports car.

Once on the road, Nixon directed Bickner to drive to a remote place. En route he overpowered her and stopped the car. Next he put her in the car boot, drove into a wooded area, removed her from the car and tied her to a tree with jumper cables. In abject terror, Bickner pleaded with Nixon to release her, offering him money.

Concerned that Bickner might identify him, Nixon decided to kill her, and kill her he most certainly did. He set fire to her personal belongings and ignited her with burning objects. Nixon drove away in the MG, and later told his brother and girlfriend what he had done. He burned the MG on Tuesday, 14 August after reading in the newspaper that Bickner's body had been discovered. The State gathered overwhelming evidence establishing that Nixon had committed the murder in the manner he described.

A witness saw Nixon approach Bickner in the mall's parking lot on 12 August and observed the woman taking jumper cables out of the boot of her car and giving them to Nixon. Several witnesses told the police they saw Nixon driving around in the MG in the two days following Bickner's death, and Nixon's palm print was found on the car's boot.

Interviewed by the police, Nixon's girlfriend, Wanda Robinson, and his brother, John, both stated that Nixon told them he had killed someone and showed them two rings later identified as Bickner's. According to Nixon's brother, John, Nixon pawned the rings and attempted to sell the car. Police recovered the rings and a receipt for them bearing Nixon's driving-licence number. The pawn-shop owner identified Nixon as the person who sold the rings to him. Subsequently, Nixon was indicted for first-degree murder, kidnapping, robbery and arson.

Given Nixon's admission of guilt, his lawyer, Michael Corin, had some major obstacles to overcome in order to sway the jury, persuading them to sentence Nixon to life instead of death. The accused was unresponsive to Corin's attempts to discuss strategy with him, believing that the State's case of premeditated murder was solid.

Another difficulty was that the prosecutor refused to accept a plea of guilty in exchange for life. As a result, Corin decided on a strategy of frank admission of guilt in order to show credibility and lead the jury towards a mercy vote of life.

However, his efforts were hampered by Nixon himself. During

the trial, he went from being unresponsive to violent and disruptive in the courtroom. He pulled off his clothing, demanded a black judge and lawyer, and threatened to act in such a way that the guards would have to shoot him. While in a holding cell, he refused to attend the trial, threatening to misbehave if they forced him to go. The judge ruled that he had voluntarily and intelligently waived his rights to be present at his trial.

Nixon was found guilty of premeditated murder, kidnapping and arson and was sentenced to death.

And it might have ended there but for the efforts of Jonathan Lang, a Manhattan real-estate attorney who took up Nixon's cause by questioning whether Corin had been rendered ineffective by conceding his client's guilt without his explicit consent. A long series of actions followed, during which Lang died from cancer.

Nixon's defence team is now headed by Eric Freedman, who argues, 'Without explicit consent, a defence lawyer has no right to interject his own wisdom for the wishes of the client. A trial should give you a high-quality outcome, rather than what's happening in the death-penalty system. As it is now, the trial merely gives us a rough draft, which is then polished through layers of post-conviction review in the hope of eventually achieving what should have been put forward in the first place. Namely, in the case of Nixon, the mitigating circumstances of lifelong physical and emotional abuse should have been brought out at trial, as well as the client's relationship with his older brother, John Nixon.'

Much has been brought up in mitigation of Nixon that wasn't disclosed at his trial. According to Lang's brief, John Nixon routinely taunted his younger brother by parading him through the streets in girl's clothing, and telling Joe Elton Nixon's friends that he was regularly raped by an uncle and aunt. John Nixon, a paid informant for the Leon County Sheriff's Department, was the principal prosecution witness against his brother at the 1985 trial.

The outcome of this unsettling case remains unresolved at the time of writing, and meanwhile Joe Elton Nixon is still a resident of the Green Mile.

James Willie Brown

On Tuesday, 4 November 2003, the State of Georgia executed 55-year-old James Willie Brown, and in doing so brought to an end two decades of controversy involving appeals and retrials. From the outset Brown's guilt was never in doubt, but what was in question was his mental condition and whether or not he should have been facing life imprisonment without parole instead of execution by lethal injection.

The crime of which Brown was convicted, the rape and murder of Brenda Sue Watson, took place not long after midnight on Monday, 12 May 1975. Around 8.30pm that evening, James Brown and Brenda Watson had gone to the Mark Inn Lounge at a motel in Gwinnett County. Watson, who had recently moved to the area from Florida, was a topless dancer in an Atlanta nightspot and she had only just met Brown. The two had brought with them a takeaway steak dinner which they ate there, before spending the next two and a half hours drinking and dancing. At approximately 11pm, they left together.

On the morning of the following day, in a wood close to a logging area and not far from Deshon Road, Lilburn, Gwinnett County, Brenda Watson's body was found near a trash pile by a man looking for collectables. Apart from a blue terry-cloth blouse that had been pulled up over her breasts, she was naked. A piece of nylon cord was tied to one of her ankles and indentations on the other ankle and both her wrists suggested that at some point she had been restrained.

It seemed very probable that she had been raped and this was confirmed at the post-mortem examination by other abrasions and contusions as well as the presence of seminal fluid in both her throat and her vagina.

Warren Tillman of the State Crime Lab testified that the cause of Brenda Watson's death was asphyxiation due to her panties having been forced so far down her throat that they were only discovered during the autopsy. Tillman also concluded, from abrasions and contusions around the victim's vagina, that she had been raped and that this had occurred before her death. An undigested meal of steak and potatoes was found in her stomach. Since a meal is usually digested within four hours, Tillman estimated that Brenda died no later than 4am.

On 15 May, police officers arrested James Willie Brown. In his car they found nylon cord that was identical to that which was tied round the victim's ankle and also a hairbrush containing hair that matched hers. At first he denied knowing Brenda Sue Watson, but after he was informed that he had been identified as being with her on the night before the body was found he confessed that he did know her. He admitted that he had gone with her to the Mark Inn but claimed that after leaving that bar they had gone on to another, off Covington Highway, and had parted company there.

Eventually, Brown came clean, saying that when they left the Mark Inn Brenda had suggested that they go somewhere quiet, out in the country. He drove her to a secluded spot off Deshon Road but, he claimed, when they got there and parked she told him that if he didn't pay her $200 she was going to call the police and claim he had tried to rape her. In response, Brown tied her up with nylon cord and gagged her. Seeing her in that position, he found that he wanted to have sexual intercourse with her and decided to do just that. He drove off, leaving Brenda behind, bound and gagged. On the way home he discovered she had left her pocketbook in the car, so when he reached a footbridge on Killian Road he stopped and threw it into the Yellow River.

It is at this point that the story of James Willie Brown evolved from an open-and-shut murder case into a cause so contentious that Amnesty International was among those who took up the cudgels on his behalf. As with the question of Brown's personality, there are two sharply contrasting positions. On the one hand, there are those who still see the man as a cunning, evil, manipulative sham, while, on the other hand, his supporters see him as a victim, a mentally ill man, the product of childhood abuse who, they argue, should never have been brought to trial but detained in an institution for the remainder of his life.

In 1975, immediately after the murder, Brown was found to have a history of severe mental illness and was deemed to be incompetent to stand trial for the murder. Instead, he was committed to a state mental institution. He remained there until

1981, when he was considered to be competent, made to stand trial, convicted and sentenced to death. In 1988, the conviction was overturned by a federal court and he was returned to an institution. However, in 1990, Brown was retried, convicted and, the following year, sentenced to death.

On appeal, the legal team promoting Brown's cause argued that he suffered from major mental illness at the time of the offence, having been diagnosed as a paranoid schizophrenic by no fewer than ten doctors, all appointed by the State of Georgia. In Brown's case, the condition evolved 'from a childhood marked by incomprehensible abuse'.

The details of Brown's upbringing, if they are true, make depressing reading. According to the USA's National Coalition to Abolish the Death Penalty (NCADP), Brown's mental illness manifested itself after a childhood of 'unrelieved and unimaginable' pain and abuse. He was born prematurely, on Sunday, 6 June 1948, to a 15-year-old mother and a severely alcoholic father who failed to provide basic food and shelter for Brown and his siblings. There was no running water, indoor plumbing or heat in the house. The children went hungry, living mostly on a single daily meal of beans and cornbread. They were bitten by rats and other vermin which infested the house.

The NCADP's report goes on to say that Brown was sexually abused as a child by his uncle, and regularly beaten and kicked by his father with fists, belts, branches and cords. Several times he was beaten to the point of unconsciousness. In 1963, Brown was diagnosed by the Emory Medical Clinic as suffering from a convulsive disorder. Doctors prescribed medication to control his seizures. Despite this, his severe headaches and blackouts persisted.

By 17, he had quit school and entered the Marine Corps. Though Brown was accepted in the service, it soon became clear that his mental health was deteriorating, and he was discharged on the grounds of mental illness after 16 months and two hospitalisations, during which he received electroshock treatment.

After his discharge from the service, Brown's mental deterioration accelerated and he became increasingly unable to hold a job. He turned to drugs, primarily LSD. He was arrested in 1968 for drug use but found mentally incompetent to stand trial. From his 1968 arrest until his trial in 1981, Brown spent 70 per cent of that time in mental-health facilities either voluntarily or involuntarily.

Without doubt, James Willie Brown did not have an easy ride in life and there is considerable evidence to support this, but it is only part of the truth. There are gaps that need filling, for it is also true that he had a record of violence.

Two years after being discharged from the military, he was charged with trying to rape and kill a woman in Fulton County. Court records show he was convicted of breaking into a home in Atlanta where he beat and stabbed the woman, on Saturday, 17 February 1968. The victim said Brown tied her up with nylon cord, shoved a washcloth in her mouth to silence her and tried to rape her. Court records also show Brown shot at a man who tried to help the woman. He was sentenced to serve ten years but released on parole three years later.

In DeKalb County, Brown was charged with an abduction and rape committed on Saturday, 29 July 1974. He convinced a woman he was an artist who needed a model for a portrait. Records show that DeKalb police officers were still searching for Brown on outstanding warrants of aggravated sodomy, kidnapping and armed robbery in the rape case when Brenda Watson's body was found nearly a year later.

Writing in the *Atlanta Journal-Constitution* in November 2002, Beth Warren recorded local opinion on the issue with comments form various sources, including Brown's younger brother, Harold:

'While Harold Brown spent most of his life saving others, older brother James Willie Brown was preying on women and fighting a death sentence. "It is hard to believe we're from the same stock," Harold Brown said Friday from his Lawrenceville home. James Willie Brown, 54, is scheduled to die Tuesday by lethal injection for the 1975 brutal rape and suffocation death of Atlanta go-go dancer Brenda Sue Watson, 21.

'Those who have fought to spare his life say James Brown, a former Marine, had an abusive childhood, has a long history of mental illness and suffers from paranoid schizophrenia. Gwinnett County District Attorney Danny Porter describes James Brown as a cunning predator who knew right from wrong when he attacked women in at least three counties.

'He was suspected of killing another woman in Gwinnett and a woman in DeKalb, but the bodies were too decomposed to make a case, Porter said. Harold Brown, 53, who spent his career in the military and as a paramedic and firefighter in Gwinnett, said he won't be in town for the execution. "And I'm not going to the funeral," he said.

'"James Brown would laugh when their father would do something mean like pluck the teeth of a possum out with tweezers," Harold Brown said. "James also followed his father's lead, hanging their neighbor's baby ducks and swinging cats in the air until their necks broke," the younger brother said. "I was easygoing and soft-hearted," Harold Brown said. "My brother was mean. I thought when my dad died the devil died, but I think he's the devil's son."

'James Brown's former attorney, Larry Duttweiler, said his client had a difficult childhood and began hearing voices and suffering severe headaches while still in elementary school. "His father beat him pretty regularly as a child and would encourage him to beat up other kids," Duttweiler said.

'Harold Brown said his father often beat him and even broke his arm. But he said he never saw brother James take a blow. Harold Brown said his mother, who declined comment, made excuses to explain away the bruises. He said he began running away from home at age 5 and finally was allowed to live with a loving and supportive family down the street beginning at age 9. James Brown had a borderline genius IQ but dropped out of high school in the ninth grade, records show.

'Harold Brown said he worked hard to get good grades and earn accolades on his high school football team. He volunteered for the Army and earned a college degree on the GI Bill. James Brown escaped going to Vietnam, leaving the military in 1966 because of "mental difficulties", court records show. Harold Brown said his older brother went AWOL and was looking for a way out. "I had some hard knocks, but I never used that as a crutch," Harold Brown said.'

So said James Brown's own brother.

There is far more detail supporting both sides of the argument, but, from whichever angle he is viewed, it is very difficult to conclude that James Willie Brown was a normal, well-adjusted man. There is no doubt that he carried out the brutal rape and murder of Brenda Watson. There is also much evidence to suggest that he had savagely exercised his predatory urges on other women. On the balance of probability, he was a monster who was always going to be a danger to women if he were free. However, the question was and still is: was he mentally ill and incapable of rational judgement or behaviour when he committed murder? If he was, he should not have stood trial and, baldly speaking, criminally insane, he should have spent the remainder of his life detained in a secure mental hospital. The issue is now academic because, madman or cunning malingerer, James Willie Brown has made his last walk along the Green Mile.

Michelle Sue Tharp

A simple definition of cruelty is the derivation of pleasure or satisfaction from inflicting pain and suffering, and among the most unpalatable of crimes is cruelty to small children.

With all crimes there are degrees of severity, or, as some see it, of wickedness, but an adult's cruelty to a small child has a repugnant quality that renders it futile to search for a motive because there cannot be one. No small child is capable of behaviour that could provoke any normal adult into retaliating with acts of cruelty. A harsh word or a smack from a parent in the heat of the moment is not an act of cruelty, because the parent derives nothing but regret from it. But when a parent inflicts on their child a life in which that child knows only pain, fear, deprivation and unremitting wretchedness, we are in the realms of cruelty. And in the level of sustained cruelty that she meted out to her tiny daughter, Tausha, culminating in the child's murder, Michelle Sue Tharp stands out as a monster.

Tausha was just seven, but those seven years had been ones in which she had known only unrelenting suffering and deprivation. She died weighing less than 12 pounds and she stood just two feet six inches tall. Despite her age, the child's feet were still small enough to wear infant shoes by the time she was murdered. Severely malnourished, she was forbidden even sandwiches or snacks. Her hunger was so great that in desperation she would steal food from pets' bowls. When she was caught doing so, she would be slapped, or struck with a long-handled spoon. Whenever she cried, which was often, she would be barricaded into a tiny alcove by the kitchen or locked in her bedroom.

Her body was found dumped in bushes by the side of a West Virginia back road, wrapped in a sheet inside black garbage bags. An autopsy concluded that she had died from malnutrition. She had been starved to death.

On the night of Friday, 17 April 1988, Michelle Sue Tharp's live-in boyfriend, Douglas James Bittinger, 25, had smacked the little girl for crying. In the morning, she was dead. The couple put the body in a car seat and, accompanied by Tharp's other three children, Tonya, nine, Ashley, three, and nine-month-old Douglas Bittinger Jr, they drove to Ohio and West Virginia, before dumping the remains in the brush.

Tharp and Bittinger then went to the Fort Steuben Mall in Steubenville, Ohio, where they reported the girl missing to security guards. She had gone missing while they went to the restroom, they said. However, while volunteers and police officers searched for Tausha, Bittinger's conscience got the better of him, and he confessed.

Tausha was born three months prematurely and had suffered the most shocking abuse almost from the day she first drew breath.

Tharp was put on trial for the murder of her daughter. However, in her craven attempt to mount a defence, she put forward the transparently spurious argument that Tausha had suffered from various medical problems, including 'failure-to-thrive syndrome', a condition which prevents a person benefiting from nutrients in food.

However, the evidence of hideous maltreatment was overwhelming. Tharp was found guilty of the murder of her daughter and the jury returned a death-penalty verdict. Before Judge Pozonsky formally pronounced the sentence, he played a song by country and western singer John Michael Montgomery entitled 'The Little Girl'. The lyrics include the line 'Oh, what a sad little life', which refers to a neglected girl born into a house filled with domestic abuse.

Sentenced to death on 19 April 2000, Tharp still sits on Death Row at the Muncy State Correctional Institute in Pennsylvania.

Tharp's mother, Michelle, was also charged with homicide, endangering the welfare of a child, and concealing the death of a child and abuse of a corpse. She is serving a long jail sentence.

For his part in the crime, Bittinger was charged with aggravated assault. Currently, he is serving 15–30 years at the State Correctional Institute, Gaterford. And with a bit of luck that's where he'll stay.

Jack Harrison
Trawick

O n the evening of Friday, 9 October 1992, Jack Harrison
Trawick followed 21-year-old Stephanie Gach from a shopping
mall near Birmingham, Alabama, and abducted her from the
parking lot of her apartment complex. He took her to an isolated
area, beat her over the head with a ball-peen hammer, strangled
her and then stabbed her through the heart. The killer threw the
girl's body down an embankment, where it was discovered the
next day.

Arrested, tried and convicted, Trawick, who had confessed to
what he had done, was sentenced in 1994 to die for the murder of
Stephanie Gach, and in 1995 he was convicted of killing Frances
Aileen Pruitt, 27, in eastern Birmingham. He had murdered her
about four months before killing Stephanie Gach.

Trawick also made a plausible confession to the killing of Betty
Jo Richards, 17, at Quinton, in Walker County, Alabama, in 1972,

but he was not prosecuted in that instance because he had already been sentenced to die.

The entire saga should have ended there, with Trawick on Death Row and, after exhausting his appeals, taking his last walk along the Green Mile and finally bringing closure to the families and friends of the young women he had so callously defiled and murdered. But that isn't where it ended. Trawick is not that sort of man.

Despite his joining the ranks of serial killers, Jack Trawick was never going to attain the notoriety held by others such as Ted Bundy, Aileen Carol Wuornos and Henry Lee Lucas. Terrible though his crimes were, it is a sad fact of life that he was only a minor player in that sanguinary league and, repugnant though he may be, there are others whose appalling deeds excelled his, making them almost household names. For some twisted reason, however, Trawick is a man who appears to crave that level of notoriety and since his imprisonment on Death Row he has taken steps to elevate himself in the hierarchy of serial killing.

In 2003, with the help of his former pen pal Neil O'Connor from New Jersey, Jack Trawick used a website from which to make public a series of writings designed to draw attention to himself and attract the notoriety that he obviously craves. The website was eventually closed down in 2004, but while it was running Trawick broadcast alarmingly loathsome material, some of which was aimed directly at Mary Kate Gach, whose daughter he murdered. He taunted her, mentioning her by name and writing in detail how he had beaten, strangled and stabbed Stephanie.

Trawick also confessed to several other murders, saying that he had killed Dr Virginia Bryant, Michelle Thomas and Susan Hill. He also claimed to have killed another woman, whom he named simply as Kim, and an unnamed mother and daughter.

Of the murder of Stephanie Gach, he wrote, 'Was it really worth it? (: I would do the whole thing again knowing that Death Row was waiting for me. Watching you die was (is) worth it all,' and he included sickening drawings of the crime, in what amounted to a how-to guide to committing murder.

'I'm mad as hell,' said Mary Kate Gach. 'Those people don't even have a right to speak my name or my child's name. There's got to be a way to keep them from funnelling this stuff out of prisons.'

The material on the website was obviously the work of a man with a serious mental disorder, but it was not harmless and it presented too much of a risk for the confessions to be ignored. Sergeant Scott Praytor of Birmingham Police's Homicide Department admitted that he and his colleagues were going to look into the matter further: 'We'll go down to the prison. We're going to follow up on it and see if we can clear up some homicides.'

However, the 'confessions' appear to have been only attempts at self-aggrandisement by Trawick. A thorough police investigation revealed nothing. The Deputy District Attorney for Jefferson County, Laura Petro, was the woman who prosecuted Trawick, and she branded his 'confessions' as 'complete and utter garbage', adding, 'He always wants to make Jack Trawick bigger and better.'

According to Ms Petro, Trawick made similar claims while he was awaiting trial for the murder of Stephanie Gach but the authorities at the time found nothing of substance behind his claims. The only confession that she believed to be true was the Richards case.

Of the man running the website for Trawick, his former pen pal Neil O'Connor, little is known. He appears to be an impressionable fool who was, and possibly still may be, dangerously in thrall to a madman. O'Connor told a visitor to the website: 'I'm going to turn Trawick into an international superstar now. I'll make sure of that... Jack and I can write what we want under the protection of the First Amendment... I like Jack. I think Jack is a literary genius. I think he is a Marquis de Sade of the 21st century.'

It is understood that Trawick told O'Connor that he has killed as many as 14 people, but he has not given names or details of all of those killings.

From his autobiographical ramblings, it is easy to picture O'Connor as an insignificant man, an inadequate non-achiever who saw in his attachment to Trawick an opportunity for some form of perverted fulfilment. It would have come as a surprise to very few when he wrote that he ran the website because he had had a fascination with serial killers since he was a boy. He added, 'The site also helps alleviate sometimes violent thoughts that come into my head that come with my obsessive-compulsive disorder. I've always been an animal lover. I have four very cute cats. The cutest of the cats a lot of times I just think about stomping on it until her eyes pop out. My website alleviates these bi-polar desires.'

Among the outpourings of the literary genius that is Jack Trawick can be found: 'Trawick philosophy 101: Never rape a woman without killing her. Never kill a woman without raping her. Eventually a raped female will tell someone.' His other thoughts include: 'Murder is deliciously, deliciously delightful.'

This gratuitously offensive material continued to be published throughout 2003 and into the following year. Eventually, however, common sense prevailed and in the early part of 2004 the authorities managed to close down the detestable website.

'It's going on all over,' said Nancy Ruhe, executive director of

Parents of Murdered Children in Cincinnati. 'People say to me all the time, "When are these [victims] going to get over it?" They can't.'

In May 2007, the State of Alabama introduced a bill designed to prevent prison inmates from being able to indulge in the sort of activity on the internet that has hitherto been enshrined in their constitutional rights. The legislation currently is pending in the Senate. Attorney General Troy King urged citizens to contact their senators and ask them to act on this important bill to make it the law of Alabama. Should this happen, and there is a strong chance that it will, it is likely that other states will follow with their own similar legislation.

'As a father, my heart breaks for Ms Gach. She should never have to read about or hear about this monster selling his twisted thoughts or drawings on the internet or anywhere else,' said King. 'I am ashamed that my state, rather than allowing Stephanie to rest in peace, we have allowed the desecration of her memory. This legislation protects her memory. As Attorney General, I am committed to finding ways to make sure that these monsters can no longer reach through the bars of our prisons to re-victimise Alabama families.'

At the time of writing, the bill has yet to be voted on. Trawick has yet to exhaust his appeals, and no date for his execution has been set.

Carlette Elizabeth Parker

It is fair to say that Alice Covington was old: she was 88. It would equally be fair to say she was slightly built, for Alice stood only five feet two inches tall and weighed 88 pounds. But it would be stretching a point to describe her as frail. Her physician, Dr Wells Edmunson, asserted that she was an especially vibrant person for her age. He testified that her overall physical and mental health was excellent and that her last physical examination revealed her blood pressure, respiration and cholesterol readings were normal.

Dr Edmunson was giving evidence because Alice Covington, who lived at Springmoor Retirement Village, 1500 Sawmill Road, Raleigh, North Carolina, had been murdered.

In contrast with Alice Covington, Carlette Elizabeth Parker, born on Wednesday, 12 June 1963, was neither old nor slightly built. At 34 years old and weighing in at a daunting 230 pounds, the registered nursing assistant was hale and hearty. From

December 1996 to March 1997, she had worked at Springmoor Retirement Village, where she looked after Charles Holtz, a neighbour and good friend of Alice Covington.

North Carolina is a very picturesque Southern State, bordered to the west by the Smokey Mountains and to the east by a spectacular coastline that includes Cape Hatteras and Cape Fear. Raleigh is the capital city. According to the promotional literature, Springmoor is a perfect and luxurious setting for the elderly; its 42 acres of beautifully landscaped grounds provide a serene backdrop for houses, villas and apartments. It boasts 'numerous activities and services allow an active, secure lifestyle. On-site Stewart Health Center provides recuperative and continuing care. An indoor swimming pool, fitness center, salon, putting green, woodshop, convenience store, and on-site banking are among the amenities.' It is also described as 'pet friendly'.

In any event, court records state that, sometime between 9 and 10am on the morning of Thursday, 12 May 1998, Parker and Alice Covington met each other at the Kroger parking lot on Creedmoor Road, Raleigh. Subsequently, but during the same time span, witnesses saw the two women engaged in a struggle on nearby Strickland Road. Parker attacked the old woman, who attempted to get away and defended herself by hitting the bigger, heavier, younger woman over the head with her purse.

Later in the day, Parker drove Alice Covington, in the old woman's own car, to the Crabtree First Union Bank on Market Street in Smithfield, a town south-east of Raleigh. She stopped at the teller's window and presented a withdrawal slip together with Alice Covington's driving licence. The withdrawal slip was made out in the amount of $2,500. Curious, the teller looked into the car and saw the old woman in the passenger seat, leaning against the car door and apparently asleep, given that she was not moving.

Now richer by $2,500, Parker took Alice Covington back to the Kroger parking lot, where her own car, a Ford Fiesta hatchback, was parked. There she transferred the old woman into the Fiesta and drove to the small town of Angier, south of Raleigh, where she had her trailer home. At the trailer she drowned Alice Covington in the bathtub. She then undressed the lifeless corpse, washed the victim's clothes, dressed the body again and then took it out to her Fiesta and locked it in the hatchback of the car.

Leaving the dead woman in the Fiesta, Parker got into another car and drove off to a family party. After leaving the party, Parker drove around for several hours before returning home.

The next morning, Parker drove the Fiesta back to the Kroger parking lot, where she transferred her victim's body back into the front passenger seat of her own car. She then drove the old woman's car for several hours around Raleigh, and hit the Greensboro road, going west to pass through Hillsborough and Burlington, before finally abandoning the vehicle and its dead owner on a dirt road in Morrisville. After making her way on foot to Davis Drive, she hitched a ride to a gas station where she summoned a cab that took her back to her car at the parking lot. She drove home and rounded off her day's corpse-conveyancing by drinking a couple of bottles of wine.

Alice Covington's car, and with it her body, was discovered the next day, 14 May, by a passer-by. The dead woman was lying across the front seat, her head propped up against the driver's door, her chest squeezed under the steering wheel and her feet on the passenger-side floor. Examination of the body revealed the amount of violence she had been subjected to at the hands of the big nurse. There was substantial bruising around her face, neck, hands, upper part of both arms, upper left back and shoulder area and left wrist. There were also lacerations on her left wrist and lower left leg.

Investigations soon led the police to Carlette Parker and they conducted a series of interviews with her. During the first interview, she told her inquisitors that she had seen Alice Covington on the afternoon of 12 May, between 1 and 3pm, at the Kroger parking lot and they had driven first to a car wash and then to the old woman's home, where she remained for only a few minutes before leaving. Parker was then told by SBI Agent M.B. East that Alice had been found dead in her car at Morrisville. Parker took the news calmly and, with no apparent emotion, said simply, 'Oh really?'

Towards the end of the interview, the nurse denied having killed Alice Covington and claimed to have no idea who the killer might be. She also flatly denied having made any recent trips to Morrisville or indeed to any bank in Smithfield. Minutes later the interview came to a close.

The second interview began in more or less the same matter-of-fact, conversational manner as the first. Then it changed. Agent East told Parker that witnesses had seen her struggling with Alice Covington on Strickland Road. The agent followed up by producing a copy of the cheque that had been used to withdraw $2,500 from the old woman's account and told her that the teller had given a description of the person who had made the withdrawal.

This revelation hit Parker like a bombshell. Immediately, her whole demeanour changed and she became visibly nervous. Her leg shook and her knee bounced up and down. Pressing home the advantage that had been established, East again asked the nurse if she had any idea who might have killed Alice Covington. Warily she replied, 'Possibly.' However, she denied assaulting the old woman or accidentally killing her.

With some progress made, East concluded the interview and drove Parker home. During the journey, East heard Parker say, 'I'm going to lose my job,' and 'I won't be able to take care of old people any more.' As events unfolded, this proved to be the wildest of understatements.

On 16 May, while being interviewed by Agent East and Detective K.W. Andrews of Raleigh Police, Parker said that she wanted to come clean about what had happened. She had a story, she said, but it would seem 'kind of far-fetched'. And so it was.

The massive care worker said she had met Alice Covington at the Kroger parking lot, although it was between 10 and 11am, not in the afternoon as she had earlier claimed. The two had then gone to a car wash. She went on to say that they had gone to Covington's house, although she was vague about whether they had driven separately. In any event, they had both returned to the Kroger parking lot, from where Parker had driven them in her own car to the bank in Smithfield. There Parker had cashed the cheque for $2,500. Alice Covington had given her the money, she said, to help her with her doll business. They had never stopped on Strickland Road.

This far-fetched account continued with Parker driving the two of them to her trailer home at Angier. She sat the old lady on the commode, she said, while she ran a bath for her and then left the bathroom. On returning to the bathroom she found Alice Covington's head had fallen into the water. She simply sat the old lady up and again left the bathroom. This time, on returning, she found the old woman's head completely submerged. Grabbing her by the hair, she pulled her from the water, tearing her shirt in the process. She slapped the old lady about the face a couple of times but elicited no response. During this flurry of activity Alice Covington's head slammed into the floor.

Parker carried her elderly guest into the living room and laid her on the floor. She undressed the unconscious woman, washed and dried her clothes and then dressed her again, minus the torn shirt. At this time, she said, the old woman was entirely unresponsive, although she thought her hand may have twitched. At no time during all of this did the trained healthcare professional attempt to perform CPR, nor did she call for assistance by simply dialling 911. Instead, she took the unorthodox step of stowing her patient in the hatchback of her Ford Fiesta and leaving her there while, in her other vehicle, a truck, she drove off to a party in Durham.

Afterwards, she drove round for a few hours before returning home. Evidently, she hadn't gone home to see how her elderly patient was getting along because she climbed into the Fiesta and drove off to see her husband, who was staying in a hotel on the Greensboro road, Highway 70 East. She didn't tell her husband about the day's events and certainly didn't mention the person she had brought with her in the back of the Fiesta.

The next morning around 6.45, Parker drove back to the Kroger parking lot, where she deposited Alice Covington's body on the front seat of her own car. As the body had begun to smell, she put two pillows on it. That done, she drove around for six or seven hours before abandoning the car on the dirt road in Morrisville and hitching a ride to a gas station.

Then the far-fetched story began to unravel. Parker admitted that she had thrown the victim's purse away near Falls Lake because she was afraid that her fingerprints might show up on it. She also had to admit that she had indeed had a confrontation with Alice Covington on Strickland Road, although at first she said that she had merely stopped the car to refuel, adjust her passenger's seat and massage a cramp in the old woman's leg. However, she then retracted this story and admitted that she had forced Alice Covington to go to the bank against her will. Moreover, during the confrontation, she had grabbed her victim by the shirt and forced her back into the car. It was then that the old lady's shirt had been torn.

Alice Covington's death had been caused by drowning and the manner of the death was homicide.

Examination of the body had revealed two small reddened patches of skin. These had been inflicted by the application of a stun gun and a stun gun was found among Nurse Parker's possessions.

The dead woman was wearing blue slacks and a lightweight pink jacket in a synthetic fabric. On the lower part of the jacket there was a reddish discoloration. After Parker's arrest, the police found a pepper spray in her car which, when tested, emitted a spray that produced similar discoloration of a fabric sample.

The case against Carlette Elizabeth Parker was overwhelming and she was convicted of first-degree murder. On April Fool's Day, 1999, at Wake County Court, she was sentenced to death.

To the question of a motive for the killing, the answer is simply that she needed money. In August 1995 Parker had been found guilty on 16 counts of obtaining money by false pretences from 85-year-old Catherine Stevenson. Here too Parker had been in a position of trust and had used it to her advantage: she had been the old woman's care worker and had been forging unauthorised withdrawals from her account to the tune of around $44,000. Parker had been ordered by the court to pay restitution at the monthly rate of $920. By 1 April 1998, she was in arrears by more than $4,000 and had told her probation officer that she was worried about how she would be able to make the amount up. She saw Alice Covington's money as a way out of her problems, and the old woman died as a result.

Nevertheless, after committing such a terrible murder, there was one thing this evil woman could bank on: the death sentence. Inmate # 0311386 Carlette Parker currently resides at the North Carolina Correctional Institute for Women (NCCI), 1034 Bragg Street, Raleigh, NC 27699-4287. If you are tempted to drop her a line, no cheques or money orders, please.

Veronica Gonzalez

Among the USA's Green Mile population of over 3,600, a mere 1.5 per cent are female. And for them to qualify for their trip to perdition the crimes have to be particularly heinous.

America is extremely reluctant to impose the death penalty upon the female gender; even less so is it inclined to carry out the death sentence. Indeed, only 10 per cent of women sentenced to death are actually executed.

In the US Supreme Court, the bias in a female's favour is given even more weight because the judges' final decision, unlike in the lower courts, is irreversible. After the Supreme Court has upheld a death sentence, only a State Governor may grant clemency – a one-off shot at that – and this is why an open phone line connects the execution chamber and the Governor's office up until the moment of execution. Contradicting Dante's 'Abandon hope all ye who enter here', every condemned inmate awaits the shrill ring on the red phone, but seldom does it come.

What we can say without any hesitation is that the ladies currently on the Green Mile have been very bad indeed. Whether they deserve to be executed is for the reader to consider, and the case of Veronica Gonzalez will no doubt stimulate debate. Nevertheless, many of the crimes committed by some of these women are so horrifically bizarre, while others are wrapped up in tragicomedies that not even the most inventive screen writer could conjure up, cases that would make even Stephen King recoil in disgust.

It is a vile reality that there are many women, such as Michelle Sue Tharp, who have carried out acts of monstrous cruelty on small children. Vile it may be, yet they do exist and, although it may be difficult to envisage a woman who could emulate Tharp's treatment of her own daughter, 29-year-old Veronica Gonzalez more than matched her when, with her husband Ivan, 38, she murdered their four-year-old niece, Genny Rojas. In doing so, they became the first married couple in California's history to be on Death Row at the same time.

The despicable crime took place on Friday, 21 July 1995, and the details of the hideous savagery inflicted on the child by two adults defy belief. Genny had been beaten with a plastic baseball bat, a belt and other blunt objects, as well as starved for months, before finally being scalded to death in a bathtub. Almost all of those involved in the investigation and prosecution of the case were profoundly affected by what they encountered.

In 1995, Genny had been sent to live with the Gonzalez and their six young children in Chula Vista, California, because her mother was in drug rehabilitation and her father was in jail for child molestation. To imagine the kind of existence this small child had experienced during those first years of her life is harrowing, but if anyone thought she was about to be placed in a situation that would relieve the problem they were horribly misguided.

For six months, Genny was abused – forced to live in a box, hanged by her hands from a hook in a closet and burned with a hairdryer. When she was not bound hand and foot with handcuffs and cord, she slept in a small, triangular enclosure behind the bathroom door. She had been blindfolded so often, and so tightly, that the skin was worn off her ears and the bridge of her nose.

On the day of the murder she was pushed into water so hot that it peeled most of the skin from her body. An autopsy showed that she had burned to death over a period of *two hours*. The medical examiner concluded that it would have taken only between three and fifteen seconds for the girl to be burned from the chest down, and it looked like 'she had been burned in acid'. Deeply moved, he told the court in hushed tones, 'She was conscious while she was in the water, because areas of her skin were spared from burns, indicating that she curled up to try and protect herself. Even with her skin burned off, if she had received immediate care she would have had a 70 per cent chance of survival. Those holding this young child down had watched her die in agony over a period of around two hours before she succumbed.'

At the Gonzales' trial, prosecutor Dan Goldstein said, 'The children didn't have any clothes because the defendants spent all the welfare money on drugs. They are going to be better off without them, and somebody needs to say that. A death sentence will be a fitting end to the worst child-abuse case in San Diego County history.' He added, 'A defendant who hangs, burns and mutilates a four-year-old child is going to suffer the worst of punishments.'

Superior Court Judge Michael Wellington echoed Goldstein's sentiments, saying, 'I have never experienced a case where this degree of continued, unrelenting torture of a single victim was presented.'

Today Veronica Gonzalez, the perpetrator of the worst case of child abuse in the history of San Diego County, has undergone the Damascene conversion common to many on Death Row. Carol Rainey, the prison chaplain at Las Colinas Women's Detention Facility in Santee, says, 'Veronica has found God. She always attends Sunday worship service and helps other inmates cope with their problems.'

Despite the words of the chaplain, it is difficult to understand how a woman who has inflicted such appalling cruelty on a small child can have become reconciled and be at peace with herself. Outwardly, however, that appears to be the case for Gonzalez, living out her days in preparation for her day of atonement when she will take her last walk.

Her husband, Ivan Gonzalez, is on Death Row at San Quentin State Prison, where he awaits the same end as his wife.

Darlie Lynn Routier

The call came from 5801 Eagle Drive, Dalrock Heights Addition, an affluent suburb of Rowlett on the outskirts of Dallas. Doris Trammell, night dispatcher for the Rowlett Police Department, was surprised when the emergency phone rang at 2.31am and a hysterical female voice yelled, 'Somebody broke into our house... They just stabbed me and my children... My little boys are dying! Oh my God, my babies are *dying*!'

Doris struggled to establish details from the woman, who kept screaming, 'While I was sleeping ... me and my little boys were sleeping downstairs ... someone came in ... stabbed my babies ... stabbed me ... I woke up ... I was fighting ... he ran out through the garage ... threw the knife down...'

The distraught caller was Darlie Lynn Routier, aged 25.

'How old are your boys?' asked Doris.

They were six and five years old, and their names were Devon and Damon.

Soon the emergency services began to arrive at the house. David Waddell, the first police officer to arrive on the scene, could not believe what he saw; he had never experienced anything like it. Lying in the room were two boys, dead or dying from deep gashes to their chests, and an adult woman soaked in blood, a bloody rag pressed to her throat. The woman was Darlie Lynn Routier. Darin Routier, Darlie's husband, was also soaked in blood from attempting to resuscitate one of the boys.

Another police officer, Sergeant Matthew Walling, arrived and also the paramedic team of Jack Kolbye and Brian Koschak, who quickly realised there was too much for them to handle alone and radioed for backup.

Darlie, who had wounds to her throat, was treated by paramedics and gave a statement to Waddell. She told him that an intruder had entered her home and mounted her on the sofa while she slept; she had woken to find him on her, screamed and, after she had struggled with him, warding off his blows, he absconded towards the garage. It was then she realised that he had left behind him the two butchered boys. Of his attack on them, she had heard nothing. She described her attacker as a man of medium to tall height, dressed entirely in black: T-shirt, jeans and baseball cap.

Darlie and her two sons were taken to Baylor Medical Center, but it was too late to save the boys. Devon had been dead almost by the time the paramedics arrived and Damon had died moments before being put into the ambulance. Darlie herself was detained in hospital until the Saturday.

The next day, Thursday, Darlie was interviewed by detectives

Jimmy Patterson and Chris Frosch. This time her statement differed in many details from the one she had given to Waddell.

'I woke up hearing my son Damon saying, "Mommy, Mommy," as he tugged on my nightshirt. I opened my eyes and felt a man get off me. I got up to chase after him. As I flipped the light in the kitchen on, I saw him open his hand and let the knife drop to the floor. Then he ran out through the garage. I went over and picked up the knife. I shouldn't have picked it up. I probably covered up the fingerprints. I shouldn't have picked it up.

'I looked over and saw my two babies with blood all over them. I didn't realise my own throat had been cut until I saw myself in a mirror. I screamed out to my husband.'

Back at the crime scene, the investigating team had found much to cast doubt on Darlie Routier's account of events. What signs there were that a struggle had taken place seemed to have been contrived. There was evidence that attempts had been made to clean bloodstains from some of the surfaces and, puzzlingly, Darlie's purse and some items of her jewellery were untouched by the intruder. In short, the investigators believed that there was no intruder. They were persuaded that Darlie had made up the story after butchering her own children. Moreover, her behaviour over the following days seemed entirely at odds with a woman who had been through such an ordeal. There were further indications that her story was not authentic, so it wasn't long before she was arrested and charged with homicide. In October of that year, Darlie Routier went on trial for a month, at the end of which the jury found her guilty. She was sentenced to death.

Darlie Routier was born Darlene Peck on Sunday, 4 January 1970 in Altoona, Pennsylvania, the eldest of three children. Her parents were Darlie and Larry Peck, who divorced seven years later. When Darlie's mother married Dennis Stahl, Darlie gained two stepsisters and the family moved to Lubbock, Texas. Marriage number two didn't work out for Darlie's mother either: she and Dennis fought constantly and again she divorced.

By the time she was 15, Darlie had grown into a very attractive young woman and started dating Darin Routier, who was two years her senior. The two lived together in Dallas until they married in August 1988. Darin worked in the computer-chip industry and eventually started his own company, Testnec, testing circuit boards. He operated his company from their home in Rowlett. The business prospered and by 1992 the couple were able to afford business premises and to have a house – 5801 Eagle Drive, Dalrock Heights Addition – built in grandiose Georgian Colonial style with colonnaded porch. Status-conscious, they also owned a Jaguar car and a 27-foot cabin cruiser. In the meantime, Darlie had given birth to two sons, Devon Rush on 14 June 1989 and Damon Christian on 19 February 1991.

Outwardly, the Routiers were a happy and successful family, living the American Dream with all the trappings of prosperity, although they may not have had the sophisticated taste to match. In fact, their taste simply reflected their craving for attention. Darlie even indulged herself in breast implants of a massive size EE. It's important to note that she was, after all, still only in her early to mid-twenties and still had some growing up to do. In any event, the couple's superficial lifestyle came at a very high cost and Darin's company was their only source of money. Friends also noted that there appeared to be a growing friction between Darlie and Darin.

Nevertheless, the two seemed to be very happy when, in October

1995, Darlie gave birth to a third son, Drake. However, that proved to be simply the beginning of the end. After the birth, Darlie suffered post-natal depression with its mood swings, sudden bouts of temper and dark, uncontrollable rages. Also, desperate to lose the weight she had put on during pregnancy, she had turned to diet pills. 'Diet pills' is generally a euphemism for amphetamine, which acts as an appetite suppressant and a stimulant, and this is a dangerous drug to be using when suffering from any depressive condition. It all came at the worst of times. Testnec was a profitable business but not enough to sustain the couple's level of spending, and they were faced with tightening their belts. The decline in their finances reached meltdown on Saturday, 1 June 1996 when their bank refused them a much-needed loan of $5,000. In May, Darlie had contemplated suicide, although this was due to more than just financial issues and there had been signs that she had begun to attempt to come to terms with her problems.

Whatever her situation, in the early hours of 6 June, the Routiers' two older sons were brutally murdered and Darlie, who sustained neck wounds, was subsequently charged with the killings and convicted at trial. However, the successful prosecution of Darlie Lynn Routier didn't mark the end of the story. Since her trial, there has been a growing body of opinion that the convicted child killer may have been telling the truth. There is much controversy concerning the conduct of both the investigation of the case by the police and the conduct of the trial, but this is lengthy and too involved to be included in depth here. However, the case has been dealt with at length by the writer Barbara Davis. In her book *Precious Angels*, Davis explained why she was convinced of Darlie's guilt, but since researching and writing it she has been persuaded that the opposite is the case: that Darlie is innocent and should not be on Death Row.

There are also several websites devoted to promoting Darlie Routier's cause which argue cogently that there was manipulation of evidence by the police investigators and also by the prosecution at the trial. It is true that many convicted murderers attract this sort of attention and their adherents put forward very convincing arguments, but they are not always proved right. Many simply turn out to be specious conspiracy theories. Nevertheless, there appears to be justification for at least a re-examination of Darlie Routier's case.

Among the more interesting allegations raised by her supporters is that a neighbour reported an intruder at her own home who matched the description of the man in the baseball cap that Darlie said had attacked her and killed her sons. It is alleged that the police failed to pursue this matter. It is also alleged that there were reports from other neighbours of a mysterious black car that was seen at the Routier home.

Moreover, it has been suggested that some of the blood evidence was mishandled by investigators and that there was evidence of the prosecution holding a 'mock' trial in order to rehearse the witnesses, especially the hospital staff, in how to give evidence. This latter point would seem to be supported by the answers given by Detective Jimmy Ray Patterson to questions put to him at the trial by defence lawyer Douglas D. Mulder.

The following is an extract from the cross-examination in which Mulder touches on the rehearsed testimony session:

Q: OK. And I take it you testified in that event?
A: No, sir.

Q: But you were there and listened to everyone else?

A: I was there, and we talked about our case, yes.

Q: OK. Was there someone on the bench in lieu of the judge?

A: Well, there was someone sitting up there in the judge's chair.

Q: OK. Well, just by coincidence or do you…?

A: Well, I don't know why.

Q: You never did figure out why?

A: No, sir.

Q: All right. Well, let's just see if we can't figure out why – you know what circumstantial evidence is, don't you?

A: Yes, sir.

Q: OK. Was there someone in the prosecutor's – at the prosecutor's desk in the courtroom?

A: Yes, sir.

Q: And was there someone at the defense table, a lawyer?

A: Yes, sir.

Q: And was there someone up on the bench in the judge's position?

A: Yes, sir.

Q: And was there someone on the witness stand where you are right now?

A: Yes, sir.

Q: And did the prosecutor ask them questions?

A: Yes, sir.

Q: And did the defense lawyers ask them questions?

A: Yes, sir.

Q: Now circumstantially, do you think that we could put those circumstances together, and figure out that they were conducting a mock trial?

A: I think what we were doing, is that we were just trying to make sure – well, we wanted to make sure that the prosecutors knew what we knew.

Q: OK. And, it helped, I guess, to make sure that the other officers knew everything that you…

A: Well, I don't know about that.

Q: You don't know about that. OK. Now, at any rate, after you had talked to the lady at the curb side there, in what you termed to be the street, and I would call an enlarged maybe elbow of the street, did you then leave to go to Baylor Hospital?

Adding weight to the allegations, some of the prosecution witnesses opted to take the fifth amendment in order to avoid having to answer questions from the defence lawyers at the trial.

One particularly intriguing aspect of the post-conviction furore has been the emergence of Darlie's husband Darin as one who has more of a connection with the crime than has been revealed. Darin is alleged to have admitted that he had attempted to arrange an insurance scam which involved someone breaking into the Routier home. This was meant to take place when nobody was in the house. The matter was not raised during the trial.

It has also been alleged that Darlie Routier's own defence attorney had conflicting interests in that he had entered into an agreement with Darin Routier and Darin's family not to pursue any line of defence that could lead to Darin being implicated.

Darlie had suffered a number of cuts and bruises to her arms that were alleged to have been sustained during the attack. Photographs of these were never brought to the attention of the jury. This led one juror to state, after being shown them, that had he been shown them during the trial he would never have returned a guilty verdict.

All of these points present serious questions surrounding the behaviour of those investigating the murders and the way in which the prosecution was conducted, which, in turn, has implications concerning the validity of the verdict that was returned. What is more, these are only a few of the allegations and concerns that have been raised. If justice is to be seen to be done, issues such as these must be acknowledged and addressed satisfactorily, particularly in a case involving the death penalty.

At the time of writing, Darlie Lynn Routier sits on Death Row sentenced to be executed by lethal injection. On the one hand, she may be a woman who, for a few minutes one night, became a homicidal monster who butchered her two young sons. On the other hand, she could equally be an innocent woman, the victim of a conspiracy intended to shield the true killer from retribution. This is a case in which neither side seems to have told the truth, the whole truth and nothing but the truth, and there is, of course, always the possibility that whatever is the truth may never emerge.

Note: A full investigation into the case of Darlie Routier can be found in *Killers on the Web* by Christopher Berry-Dee and Steven Morris (John Blake Publishing, London, 2006, ISBN 184454 188 6).

Kenisha Eronda Berry

If Quentin Tarantino were to include in a film a scene in which a mother leaves her newborn baby to be eaten to death by ants, it is doubtful that it would be granted a certificate of release. Such a scene would be considered too far-fetched and gratuitously violent for public consumption. Yet such an incident did take place and it was carried out by Kenisha Eronda Berry. Nor was it this woman's first connection with infanticide.

A former prison guard, Berry was just 21 when, towards the end of November 1998, she suffocated her three-day-old son by placing duct tape over his mouth. The baby boy, whom she had named Malachi, was still alive when his mother taped his tiny arms across his chest, placed him in a black plastic garbage sack and left him in a dumpster at an apartment complex in Beaumont, Jefferson County, Texas.

In the early hours of Sunday, 29 November, Roy Black and his wife, Ima, were wandering the streets of Beaumont, looking for aluminium cans. When he opened a trash bag that he had taken from the dumpster, Roy found that it contained what at first he thought to be a baby doll's leg. His curiosity turned to horror when he found that he was holding the remains of a dead baby. The couple alerted the police.

Ima named the child Baby Hope and neighbours held candles, prayed and sang 'Amazing Grace' in his memory. Nobody came forward with information on the identity of Baby Hope or his mother and, as the years passed, many came to believe that whoever had killed the infant would never be found.

The case remained unsolved until the summer of 2003, when Debbie Beavers, of Jefferson County Sheriff's Department, was investigating another case involving an abandoned baby. This concerned a newborn girl who had been found lying in an ants' nest on Hillebrandt Road, Beaumont. The baby was covered with ant bites, but somehow she survived.

A connection was made between the abandoned baby girl and Kenisha Eronda Berry. Detective Beavers called to see Berry at her modest one-storey home, but her mother, Ruby Sherman, said her daughter was out, so Beavers left her business card.

On 12 June, Berry called in at the Sheriff's Department, where she acknowledged that she had abandoned her baby daughter, Parris. She took detectives to a dumpster a few miles away and showed them where she had thrown some of the evidence from the little girl's birth. It lay in the squalid surroundings of a road littered with old furniture and tyres. However, what rang alarm bells in the mind of Detective Beavers was that this was the same dumpster in which, five years earlier, the body of Baby Hope had been found.

Beavers brought her discovery to the attention of Sergeant John Boles of Beaumont Police, who compared Berry's fingerprints with those found on the duct tape and trash bag that had held Baby Hope: they matched. DNA testing indicated a 99.8 per cent probability that Kenisha Eronda Berry was the mother of the dead infant. Sergeant Boles said, 'We knew eventually we would have a suspect for Baby Hope's murder. I had been hoping and praying for years. A lot of us had. Nobody likes to have a case that you can't solve. It bothers you. It gnaws at you.'

Berry was charged with the murder of her baby son.

Although she abandoned her initial story that the baby had been stillborn, at trial she insisted that she did not kill her baby and that he had been dead when she had taped him up and thrown him into the dumpster.

According to the court records, she said that she knew that she was pregnant in 1998, but not how far advanced her pregnancy was. The baby's father was a man named Nicholas Beard. She did not tell her family or anyone else that she was pregnant. She had given birth at home by herself and named the infant Malachi. Afterwards, she had thrown away the placenta and cleaned the place up with water and bleach.

Malachi appeared to be healthy when he was born and she fed him milk from a bottle. His nose started running the next day, and she went to the store that morning to buy more milk. When she returned from the store, he was still asleep on the bed in her bedroom. She lay on the couch to watch television and later checked on him because she was concerned that he had not yet woken. When she went into the bedroom, he was 'limp' and was not moving or breathing. She realised that he was dead, but did not call for help because she was 'scared' and did not know 'if it was against the law to have a baby at home'. She wrapped duct tape around his arms because they were stiff and sticking out and she 'wanted them in front of him'. She put duct tape over his mouth because it bothered her that his mouth was open.

With Malachi in a bag, she then left her apartment, borrowed her grandmother's car, placed the infant, 'which was already inside the trash bag', in the boot and transported him to a dumpster without anyone's knowledge. She stated that 'the baby was not kicking or moving' when she put him in the dumpster.

However, the forensic pathologist who had performed the autopsy on Malachi gave a damning testimony in court. In his statement Tommy Brown said that he estimated that the boy was: 'two to five days old. Duct tape had been used to cover his mouth and to constrain his arms around his abdomen, and he had been placed inside a plastic trash bag. His stomach contained a "milk-like product", which indicated that he had been fed before death, and there was fecal matter inside the plastic trash bag. He had "petechiae of the pleural surfaces of the lung", which was consistent with oxygen deprivation. The combination of being duct taped and covered with a plastic trash bag was also consistent with oxygen deprivation.'

According to the court records, 'Brown observed no indications of an infection or sudden-infant-death syndrome. He determined that the infant "died from asphyxia due to smothering", and he ruled the death a homicide. Brown opined that the infant was still alive when he was placed in the plastic trash bag, and "as the baby died, then there was a large release of fecal material from the rectum".'

The pathologist further stated that 'The baby would have released his bowels before or during death, but not after' and that 'the death wasn't consistent with sudden infant death syndrome, and a stillborn infant couldn't have drunk the milk found in his stomach, and the baby had been fed at least twice'. The court records report that Brown said, 'The lividity on the anterior and posterior sides of the body led him to conclude that the infant was lying on his stomach when he died and that after he was discovered he was turned over and placed on his back for a short period of time.'

It appears that Berry had been able easily to conceal two pregnancies, those of Malachi and Parris, from her friends and family. Tracy Redeaux, a foster-care supervisor for Child Protection Services, testified that Berry told her that Malachi's delivery was easy and that she kept it secret from everyone. After the birth, Berry told her family she had purchased a bottle of formula for the baby, who was a friend's newborn that she was babysitting.

What else emerged during their investigation is that Berry had four living children, including Parris, the baby she left to be bitten to death by ants. The father of three of her children is Joskin Love. The problem, it would appear, is that Love is not the father of Parris, nor was he the father of Malachi. These two children were the result of Berry's relationships with two other men, Leonard Carrier and Nicholas Beard, respectively.

When asked at trial whether she had killed Baby Hope and abandoned Parris because she didn't want Love to know about the other men, Berry denied it. However, her reason for committing her crimes matters little as the jury took only an hour to find her guilty of murdering the baby they called Hope, and she sits on Death Row at Mountain View Prison, Gatesville, Texas.

Summing up the case, Sergeant John Boles said, 'It's a great relief … tinged with sadness. I feel bad for the family because I don't really think in 1998 they really knew about Baby Hope. To find out that you had a grandchild that was thrown away into the trash must be heartbreaking.'

Lisa Jane Coleman

On Thursday, 22 June 2006, Lisa Jane Coleman took up residence on Death Row, and a Fort Worth jury had taken less than an hour to deliver the verdict that put her there. The crime for which she had stood trial was that of capital murder and it involved the starving to death of a nine-year-old boy, Davontae Williams.

Coleman lived at Arlington, in Tarrant County, Texas, where she shared an apartment with her friend Marcella Williams, the mother of the dead boy. On Monday, 26 July 2004, paramedics were called to the apartment. When they arrived, they found the body of Davontae Williams, who at his death weighed barely 35 pounds.

A 'busted lip' and some 250 scars visible on his body made it clear that this was the victim of an extreme case of child abuse. An autopsy concluded that Davontae Williams was severely malnourished at the time he died. Coleman and Williams were arrested and charged in connection with the child's death.

Coleman was the first of the two women to be tried. At her trial, it emerged that she and Williams were found to have tortured Davontae over a period of time and deprived him of food. The court was told that the child had been forced to live in an empty pantry and starve to death, while no one else in the house went hungry.

Records also showed that Child Protection Services (CPS) had made six calls to the home where Davontae lived. In 1999, CPS had removed the boy and his sister, who was a toddler, after finding that the boy had been beaten with an extension cord. The children were later returned to the family home. This raises questions of negligence by CPS but doesn't diminish the enormity of Coleman's actions.

The evidence against Lisa Jane Coleman was overwhelming and she was convicted of Davontae's murder. However, it appears that Coleman herself had been subjected to serious childhood abuse. Her defence attorney pleaded to the jury for clemency, offering in mitigation the story of Coleman's own upbringing, which was itself tragic and prompted the *Dallas Morning News* to comment after her sentence: 'Lisa Jane Coleman's tragic life was not enough to keep her off Death Row for the starvation of her girlfriend's son, 9-year-old Davontae Williams. A Tarrant County jury rejected defense attorney's emotional pleas to spare the life of a woman he said was the product of incest, neglected by her mother, bounced through foster homes and repeatedly raped by an uncle.'

Lisa Jane Coleman was born on Monday, 6 October 1975. Short, overweight and with the educational level of a ten-year-old, she claimed that she had had to live throughout her childhood with the nickname 'Pig' and that children at school would tease her by making snorting noises. What is more, as a child she had been made to go for long periods without food. She had begun using marijuana at 13 and later moved on to cocaine and ecstasy. Doctors diagnosed her as bipolar, often described as manic depressive. This may indeed have been a powerful argument, but in the eyes of the jury it did not carry sufficient weight to mitigate the cruelty that Coleman had inflicted on little Davontae. They returned from their deliberations to recommend the death penalty.

On Death Row, Coleman lives in denial of her guilt. This prompted Davontae's great-aunt, Tracey Binder, to say that she agreed with the guilty verdict: 'One down, one to go … there is no excuse for what happened to this kid. Justice was done. I've forgiven both of them. The hardest thing I've ever done was forgive them. Lisa needs to fess up. How can you torture someone and act like nothing has happened? Lisa, if you are really sorry, you need to fess up.'

With her deprived background and her limited intelligence, there is the possibility that prisoner # 999511 Lisa Jane Coleman may one day walk the Green Mile never having come to terms with what she has done.

John E. Robinson

In Kansas City in the 1980s, the dust had barely settled after the horrifying case of the sexual torturer and serial killer Bob Berdella when the ghastly discovery by the police of several rotting bodies in barrels at sites straddling the Kansas–Missouri border heralded the emergence of yet another bizarre multiple murderer. And the man accused of the murders of six women is arguably the world's first cyber-sex serial killer, whose arrest has exposed a strange, dangerous and secret world of bondage and sado-masochistic sex which has burgeoned within the internet's chatrooms and websites.

John E. Robinson, known to his friends as J.R., was born on Monday, 27 December 1943 in Cicero, Illinois, a working-class suburb of Chicago. As one of five children in a devout Roman Catholic family, he lived and grew up at 4916 West 32nd Street. His father, Henry, worked as a machinist for Western Electric and, although respectable enough, was given to occasional bouts of heavy drinking.

Alberta Robinson, John's mother, was the backbone of the family and ensured that their five offspring had a respectable upbringing. John became an Eagle Scout on 13 November 1957, at the age of 13, and was chosen as leader of 120 boy scouts who flew to London that year and appeared before the Queen at the London Palladium. According to the *Chicago Tribune*, John was singled out for the honour 'because of his scholastic ability, scouting experience and poise', and the piece went on to say that 'he also has an engaging smile'.

John Robinson's engaging smile seems to have served him well, for, by the time he was 21, he had married Nancy Jo Lynch and moved to Kansas City. There he was employed as a lab technician and office manager by Dr Wallace Graham, who for many years had been the personal physician to former President Harry S. Truman. It was during his time in this job that Robinson, the former Eagle Scout, began his criminal activities. In 1967, he was convicted of embezzling $33,000 from Dr Graham and placed on probation for three years.

Robinson's next job was as a manager of a TV rental company. Here he developed his incipient career in crime by stealing merchandise from his employers. They fired him but did not prosecute.

In 1969, Robinson got a job as a systems analyst working for Mobil Oil, although he neglected to tell them that he was still on probation. This job ended in September of that year when it was discovered that the systems analyst had stolen more than six thousand postage stamps, worth $372, from the company. This time his employer, impervious to his engaging smile, reported him to the police and he was charged with theft.

After moving back to Chicago, Robinson worked for a company called Illinois R.B. Jones, where he quickly began helping himself to his employer's money. After embezzling more than $5,500 in six months, he was caught and fired. His father paid money to the company in restitution and Robinson avoided criminal charges.

He returned to Kansas City and there he was arrested for violating the terms of his probation. This resulted in his spending a few weeks in jail and having his probation extended by five years, to 1976. Despite this, the probation board had formed a good opinion of the habitual thief and he was discharged from his probation two years early, in 1974.

Unknown to the probation department, Robinson had indulged in his favourite pastime while still on probation: his next-door neighbour, a retired schoolteacher named Eva Lee McKnight, labouring under the misguided notion that Robinson was as honest as the day is long, entrusted him with $30,000 to invest on her behalf, and never saw the money again. Her 'investment adviser' somehow escaped prosecution.

Having formed a company called Professional Services Association Inc, or PSA, Robinson began offering financial consultation services to the medical profession. He was appointed by two groups of doctors at the University of Kansas Medical School and set about managing their financial affairs. However, he was dismissed after a few months because of irregularities in the way he was handling the doctors' finances. According to a report in the *Kansas City Star*, one of the doctors, who had interviewed Robinson for the job, said, 'He made a very good impression; well dressed, nice looking ... seemed to know a lot, very glib, good speaker.'

Undaunted, Robinson promoted PSA with vigour and employed

some extremely dishonest means in order to attract investment. Letters were sent to people whom he saw as potential investors informing them that the company was a thriving concern and was in the process of being bought by Marion Laboratories. None of this was true. The result of these nefarious activities was that Robinson was indicted on four counts of securities and mail fraud, fined $2,500 and once again placed on probation, this time for three years.

A year later, in 1977, Robinson bought a large house set in four acres in Pleasant Valley Farms, an affluent neighbourhood in Johnson County, Kansas. By now, he and Nancy had four children. It was in these picturesque, rural surroundings that the confidence trickster and embezzler formed another company, Hydro-Gro Inc. This specialised in hydroponics, a method of growing plants and vegetables under lights and one widely used by those who grow marijuana indoors. The company's publicity material, a 64-page brochure, portrayed the founder as a sought-after lecturer and author and 'one of the nation's pioneers in indoor home hydroponics'. Robinson even employed the services of his five-year-old twins, who appeared in a photograph in the brochure wearing T-shirts with the legend 'Grow your own'.

In addition to his business activities, Robinson was throwing himself into becoming a high-profile pillar of his community. The philanthropic president of Hydro-Gro Inc somehow managed to engineer his appointment to the board of governors of a workshop for disabled people. He had been involved with the workshop for scarcely more than two months when he was named 'Man of the Year' for his work with handicapped people, amid much publicity. Headlines in the *Kansas City Times* proclaimed his virtues and, at a special dinner and presentation ceremony, he received a certificate in the form of a grandiose proclamation signed by the mayor. A short time later, the meritorious award was exposed as having been fraudulently obtained. It had been made as a result of fake letters of commendation sent to City Hall, all written by Robinson himself.

In 1980, the 'Man of the Year' became Director of Personnel with a company which was a subsidiary of Borden Inc. Nobody questioned his references and very soon he homed in, like a heat-seeking missile, on the company's money, which he was manipulating in the direction of his own bank account. He diverted $40,000 to PSA, the company which he still owned.

Robinson founded another company, Equi-Plus. This newcomer to the portfolio specialised in management consultancy services and was very soon engaged by Back Care Systems, a company which ran seminars on the treatment of back pain. Equi-Plus was asked to prepare a package which included a marketing plan, printed publicity material and videos. However, what it actually provided was a string of inflated, and in some cases bogus, invoices, and once again a criminal investigation was begun into Robinson's business activities. He responded by producing a series of faked affidavits which attested to the legitimacy of the invoices.

While the investigation was going on, Robinson founded Equi-II, and it was under the auspices of this new outfit that he moved into a world of activities far more sinister than mere fraud and embezzlement.

The $40,000 that Robinson had embezzled from Borden allowed him to acquire an apartment in the town of Olathe, south of Kansas City. Here he was able to enjoy sexual affairs with two women whom he had met while working for Borden, one of whom has been quoted as saying, 'John kind of swept me off my feet. He treated me like a queen and always had money to take me to nice restaurants and hotels.'

Nevertheless, there is no such thing as a free lunch and retribution loomed on the horizon for the thieving and libidinous Robinson; the theft of the money resulted in his being convicted and, in view of his criminal record, he faced a possible prison sentence of seven years. However, he spent only a couple of months behind bars and once more found himself placed on probation, this time for five years.

In 1984, an attractive young woman named Paula Godfrey went to work for Robinson at Equi-II. She was told by her new boss that she was going to be sent to Texas on a training course paid for by the company. Accordingly, Robinson collected Paula from her parents' home in Overland Park to drive her to the airport, and that was the last time that she was ever seen by her family.

Not having heard from her for several days, Paula's parents became anxious and eventually contacted the police to report her missing. When the police questioned Robinson, he professed ignorance of Paula's whereabouts and they went away. Not long afterwards, they received a letter which bore Paula Godfrey's signature and began: 'By the time you read this I'll be long gone. I haven't decided on Cleveland, Chicago or Denver, oh well.' In the rest of the letter Paula seemed to be saying that she was perfectly fine but didn't want to remain in touch with her family. At the time this was good enough to satisfy the police, who closed their investigation.

It is now widely believed that Paula Godfrey was Robinson's first murder victim as she has never been seen again.

In the pursuit of his new vocation as a philanthropic helper of young women, Robinson approached the Truman Medical Center, a hospital in Kansas City. There he spoke to social workers, telling them that he, together with some other local businessmen, had formed Kansas City Outreach, a charitable organisation which, he said, provided young unmarried mothers with housing and career training along with a babysitting service. He also approached Birthright, an organisation which gave help to young pregnant women, and pitched them the same story.

The writer David McClintick quotes Robinson as telling the two organisations that Outreach was likely to receive 'funding from Xerox, IBM and other major corporations'. In any event, the great philanthropist asked the social workers to submit candidates that they felt would be suitable for the Outreach programme and, in January 1985, he was contacted by the Truman Medical Center and put in touch with Lisa Stasi.

Nineteen-year-old Lisa had a baby daughter of four months named Tiffany. She had married the child's father, Carl Stasi, in August 1984 and given birth to Tiffany on 3 September. However, by the end of the year, the marriage had fallen apart and Carl Stasi had left his wife and daughter to join the US Navy.

Lisa and the baby were staying at Hope House, a shelter for battered women, when Robinson, using the name John Osborne, arrived on the scene, offering her free accommodation and career training. He explained that this involved helping her to gain her High School Equivalency Diploma, after which he would arrange for her to go to Texas, where she would be able to train as a silkscreen printer. He went on to say that, after she had completed her training, there would be job opportunities for her in Chicago, Denver or Kansas City. In the meantime, her new mentor told her that, as well as paying for her accommodation and living expenses, he would pay her a wage of $800 a month. It was an offer she couldn't refuse.

The kindly benefactor then took Lisa and Tiffany out of the battered women's refuge and installed them in Room 131 at the Rodeway Inn, a motel in Overland Park, telling her that she and her baby would be travelling to Chicago within a few days. He then got her to put her signature to four blank sheets of paper and to provide him with the addresses of her immediate family, saying that, as she would be too busy to write letters when she got to Chicago, he would write them for her, to inform her relatives of her whereabouts. After Robinson left the motel, Lisa went to see some relatives in Kansas City and discussed the matter with them.

The following day, 9 January, Robinson collected Lisa and Tiffany from Lisa's sister-in-law's home. After expressing anger that she had left the motel, he insisted that they leave with him immediately and so they drove off in a heavy snowstorm. Like Paula Godfrey, Lisa was never seen again by her family.

Lisa's sister-in-law, Kathy Klinginsmith, wasn't very happy about 'Osborne', so the following morning she telephoned the Rodeway Inn. She was told that Lisa had checked out and that the bill had been paid by a John Robinson, using a corporate credit card in the name of Equi-II. Kathy drove to the Overland Park Police Department and reported Lisa and Tiffany missing. That same morning Kathy's husband, Dave, had gone to the offices of Equi-II and confronted Robinson, but had been physically ejected from the building. Later the same day, Dave received a phone call from a man who called himself Father Martin and claimed that he was a priest from the City Union Mission. The cleric said that he was calling on behalf of Lisa to let the Klinginsmiths know that she and her baby were fine. Before hanging up, he left a number for Dave to call should the need arise. However, when Dave rang the number, it turned out to be someone's home and they certainly didn't know 'Father Martin'. Moreover, the City Union Mission advised Dave that they had no priests attached to their organisation.

On the evening of 10 January, Robinson's brother Don and his wife Helen arrived at Robinson's home and were handed a four-month-old baby girl. The childless couple had been trying to adopt a baby for some years when Robinson had suddenly announced that he had influential contacts who might be able to help them. So that morning they had flown into Kansas City and were met at the airport by Robinson, who drove them to the offices of Equi-II. There they had signed what appeared to be adoption papers and handed over $5,500 in cash before being driven to the Robinsons' home, where Nancy Robinson was waiting with the baby. According to testimony given by Nancy years later in court, her husband had brought the baby home the previous night. She recalled that it was snowing heavily when he arrived home with the infant and that the child was not very clean. Apart from the clothes she was wearing, the infant had arrived with just some spare nappies and some baby food.

Don and Helen were told by Robinson that the baby had suddenly become available for adoption because her mother had committed suicide at a women's shelter. In any event, they were delighted with their new baby, whom they named Heather, and the next day they flew home completely unaware that the child was in fact Tiffany Stasi, who, with her mother, had been reported missing the previous day. It was to be 15 years before Heather Robinson's true identity would be revealed, in the most shocking circumstances imaginable: when the man she knew as 'Uncle John' would stand in court accused of murdering her mother.

At the time that Lisa and Tiffany Stasi disappeared, Ann Smith, an employee of Birthright, began to check up on the details that Robinson had provided concerning Kansas City Outreach and himself. She discovered that almost all of his story was untrue and decided to discuss the matter with Stephen Haymes of the Missouri Board of Probation and Parole. Haymes examined Robinson's file and interviewed him himself, but, although there was much about the man that he didn't like and found suspicious, there was nothing of substance for him to take further. Nevertheless, with two women and a baby missing, he was deeply concerned and contacted the FBI. As a result, two FBI agents, Thomas Lavin and Jeffrey Dancer, were assigned to investigate Robinson, and teamed up with Haymes.

Among the information that began to emerge about Robinson was the fact that Johnson County's District Attorney was investigating his company Equi-II in connection with forceful allegations that it had defrauded its client Back Care Systems. Not only that, but Robinson and a fellow ex-convict, Irvin Blattner, were being investigated by the US Secret Service for forgery involving a government cheque.

None of this, however, was connected to the disappearances of the two women and the baby, and the trail was in danger of becoming cold.

Shortly after Lisa's disappearance, a letter turned up at the women's shelter, signed by Lisa and saying that she had 'decided to get away from this area and to try to make a good life' for herself and Tiffany. A similar letter was received by the Klinginsmiths, who viewed it with great suspicion, particularly since they knew that

Robinson had persuaded Lisa to sign four sheets of blank paper before she had disappeared. In addition, both letters were typewritten and the Klinginsmiths knew that Lisa could not type. The FBI investigators and Haymes could do little, despite their own strong suspicions. Nevertheless, Haymes ordered Robinson to turn up at his office for further questioning. During the interview, the wily Robinson protested about being harangued over the matter and insisted that Lisa and the baby were in fact alive and well. He claimed that a woman who lived in the Kansas City area, and for whom Lisa had recently done some babysitting, had told him this. However, when FBI agent Lavin questioned the woman, she confessed that the story about Lisa having babysat for her was not true. She said that Robinson had made her go along with the story because she owed him money and he had photographed her nude in order to promote her services as a prostitute. With this new angle to pursue, the FBI investigators arranged for a female agent, posing as a prostitute, to approach Robinson on the pretext of looking for work.

According to David McClintick, it was around this time that Robinson developed a taste for sado-masochistic sex. However, he not only engaged in it himself, but also saw in it the potential to make a lot of money and was very soon running a thriving business exploiting this lucrative niche in the market. He organised a string of prostitutes to cater for customers who enjoyed S&M. To satisfy his own appetites, he employed a male stripper, nicknamed M&M, to find suitable women for him.

The female FBI agent, wired to record any conversation, arranged to meet Robinson at a restaurant in Overland Park. Over lunch, Robinson told her that, working as a prostitute for him, she could earn up to $3,000 for a weekend travelling to Denver or Dallas to service wealthy clients. She could also earn $1,000 a night just working in the Kansas City area. His clients, he said, were drawn mainly from the ranks of doctors, lawyers and judges.

Robinson went on to explain that as an S&M prostitute she would have to allow herself to be subjected to painful treatment such as having her nipples manipulated with pliers. When they heard this part of the recording of the conversation, the FBI investigation team decided to end the undercover operation out of fear for the female agent's safety. It is doubtful that the young woman herself would have been particularly enthusiastic about continuing after hearing that aspect of the job description.

Robinson maintained an apartment on Troost Avenue in Overland Park, and it was here, during April 1985, that he installed a young woman named Theresa Williams. Theresa, 21 and attractive, had been introduced to him by the male stripper M&M as a suitable candidate for prostitution. She had been working at various odd jobs around Kansas City and jumped at the chance. After photographing her nude in a hotel room, Robinson initially offered her the position of his 'mistress'. This involved her being given an apartment with all her expenses paid, and there was the added attraction that Robinson would keep her well provided with amphetamines and marijuana. She would also be expected to provide sexual services for others, for which she would receive prostitution fees. Theresa took the job and moved into the Troost Avenue apartment.

However, life wasn't all roses for Theresa. One night towards the end of April 1985, after being given $1,200 and a new outfit by

Robinson, she was taken blindfold in a limousine to a mansion. There she was introduced to a distinguished-looking man of about 60, who led her down to a basement which was fitted out as a medieval torture chamber. Her host instructed her to remove her clothes and moments later she found herself being stretched, naked, on a rack. Theresa panicked and demanded to be allowed to leave. Blindfolded once again, she was driven back to her apartment. Robinson reacted angrily and a few days later she had to give back the $1,200.

On another occasion, Robinson took Theresa to task for entertaining a boyfriend at the apartment. But the worst was yet to come. In late May, he paid her a visit during which he did something that caused her more fear than she had ever known in her life. She was asleep when he let himself into the apartment. He burst into the bedroom, dragged her out of bed by her hair and spanked her until she began to scream. After throwing her to the floor, he drew a revolver, put it to her head and pulled the trigger. Instead of an explosion, there was only a click. The chamber was empty.

By now, Theresa was whimpering with fear but she went rigid in utter terror as Robinson slid the revolver slowly down her stomach before inserting the barrel into her vagina. He left it there for several terrifying seconds before withdrawing it, replacing it in its holster and, without another word, leaving the apartment.

About a week after the incident with the gun, FBI agents Lavin and Dancer called unannounced at Theresa's apartment. She told them that she worked for Equi-II as a data processor, but, when they made her aware that they were investigating the disappearance of two women and that Robinson was the suspect, she decided to tell the truth. That, of course, involved telling them about the drugs that Robinson was supplying to her as well as the incident with the gun. When the agents learned that she had been asked by Robinson to sign some blank sheets of paper, they felt that they had grounds to believe that her life was in danger, so they moved her to a secret location.

Together with Stephen Haymes, the two agents filed a report with the Missouri court which claimed that Robinson had violated his probation conditions by carrying a gun and supplying drugs to Theresa Williams. They asked the court to revoke Robinson's probation and put him in prison.

Once more, however, Robinson evaded justice and avoided prison, this time on a technicality. His lawyer argued successfully that, because he had not been allowed to confront his accuser, Theresa Williams, his constitutional rights had been violated. Nevertheless, his liberty was soon to be curtailed, as the investigation into his fraudulent business practices was drawing to a conclusion in Johnson County. There the district attorney charged him with fraud in his dealings with Back Care Systems and in January 1986 he was found guilty. Shortly afterwards, he was convicted of a second fraud, involving a real-estate deal, and in view of his abysmal previous criminal record he was sentenced to serve between six and nineteen years in prison. Despite mounting an appeal, John E. Robinson went to prison in Kansas in May 1987.

At the time that Robinson was heading for prison, the police were searching for a missing woman, Catherine Clampitt, aged 27. Born in Korea but adopted and raised by the Bales family in Texas, Catherine was a one-time drug user now seeking rehabilitation. Early in 1987, in an attempt to get away from the influence of her friends and leaving her infant son, Ryan, in the care of her parents, she moved from Wichita Falls, Texas, to the Kansas City area, where she was employed early in 1987 by none other than John E. Robinson's company Equi-II. At first Catherine lived at the Overland Park home of her brother, Robert Bales. However, a few months after her arrival, she simply disappeared. Bales went to the police and reported his sister missing. However, it would be some years before the mystery of Catherine's disappearance would be solved. There was no apparent evidence to link her to Robinson, who in any case was on his way to jail.

Ironically, Robinson's time in prison seemed to bring out the best in him and he became a model prisoner. Mental tests and a psychological examination showed him to possess an above-average intelligence, and as a result he was given a position coordinating the prison's maintenance-operations office. For once Robinson was in a job in which embezzlement and theft were out of the question and he put his undoubted talents to good use. The computer programs that he put in place saved the prison system almost $100,000 a year.

During his time in prison, Robinson suffered a series of minor strokes. Nevertheless, he made a full recovery and, while he was undergoing treatment, he created a very favourable impression among the medical staff. In fact, two senior doctors produced a glowing endorsement of the pathological confidence trickster which would have astonished anyone who knew the real Robinson. They described him as 'a model inmate who has made the best of his incarceration. He is a non-violent person and does not present a threat to society.'

The 'model inmate' made such a good impression on the prison authorities and the parole board that he was released on parole in

January 1991, having served less than four years. However, he still had to go to prison in Missouri for having violated the terms of his probation from the $40,000 fraud he had perpetrated against Borden when he worked for the company in 1980. Stephen Haymes, who was Robinson's probation officer, was adamant that his client should go back to prison, despite the fact that prison doctors in both Kansas and Missouri agreed that he should go free. In the end, the Missouri court listened to the probation officer and Robinson went inside for a further two years.

It is interesting to read Haymes's assessment of Robinson in a memo that he wrote to a colleague in 1991. The memo was seen by David McClintick and in it Haymes says, 'I believe him to be a con-man out of control. He leaves in his wake many unanswered questions and missing persons… I have observed Robinson's sociopathic tendencies, habitual criminal behaviour, inability to tell the truth and scheming to cover his own actions at the expense of others.' The probation officer went on to say, 'I was not surprised to see he had a good institution adjustment in Kansas considering that he is quite bright and a white-collar con-man capable of being quite personable and friendly to those around him.'

While in jail in Missouri, the 'white-collar con-man' forged a friendship with William Bonner, the prison doctor. He also developed a relationship with Bonner's wife, Beverly. She was the prison librarian and Robinson very soon found that he had a job in the library.

On the outside, Nancy Robinson had found the going tough without her husband's income and eventually she had had to sell their palatial home at Pleasant Valley Farms. What is more, she had needed to take a job in order to keep body and soul together, and she was fortunate in getting one which provided living accommodation. She became the manager of a mobile-home development in Belton, a suburb of Kansas City, on the Missouri side of the State line. Ironically, the mobile-home development was called Southfork, like the Ewing family home in the TV series *Dallas*, the home of the original J.R. The streets on the development were named after characters in the series, one being Sue Ellen Avenue.

It was to these much reduced living quarters that Robinson went when he was released from prison early in 1993. The two elder children had grown up and left home and the twins were at college, so the Robinsons had the place to themselves. They rented storage lockers to house their surplus belongings at a place nearby.

Robinson set to work restoring the family fortunes and had soon resurrected his old company, Hydro-Gro Inc. There was never any real likelihood that he would stay on the straight and narrow path and it wasn't long before he had returned to his old ways.

Back at the prison in Missouri, Beverly Bonner had left her husband and begun divorce proceedings. A few months later, she moved to Kansas City and went to work for Robinson, who appointed her a director of Hydro-Gro. At this time she was in correspondence with her mother – or someone was. Letters signed by Beverly Bonner arrived at her mother's home, saying that her new job required her to travel abroad. None of the letters bore a return address. Moreover, they contained instructions that all of Beverly's mail, including her alimony cheques, should be redirected to a box number at the Crossroads Shopping Center, Santa Fe Street, Olathe. However, it was not Beverly who collected the mail from the mail collection office, it was Robinson. Beverly Bonner was never seen or heard from after January 1994.

Robinson's next victim was a widow named Sheila Dale Faith. When her husband, John, had died of cancer in 1993, Sheila was left to bring up their teenage daughter, Debbie, alone. Debbie had been born with spina bifida and spent her life in a wheelchair. Life was not easy for the two, who had moved from California to live in Pueblo, Colorado, and depended on Social Security payments for their livelihood.

It isn't certain exactly how Sheila met Robinson, although it may have been through a newspaper ad, but after being in Pueblo for only a few months she and Debbie moved to Kansas City. Sheila told her friends that she had met her 'dream man', John, who had promised to take her on a cruise. He had also assured her that she would never have to work or worry about Debbie as he would look after them both and that money was no problem.

One night in the summer of 1994, with no prior warning, Robinson called at Sheila's home and took her and Debbie away to live in 'the Kansas City area'. As was the case with so many other women who were befriended by Robinson, Sheila and her daughter were never seen again.

Sheila Faith was receiving disability benefits from the Social Security Administration for herself and Debbie and soon these were being sent to a mail centre in Olathe, where they were collected by Robinson. In the autumn of 1994, according to court documents, Robinson filed a medical report to the Social Security Administration in which he claimed that Debbie was 'totally disabled' and would require care for the rest of her life. The report somehow bore the signature of William Bonner, the doctor with whom Robinson had been friendly while in prison and who until recently had been Beverly Bonner's husband. When he was eventually questioned on the matter, Dr Bonner denied ever having met Sheila or Debbie Faith and had certainly never treated either of them. In any event, Robinson collected the Faiths' disability cheques for almost six years. Records show that these were deposited in accounts in the names of two Robinson companies, Hydro-Gro and Specialty Publications Inc.

In July 2000, Cass County Prosecutors alleged that, between 1994 and 1997, Robinson defrauded the US government of more than $29,000 in Social Security and disability payments by forging documents to suggest that Sheila and Debbie Faith were alive. It was also alleged that he received more than $14,000 in alimony cheques which were meant for Beverly Bonner. The owner of the mail centre from which Robinson retrieved the cheques told the police that he knew him as 'James Turner'. The incorporation papers for Hydro-Gro show no mention of Robinson, but they list James Turner as company secretary.

Meanwhile, Robinson's interest in sado-masochistic sex continued to flourish. He began placing adverts in the personal columns of a Kansas City newspaper called *Pitch Weekly*, seeking others interested in bondage and sado-masochism, activities often referred to jointly as 'BDSM'.

One such contact, whom David McClintick calls Chloe Elizabeth, a businesswoman from Topeka, Kansas, claimed that Robinson sent her a host of publicity material designed to show him in a good light. He included newspaper clippings describing his appearance before the Queen when he was a Boy Scout, as well as his hydroponics brochure, details of his Man of the Year award and a Kansas University brochure containing pictures of two of his children: an unlikely portfolio for someone wishing to engage in a relationship involving bondage and sado-masochism. Unsurprisingly, his lengthy and distinguished criminal record received no mention whatsoever.

In an interview with McClintick, Chloe Elizabeth said that after a few weeks of conversations with Robinson about their sexual preferences she knew just what her new 'dominant', or master, wanted of her, and she invited him to her home on the afternoon of 25 October 1995.

'I was to meet him at the door wearing only a sheer robe, a black mesh thong, a matching demi-cup bra, stockings and black high heels. My eyes were to be made up dark and lips red. I was to kneel before him,' she recounted.

On arriving, Robinson took a leather-studded collar from his pocket, placed it around Chloe Elizabeth's neck and attached a long leash to it. After a drink and some small talk he made her remove all her clothes, except for her stockings, before he took from his pocket a 'contract for slavery' in which she consented to let him use her as a sexual toy in any way he saw fit.

'I read the contract and signed it. He asked if I was sure. I said yes, very sure,' said Chloe Elizabeth.

After he had tied her to the bed, whipped her and carried out a variety of acts on her breasts with ropes and nipple clamps, Robinson concluded their first date by making her perform oral sex on him. Chloe Elizabeth was delighted with her new master and he was pretty much delighted with her. Their first date was 'sensational', she told McClintick. 'He had the ability to command, to control, to corral someone as strong and aggressive and spirited as I am.'

Before he left, Robinson told Chloe Elizabeth that she had been stupid for allowing him to do all that he had done to her. 'I could have killed you,' he said.

However, she wasn't as naive as he may have thought. Unknown to him, she had taken the sensible precaution of having a male friend stationed in another room of her house, listening vigilantly for any sound of excessive behaviour. The man also noted down the licence number of Robinson's car.

The relationship between Chloe Elizabeth and Robinson burgeoned and they began meeting at least twice a week. However, she began to distrust him, suspecting that he wasn't all that he said he was. He had told her that he was divorced from his wife, but she was soon disabused of that notion. When she got a friend in local government to run a check on his licence plates, she discovered that his car was registered in his wife's name as well as his own.

It is not unusual in BDSM relationships for the dominant to take control of the submissive's assets and financial affairs: this is sometimes included in the master–slave contract. Naturally, given his passion for other people's money, Robinson broached this issue with Chloe Elizabeth and suggested that they exchange lists of their assets. She wisely refused to have that sort of involvement, suspecting that he was after her money. Given that he was, on the face of it, the unemployed husband of a woman who was the manager of a mobile-home park, it would have been interesting to have seen just what those assets were that Robinson had intended listing, apart from Beverly Bonner's alimony cheques and the Faiths' welfare payments.

Robinson invited Chloe Elizabeth to travel with him to Europe. Although unsure about him, she tentatively agreed and it was then that events assumed a more sinister complexion. He tried to persuade her to sign some blank sheets of paper and to provide him with a list of names and addresses of her relatives, whom he intended to keep informed of her whereabouts. At this point, Chloe Elizabeth sensibly cancelled any plans to travel with him.

If Robinson had imagined that Chloe Elizabeth's submissiveness extended beyond her sexual inclinations, he was badly mistaken; she was an intelligent and successful businesswoman, not an ill-educated teenage mother desperate for help and support. Relations between the two were by now moving in the wrong direction and she began to 'find him out' more and more. He told her that he was going to Australia and would be away for some time. However, she discovered that he had not even left Kansas. When she telephoned his office, the phone was answered but remained utterly silent. About an hour afterwards, her phone rang and she found herself being berated by a furious Robinson, who accused her of checking up on him and, in very unpleasant tones, warned her against that sort of thing. The final straw for Chloe Elizabeth was when she found out about Robinson's criminal record, and in February 1996 she ended their relationship.

During that same year Robinson and Nancy left Southfork mobile-home park and went to live near Olathe, just inside Kansas. The development they moved to was called the Santa Barbara Estates, and again Nancy was the estate manager. The new place was not dissimilar to Southfork except that here the streets were all named after Californian cities. The Robinsons' new address was 36 Monterey, and here they certainly didn't opt for inconspicuous anonymity. They erected a statue of St Francis of Assisi in the yard at the front of their house, hung wind chimes at their front door and at Christmas they earned quite a reputation for their spectacular display of decorations.

The couple also bought some farmland near the small town of La Cygne, south of Olathe. The 16 acres contained a fishing pond to which Robinson invited friends from time to time. They improved the place by putting a mobile home and a shed on the site.

By now, Robinson, in pursuit of his BDSM activities, had graduated from newspaper advertisements to the internet. Using 'Slavemaster' as his 'handle', he was, according to David McClintick, maintaining five computers and spent hours trawling BDSM websites. Ultimately, however, it would be two of his internet contacts who would be instrumental in bringing his world crashing around his ears, but in 1996 that was still some years ahead.

The following year, Robinson encountered a young, Polish-born undergraduate on the internet. Her name was Izabel Lewicka and she was studying fine arts at Purdue University in Indiana. Izabel had moved from Poland to the United States with her parents when she was about 12. The family had settled in Indiana and in 1996 Izabel graduated from high school in West Lafayette.

As well as fine arts, Izabel was very interested in computers and spent much time trawling the internet, eventually coming into contact with Slavemaster.

Izabel's parents were very concerned when, in the spring of 1997, she told them that she was moving to Kansas, having been offered an 'internship'. She wasn't forthcoming with details, doing nothing to allay their misgivings, other than to leave an address on Metcalf Avenue in Overland Park. In June, she abandoned her place at

Purdue University and drove off to Kansas. Her parents were never to see her again.

After receiving no reply to their letters, they grew extremely anxious about their daughter and in August drove to Kansas to find out what was the matter. However, when they reached Overland, they found that the address on Metcalf Avenue was simply a mailbox: their daughter didn't live there. When they asked the manager of the place for Izabel's forwarding address, he refused to divulge the information. Despite their anxiety, Izabel's parents did not bother to contact the police, instead simply driving back to Indiana.

In fact, Izabel was still alive at that time and enjoying a life far removed from the one she had known in Indiana. However, she had good reason to be keeping it a secret from her parents. Her new friend Robinson had provided her with an apartment in south Kansas City and there they enjoyed a BDSM relationship. They even had a 'slave contract' which contained more than a hundred clauses governing their conduct; she was the slave and he the master.

In return for her submission, Robinson maintained Izabel financially, paying all her bills. When she wasn't engaged in sexual activity with him, she led the life of a lady of leisure. Her main interest lay in reading gothic and vampire novels, bought from a specialist bookshop in Overland Park that she visited frequently. Nor did she abandon her studies completely; in the autumn of 1998, using the surname Lewicka-Robinson, Izabel enrolled at Johnson County Community College. The adoption of Robinson's surname reinforces some reports which infer that the young woman was under the impression that they were going to be married. In any event, in January 1999, a few moths after Izabel enrolled at college, Robinson moved her into another apartment, in Olathe. This was closer to his own home, which may account for his sometimes describing her as a graphic designer employed by his company Specialty Publications. On some occasions, however, he is known to have referred to her as his adopted daughter, while at other times he described her as his niece.

Whatever the relationship between them, it didn't have much longer to run. During the summer of 1999, Izabel introduced Robinson to her friends at the specialist bookshop. She informed them that she would be moving away soon and that he would be buying her books for her in future. Within days, she had disappeared. The only explanation offered by Robinson, in conversation with a business associate, was that she had been deported after being caught smoking marijuana. There was no trace of Izabel ever having been in the apartment, and when Robinson returned the keys to the managing agent the place had been cleaned thoroughly and was in immaculate condition.

Slavemaster returned to the world of sado-masochistic chatrooms and within a few weeks made contact with a 27-year-old woman from Newport, in Monroe County, Michigan. Her name was Suzette Trouten and she worked as a nurse. Suzette, whose non-sexual interests were collecting teapots and doting on her two Pekingese dogs, enjoyed a highly active BDSM lifestyle. David McClintick writes that she carried on relationships with four dominants at once. She had pierced not only her nipples and her navel but also five places in and around her genitalia, piercings which could accommodate rings and other devices used in BDSM rituals. A photograph of Suzette with nails driven through her breasts had been circulated on the internet. She certainly appealed to Robinson and a relationship developed during the ensuing weeks.

In fact, he was so enamoured of his new submissive friend that he concocted a very attractive job offer with which to entice her to Kansas, and he invited her to fly down from Michigan for an interview. He paid for her flight and when she arrived at Kansas City a limousine met her at the airport. The job, Robinson told her, involved being a companion and nurse to his very rich, elderly father, who travelled a lot but needed constant care. He went on to say that his father did most of his travelling on a yacht and that her duties would involve her sailing with them between California and Hawaii. For this she would be paid a salary of $60,000 and provided with an apartment and a car. Robinson neglected to mention that the only way to have contact with his father would have to have been through the use of a Ouija board, or a medium, as the old man had been dead for some ten years. However, Robinson was not a man to let such details inhibit his designs and he gave Suzette to understand that the interview had gone well and that the job was hers. She returned to Michigan and began putting her affairs in order before moving to Kansas.

While she was making ready to move, Suzette spoke to her mother, Carolyn, to whom she was very close, telling her all about her new job. She also discussed the matter with Lori Remington, a Canadian friend whom she had met via an internet chatroom and with whom she shared an interest in the BDSM lifestyle. In fact, she later introduced Lori to Robinson on the internet and they too developed a long-distance, dominant–submissive, cyber-relationship.

In mid-February 2000, Suzette rented a truck, loaded it with her belongings and headed off to her new life in Kansas. With her she took her clothing, books, collection of teapots and the two Pekingese dogs, along with her array of BDSM accessories, including whips and paddles.

Lenexa is a suburb of Kansas City, lying west of Overland Park and north of Olathe, and it was there that Robinson took Suzette when she arrived on 14 February. He had reserved accommodation for her, Room 216 at the Guesthouse Suites, an extended-stay hotel, and arranged for her dogs, Peka and Harry, to be boarded at the kennels of Ridgeview Animal Hospital in Olathe; the dogs would be able to go with her on the yacht, he explained, but the Guesthouse Suites didn't allow dogs.

Almost immediately after Suzette had settled in, Robinson told her to get herself a passport, as they would be leaving in a fortnight. He also produced a 'master–slave' contract to cover their BDSM activities, which she duly signed. Then, ominously, he got her to attach her signature to 30 sheets of blank paper and to address more than 40 envelopes to relatives and some friends. Just as he had done with other women, he told Suzette that he would take care of her correspondence while they were travelling, as she would be too busy to do so herself.

Suzette was the youngest of a family of five children and, according to Carolyn Trouten, 'She was a kind of a Mama's girl.' While she was in Kansas, she phoned her mother every day, keeping her informed of how things were going and, although she had at first worried that she would be homesick, she seemed to be in good spirits and was certainly happy with her employer, John Robinson. And he was evidently happy with her. Company records lodged with the Missouri authorities show that Suzette was listed as the registered agent in the articles of incorporation for Hydro-Gro.

Everything appeared to be fine when daughter and mother spoke to each other in the early hours of 1 March. Carolyn later testified that Suzette was happy and told her that she was looking forward to her impending yacht cruise with her wealthy boss and his father and she promised to phone her mother regularly while she was away. Later that same day Suzette contacted Lori Remington on the internet and told her much the same. That was the last time either woman spoke with her. Like Lisa Stasi and others, Suzette Trouten simply disappeared.

That same afternoon, using his MasterCard, Robinson paid Suzette's bill at the Guesthouse Suites. According to the General Manager, Janis Munn, she saw him loading some things into a pickup truck. He was alone and there was no sign of Suzette. He then went to Ridgeview Animal Hospital and settled the bill and checked the dogs out of the kennels. Vicki Ebenstein, the office manager at Ridgeview, said she remembered Robinson collecting the dogs on 1 March because he had complained that the bill, for $470, was too high. Not only that, but he was two days later than expected in retrieving them. Later in the afternoon, according to various reports, an animal-control officer was called to the Santa Barbara Estates, where Robinson lived, because someone had left a portable kennel outside the main office. In the kennel were two Pekingese dogs and neither was wearing an identification collar.

Having heard nothing from her daughter for a few days, Carolyn Trouten began to feel anxious. Then other family members began receiving emails, purportedly from Suzette, but when she read them Carolyn knew they were not from her daughter: Suzette's spelling and punctuation were poor, unlike the emails, and the general style was nothing like hers. Lori Remington also had received emails and she too believed them to be counterfeit. Carolyn had Robinson's phone number, so she decided to call him. He told her that at the last minute Suzette had changed her mind about her job and instead had left with a man named Jim Turner on a sailing trip around the world. Carolyn didn't believe a word of the story and, as her fears grew, she contacted the Lenexa Police and reported her daughter missing.

After Suzette's supposed departure, Lori Remington had remained in email contact with Robinson, who wanted her to be his slave. He sent her pictures of himself posing outdoors in denim. All this time Lori was receiving emails and letters, supposedly from her friend, but she knew that they were not from Suzette. She believed that someone else had written them and she had a strong suspicion as to the writer's identity. She called Robinson and asked him about Suzette, but he told her the same story that he had told to Carolyn Trouten. Lori didn't believe it either.

Carlos Ibarra was employed as a maintenance man at the Santa Barbara Estates mobile-home park. He later testified that during May, a couple of months after Suzette's disappearance, his mother had been visiting from Mexico. Before she left, Robinson had requested a favour from her; he asked her if she would take some letters and mail them from Mexico, which she did. Ibarra remembered clearly that the envelopes were pastel shades of yellow and pink. He also remembered Robinson showing him a photograph of a naked woman whose arms and legs were tied to a table. Robinson described the woman as his girlfriend. There is little doubt that Ibarra was telling the truth, because it was shortly afterwards, according to Carolyn Trouten, that some of her relatives received letters posted from Mexico purporting to have come from Suzette. They were in envelopes of pastel shades of yellow and pink.

When the Lenexa Police received notification of Suzette's disappearance, Detective David Brown began an immediate and thorough inquiry into the man whom he saw as the prime suspect, John E. Robinson. He got hold of Robinson's rap sheet and contacted the Overland Park Police. This acquainted him with the other reports of missing women and he soon saw the possible connection. After two detectives had spoken to Stephen Haymes, the Missouri probation officer, it became clear that they could be investigating a serial killer. David Brown instructed the Trouten family to tape record their telephone conversations with Robinson and pass to the police copies of all emails from him. He also asked Lori Remington to maintain her email correspondence with the suspect and to keep the police similarly informed.

At the time that Suzette Trouten had been preparing to move to Kansas, Robinson, using the name James Turner, had established two more BDSM friendships on the internet. The first woman, whom David McClintick calls Jeanne, was a psychologist from Texas who had placed an ad on a BDSM website. She had recently lost her job and when Robinson became aware of this he promised to help her to find work in the Kansas City area. Jeanne arrived in Lenexa on 6 April and, staying at the Guesthouse Suites, spent five days getting to know Robinson. During that time, Jeanne signed a slave contract in which she consented to 'give my body to him in any way he sees fit'. They also discussed her working for Hydro-Gro and Robinson told her to return to Texas and prepare to move to the Kansas City area.

On 26 April, Jeanne returned for another long weekend, and it was then that she found that Robinson was eager to pursue more severe and violent forms of bondage sex than she wanted, but she believed that he was going to find work for her and so she consented to his demands, allowing him to brutalise her way beyond anything she had intended. She later testified that he took photographs of her while she was bound and nude, and that he slapped her hard about the face. 'I had never been slapped that hard by anybody before,' she told the court. She also stressed that the photographs were taken against her wishes and despite her protests.

Fortunately for Jeanne, the promised move to Kansas never took place and she demanded the return of her sex toys, which were worth more than $500. Robinson chivalrously refused. Moreover, he threatened to publicly reveal the slave contract and the explicit, compromising photographs. Jeanne's response was to report the matter to the police.

The second woman was also from Texas and she turned out to be the last one to fall foul of Slavemaster. Kate was an accountant and, after some weeks of preamble on the internet, had agreed to become Robinson's slave. In mid-May, she too journeyed to Kansas for a few days with him and was installed in an apartment at the Guesthouse Suites. Kate recalled that on Friday, 19 May she received a phone call from Robinson telling her that he would be coming around to see her and he instructed her that, when he arrived, she was to be kneeling in the corner of the room completely naked with her hair tied back.

Kate was submissive, as instructed, when Robinson arrived. But she wasn't prepared for what followed. He grabbed her by the hair and flogged her brutally across her breasts and back. Like Jeanne before her, Kate was discovering that Robinson was interested in a much rougher relationship than she wanted. She, too, didn't like being photographed during sex, but he insisted on doing so; he seemed excited by photographing the marks his beatings made on her body. However, Kate's genuine distaste for that level of treatment must have spoiled his enjoyment, because he told her he didn't like her attitude and wanted to end the relationship. Her body burning and bruised from the flogging, Kate became hysterical and after Robinson left she got dressed and made her way, in tears, to the reception desk. There she asked for the registration card and it was then that she discovered that her new acquaintance's name was not James Turner but John Robinson. Worried and distraught, Kate called the Lenexa Police, who, on hearing that Robinson was involved, afforded her complaint the utmost priority.

The detective who arrived at the hotel in response to Kate's call was David Brown, who had been investigating Robinson since the disappearance of Suzette Trouten more than two months earlier. Convinced that Robinson was a killer, Brown was not going to risk leaving another woman in the position of being a potential victim. When he had heard Kate's tearful story, he got her to collect up her belongings and moved her to another hotel.

The next day, 20 May, Kate gave Brown a full interview in which she recounted how she had met 'James Turner' via the internet, and how she had been invited to Kansas to embark on a master–slave relationship. She told him that Robinson had beaten her with a violence far beyond her desires, explaining that she didn't go in for pain and punishment or marks on her skin. 'I'm a submissive, not a masochist,' she said.

The complaints and statements from Jeanne and Kate gave the

police justification to arrest the man who had been the subject of their investigation into the unexplained disappearances of several women. On Friday, 2 June, nine police cars drove to the Santa Barbara Estates and surrounded 36 Monterey. Detectives from one car arrested John E. Robinson and charged him with sexual assault. By the end of the following few days, he would willingly have settled for such a simple charge. Visibly shocked, Robinson was handcuffed and driven to the Johnson County Jail. At the same time police officers and detectives spilled from the other cars and began to execute a search warrant for the Robinson home.

There, as well as seizing all five of Robinson's computers, the police discovered a blank sheet of paper which had been signed by Lisa Stasi more than 15 years earlier, in January 1985. Also found were receipts from the Rodeway Inn, in Overland Park, which showed that Robinson had checked Lisa out of the hotel on 10 January that year, the day after she and her baby Tiffany had last been seen alive by the Klinginsmith family. However, those first scraps of evidence were only the tip of a gigantic iceberg. Much more was to come to light over the next few days and it would horrify those who found it.

The police investigation had been thorough and had revealed all property owned or rented by Robinson. Consequently, a second search warrant had been obtained for that morning and, while Robinson was being driven to jail, detectives were busy searching his storage locker in Olathe. There they found a cornucopia of items connecting him to two of the missing women, Izabel Lewicka and Suzette Trouten. They found Suzette's birth certificate, her Social Security card, several sheets of blank paper signed 'Love ya, Suzette' and a slave contract signed by her. Along with these they found Izabel's driving licence, several photographs of her, nude and in bondage, a slave contract and several BDSM implements. They also found a stun gun and a pillowcase.

On the following day, Saturday, 3 June, another search warrant was served. This time the search team descended on the Robinsons' farmland near La Cygne. They found two 55-gallon metal barrels near a shed and opened one. Inside was the body of a naked woman, head down and immersed in a fluid which had resulted from the body's decomposition.

The detective who opened the barrel, Harold Hughes, a forensic crime-scene investigator, turned his attention to the second barrel and prised open the lid. Inside he found a pillow and a pillowcase, which he removed. Underneath he found another body. Again it was that of a woman, but this one was clothed. Like the first body, however, it was immersed in the fluid of its own decomposition. Hughes completed the customary procedures of photographing and fingerprinting the barrels before resealing them and marking them 'Unknown 1' and 'Unknown 2'.

Later that day, Stephen Haymes, Robinson's former probation officer, was told of the discovery of the bodies. After so many years of suspicion, his judgement of Robinson was vindicated. He later told David McClintick, 'It confirmed what I had always believed, but the move from theory to reality was chilling.'

At the time that Haymes was learning of the Robinson arrest, the District Attorney for Johnson County, Paul Morrison, was contacting his counterpart in Cass County, across the border in Missouri, in order to negotiate the issue of another search warrant. Detectives had discovered that Robinson maintained a locker at the Stor-Mor-for-Less depot in Raymore, a Missouri suburb of

Kansas City. As an influential figure Morrison was given the utmost cooperation in cutting through the red tape involved when issues of this sort are handled by more than one State. As a result of his discussion, he and a group of detectives from Johnson County arrived at the office of Cass County's Deputy Prosecutor, Mark Tracy, early the next morning. They carried with them the longest affidavit in support of a search warrant that Tracy had ever seen. It asserted that Robinson was believed to have killed several women and that it was suspected that evidence, connected with the killings, was hidden in the storage locker at Raymore. He had paid for the rental of the locker with a company cheque, in order to conceal his identity. It also mentioned that he had lured his victims via the internet.

At 8am on the Monday morning, Tracy served the search warrant at the storage depot and the Johnson County detectives were led to Robinson's locker. Inside was a lot of clutter and the task force had spent more than half an hour sifting through it when, hidden at the back, they saw three barrels. Wafting from the barrels came the nauseating, unmistakable smell of decomposing flesh.

As it was virtually certain that the barrels contained dead bodies, Tracy summoned his boss, Christopher Koster, and the State of Missouri assumed immediate control of the crime scene. A new team of police investigators arrived and the locker was emptied of all its contents except the three barrels. These were found to be standing on piles of cat litter: obviously a futile attempt by Robinson to reduce the smell which was emanating from them.

The first barrel was opened, to reveal a light-brown sheet, a pair of spectacles and a shoe. When the crime-lab technician had removed the sheet, he took hold of the shoe, only to find that there was a foot inside it and the foot was still attached to a leg. On the assumption that the storage depot was not the best place to investigate the barrels and their contents, it was decided to reseal them and take them to the Medical Examiner's office in Kansas City. This was not as simple as it seemed. There was a real fear that the bottoms of the barrels might have corroded and would give way, so a police officer was sent to a nearby Wal-Mart to buy three children's plastic paddling pools and these were slipped underneath the barrels before they were loaded on to a truck.

Back at the Medical Examiner's office, the barrels were opened and, as expected, each contained the severely decomposed body of a female. Each had been beaten to death with an instrument, probably a hammer, and had been dead for some years. The first body was fully clothed but the second was wearing only a T-shirt. In its mouth was a denture which was broken in two. Body number three was that of a teenager and was wearing green trousers and a silver beret. Identification was not immediately possible and was going to take some days.

Over in Kansas, in Topeka, the two bodies found on the Robinson property were identified, through a forensic odontologist, as Izabel Lewicka and Suzette Trouten. Both women had very recently been reported missing and were easier to trace.

A few days later, again with the help of a forensic odontologist, two of the bodies that had been found at the storage depot were identified. One was Beverly Bonner and the other was Sheila Faith. Sheila's daughter, Debbie, who suffered from spina bifida, was identified as the third body, by means of a spinal X-ray.

It was more than a year after his arrest before John E. Robinson stood trial in Kansas for the three murders that had been committed in that State's jurisdiction. The trial lasted for six weeks and the jury found him guilty. In January 2003, Judge John Anderson III sentenced Robinson to death for the Lewicka and Trouten murders and to life imprisonment for the murder of Lisa Stasi.

In October that year, after some prolonged bargaining, Robinson was brought to trial in Missouri pleading guilty to the murder of Beverly Bonner and Sheila and Debbie Faith, whose bodies had all been found in barrels. He also pleaded guilty to having murdered Paula Godfrey and Catherine Clampitt, neither of whose bodies has been found. In return for the plea of guilty, Robinson received life sentences without parole for all five killings. The plea arrangement had allowed him to escape the death penalty for three of the murders. Given that Missouri is more likely to execute than Kansas, that was important to Slavemaster.

Missouri Prosecutor Christopher Koster acknowledged that many people had wished for Robinson to receive the death penalty but he asserted that it had been important to resolve the deaths of Paula Godfrey and Catherine Clampitt. A guilty plea would not have been forthcoming had the death penalty been in the equation and in this way it had brought closure to the families of the two women.

Paula Godfrey's father, William, described his daughter fondly and said of the effect her disappearance had had on his wife, who died from cancer in 1993, 'After she disappeared, my wife was a changed woman. A big part of her was ripped away. John Robinson, you took away from our family our oldest daughter that we all loved so much.'

John E. Robinson now lives on Death Row in Kansas.

Patricia Joann Wells Jennings

When one checks out an offender's Department of Corrections status and it highlights 'Total Term – Death', the succinctness has an uncompromising quality that speaks volumes. In the case of Patricia Jennings, it relates to her having murdered her husband in a violent and savage manner.

On Tuesday, 19 September 1989, Patricia beat and tortured her husband, William Henry Jennings, aged 80, to death in a hotel bedroom in Wilson, North Carolina. At trial, she claimed that he suffered dementia and had inflicted the wounds himself.

The oddly matched couple had met in June 1983, while Patricia was employed as a nurse at Westwood Manor Nursing Home. Jennings, a retired businessman, was an active member of Alcoholics Anonymous and had been called to the nursing home for a consultation. It is doubtful if it was love at first sight, but a relationship developed between the two over several years and in February 1987 they married. She was 44 and he was 77.

It was transparently obvious that the new Mrs Jennings didn't anticipate that she would ever be celebrating a Silver Wedding anniversary. Shortly after their marriage William agreed to take his wife to see George Henry, a financial consultant at Merrill Lynch. The two men had known each other for 20 years. The purpose of the meeting, as Henry later testified, was to transfer half of Jennings's assets, which then totalled about $150,000, into his new wife's name. A bank account was opened and half of Jennings's assets were deposited in it. Betraying a sign or two of greed, Patricia attempted to persuade her far from sprightly husband to make out a will. By its terms, in the event of his death the remainder of his estate would pass to her as sole beneficiary. However, William wasn't happy with the proposed arrangement and refused to comply.

This show of defiance incensed Patricia and she started abusing and beating her elderly husband. Jennings became terrified that she might kill him, or have him committed to an institution, if he didn't sign the will, so he consulted his lawyer, Knox Jenkins – later a Superior Court Judge – who had a practice in the town of Smithfield.

Sitting in the lawyer's office, Jennings described how his wife had physically beaten him, dragged him across the room and stamped on him with her cowboy boots. 'She threatened to stomp me to death,' the frail man added, 'so I have to sign the will, so please draw it up for me.'

The will remained unsigned because Jennings never returned to Jenkins's office owing to his having been murdered.

On 19 September 1989, William and Patricia Jennings were staying at the Hampton Inn, South Tarboro Street, Wilson. At about 9.30pm, Patricia called the desk and said she had a 'Code Blue'. The hotel manager called 911 and an ambulance arrived five minutes later. The paramedics went to the room and found Patricia performing CPR on her husband, who was lying nude on the floor. When technician Larry Parnell asked her, 'How long has he been down?' she replied, 'Between five and ten minutes.' This puzzled the paramedics as it was very much at odds with the man's condition; his skin was cool and his body was generally stiff. Paramedic Lee Fowler noted, 'Mrs Jennings was wearing a flimsy black nightgown and brown cowboy boots.'

Cold and stiff as a board, William Jennings was rushed to the Wilson Memorial Hospital, where he was pronounced dead. In fact, the local Medical Examiner, Dr Andrew Price, having immediately examined the man's body, suggested that he had been dead between six and eight hours.

Dr Page Hudson, forensic pathologist and former Chief Medical Examiner for the State of North Carolina, performed an autopsy on Jennings on 20 September and found multiple bruises and scrapes on various parts of his head, scalp, face, legs, arms and hands. All the injuries appeared fresh.

There was a large bruise in the mesentery of the abdominal cavity – the tissue which holds in and supports the intestines and contains blood vessels to the intestines. Dr Hudson formed the opinion that a blunt-force impact to the abdominal wall caused the tears in the mesentery, and the resultant blood loss was the cause of death. Patricia had lived up to her threats and had stamped her husband to death wearing her cowboy boots.

The autopsy also revealed evidence of even greater levels of savagery in the treatment that she had meted out to William

Jennings. On examining the man's penis, Dr Hudson found injuries in the form of skin-peeling, scrapes and cuts around the head and along the shaft – his wife had used forceps to skin his penis while he was still alive.

Unable to persuade the jury that her husband had beaten himself to death, Patricia Jennings was convicted of first-degree murder and now sits on North Carolina's Death Row.

Christina Marie Riggs

'I'll be with my children and with God.
I'll be where there is no more pain.
Maybe I'll find some peace.'

Christina Riggs before her execution

At 9.28 on the evening of Tuesday, 2 May 2000, Christina Riggs was executed by a lethal injection of potassium chloride. Her crime was the murder of her children, five-year-old Justin Thomas and two-year-old Shelby Alexis. Potassium chloride was the very same drug that she had used when killing her son and with which she had attempted to take her own life on Tuesday, 4 November 1997 at her home in Sherwood, Arkansas.

On the morning of the murders, 26-year-old Riggs had obtained the anti-depressant Elavil from her pharmacist. She then obtained the painkiller morphine and the toxic potassium chloride from the hospital where she worked as a nurse. She gave each of the children a small amount of Elavil to put them to sleep. Then she placed them both in their beds. About 10pm, she injected Justin with undiluted potassium chloride. However, she didn't know that unless diluted this drug, as any condemned person strapped to an execution gurney will confirm, causes intense burning and excruciating pain. One person who survived such an injection described it as 'having the fires of hell burning through your veins'. As the drug took effect, Justin woke up and screamed in pain and terror. Horrified at this, his weeping mother administered morphine to quell the pain and then smothered the little boy to death with a pillow.

Moving to two-year-old Shelby, and still in shock from the agony she had caused to her son, Riggs suffocated her daughter with a pillow. She then placed the bodies of her two dead children side by side on her bed and covered them with a blanket. That done, she set about ending her own life. After writing suicide notes, she took 28 Elavil tablets, an amount considered to be a lethal dose, and then injected herself with undiluted potassium chloride in a dose sufficient to kill five people. Shortly after this, the Elavil took effect and she collapsed unconscious to the floor.

The following morning Riggs didn't arrive for work. Her mother, Carol Thomas, phoned her but, after getting no reply, drove round to her daughter's home and let herself in.

Waiting for her inside the house was a nightmare. She found her two grandchildren dead. Then she saw her daughter lying on the floor and thought that she too was dead. The woman was profoundly shocked. 'All I could do was turn around and around and scream and holler, "No. No. No,"' Carol Thomas said. 'There's no way to describe how I felt.' She punched 911 into her mobile phone. 'My daughter and her babies are dead!' she cried.

Police officers David Smith and Steve Henker arrived and found that Christina Riggs was still alive. As she had lain unconscious, the undiluted potassium chloride had burned a hole in her arm that was described as being as big as a silver dollar. Barely alive, she was taken to the Baptist Memorial Medical Center emergency room in North Little Rock. Doctors stabilised the woman and later moved her to intensive care. The police, who had found the syringes and the suicide notes, kept her under guard.

The next day, when it was considered that she was sufficiently recovered, Riggs was arrested and charged with the murder of her two children. Her trial took place in June 1998, some seven months after the event, at Pulaski County Circuit Court. She entered a plea of not guilty by reason of mental disease or defect.

Her defence attorneys did not dispute the charge that she had killed her two children. They argued that she had been driven to the terrible act through circumstances. She had a long-standing history of depression and very low self-esteem. Here was a struggling single mother who was very poor. She was also very overweight at around 280 pounds and could see no way out of her life of perpetual hardship. It also seemed manifestly clear that, at the time she killed her children, she had every intention of killing herself too. One psychiatrist testified that she was a mentally ill woman who suffered severe depression which led her to believe that it was 'an act of love' to take her children with her. The jury found Riggs guilty and she was sentenced to death.

Christina Riggs's life was one of years of abuse, severe depression and failed relationships with men. Born in Lawton, Oklahoma, she grew up in Oklahoma City. Between the ages of seven and thirteen, she was sexually abused by her stepbrother and had also suffered sexual abuse at the hands of a neighbour. When she was 14, she began drinking and smoking marijuana. At this time she began to be sexually promiscuous. She later wrote in her prison journal, 'I felt that no boy liked me because of my weight, so I became sexually promiscuous because I thought that was the only way I could have a boyfriend.'

At the age of 16, Christina became pregnant. She gave birth to a baby boy in January 1988 and gave the child up for adoption.

After leaving high school, she became a licensed practical nurse. She found part-time work as a home-care nurse and full-time work at a Veterans Administration hospital.

Riggs dated several men before she settled into a relationship with Timothy Thompson, who was stationed at Tinker Air Force Base. In late October 1991, she learned she was pregnant again. She told Thompson about the baby the day before his discharge from the service. Unable to accept that he was the father, Thompson abandoned her and moved back to his home State of Minnesota.

Riggs's mother later said, 'Chrissie's luck with men was about zero to nothing.'

Following Thompson's departure, the pregnant Christina rekindled an old relationship with a sailor, Jon Riggs, while he was home on leave. On 7 June 1992, the baby, a boy, was born, and he was given the name Justin. Jon Riggs eventually moved in with Christina and after she again became pregnant they married in July 1993. However, tragedy struck on the wedding night when Christina miscarried.

The relationship had been a troubled one and the marriage

continued in that vein, always veering in the direction of divorce. Christina suffered from depression, which she attributed to prescribed birth-control medication. She was prescribed Prozac to combat the depression, but when she began to feel better she stopped taking it. After becoming pregnant again, in December 1994 she gave birth to a little girl, Shelby Alexis.

The following year the couple moved to Sherwood to live beside Christina's mother, Carol Thomas. Both children had health problems and it was hoped that their grandmother would help in looking after them during the day so that Christina could go to work. Shelby had a series of ear infections, and Justin's attention deficit disorder and hyperactivity made him more than a handful, Thomas said. In any event, Christina got a job at the Baptist Memorial Medical Center.

Almost inevitably, however, the Riggs's marriage fell apart. They divorced and Jon Riggs moved back to Oklahoma City after he had punched Justin in the stomach so hard that the boy required medical attention. Justin was crushed: 'My daddy hurt me, and then he went away,' he sobbed to his grandmother.

That seems to have been the point at which Christina Riggs's life accelerated downhill. Child support payments from Jon were only spasmodic and, despite working extremely long hours, she found herself losing the struggle to keep on top of her finances. By the time she came to the decision to end her life and the lives of her children, she had lost all belief in her ability to continue. Her car registration and insurance had expired and she could not afford to renew them. She was writing cheques that would bounce and the pressure on her showed no sign of letting up. She said later in prison, 'I started out in a boat with a small hole. But the hole kept getting bigger and, no matter how hard you bail, you keep sinking. I was tired and I gave up. Suicide seemed like the only thing.'

Three days before her execution, Christina Riggs was taken to the Cummins Unit at Pine Bluffs. She had waived her right to appeal against the death sentence and had spent almost two years in isolation on Death Row. On Tuesday, 2 May 2000, of her own free will, she walked to her execution. Her last words, strapped to the gurney, were: 'There is no way words can express how sorry I am for taking the lives of my babies. Now I can be with my babies, as I always intended.' She also said, 'I love you, my babies.'

The execution went smoothly and she was certified dead nine minutes later.

Robert Lee Yates

'Bobby is a loving, caring and sensitive son, a fun-loving and giving brother, an understanding, generous and dedicated father, who enjoys playing ball, fishing and camping with his kids. We feel deeply for the families who have experienced loss,' the statement said. 'We ask that all judgments be reserved until the timely due process of law has been completed.' It was signed: 'the Robert L. Yates family members'.

Patrick Oliver, Susan Savage, Yolanda Sapp, Melinda Mercer, Stacey Hawn, Patricia Barnes, Connie LaFontaine Ellis, Shannon Zielinski, Jennifer Joseph, Heather Hernandez, Darla Sue Scott, Shawn Johnson, Laurel Wason, Sunny G. Oster, Linda Maybin, Melody Murfin, Michelyn Derning and Shawn McClenahan: one man and 17 women with an unenviable common bond. They are all believed to be murdered victims of Robert Lee Yates, known as the 'Spokane Serial Killer'. Chillingly, it is very probable that the list is incomplete.

Robert Lee Yates was born on Sunday, 27 May 1952 in Spokane, Washington State, and grew up in the town of Oak Harbor on Whidbey Island, situated in Puget Sound, roughly halfway between Seattle and Vancouver Island.

His upbringing was middle-class and his family were regulars at a local Seventh Day Adventist church. Although there are reports that at the age of six he was sexually molested by an older brother, Robert's early life seemed otherwise normal.

In 1970 Yates graduated from high school and enrolled in college at Walla Walla, one of the so-called Tri-Cities in the lower east of the State. Here he earned a diploma, but dropped out after a mere two years. On Sunday, 27 August 1972, he married his first wife, Shirley Nylander; it was to last until March 1974, when they separated. However, that same year, on 14 July, he tied the knot with Linda Dawn Brewer and they went on to have four daughters and a son.

In the summer of 1975 Yates began employment at the Washington State Penitentiary as a correctional officer. Four months later he enlisted in the US Army and became a helicopter pilot flying OH-58D Kiowa reconnaissance aircraft. And, to his credit, he also qualified to fly civilian transport planes and helicopters. In July 1980, he was promoted to Warrant Officer and was based at Fort Rucker, Alaska.

During his 19 years in the Army, Yates served overseas. He was in Germany from August 1980 to February 1984, and again from May 1988 to May 1991. He fought in Iraq in 1990 and was seconded to the ill-fated UN peacekeeping mission in Somalia during the early 1990s.

Throughout his military career, he served with distinction, receiving three meritorious service medals, three Army commendation medals, three Army achievement medals and two Armed Forces expeditionary medals, as well as a Humanitarian Service Medal for participating in a relief mission to South Florida to help clean up the devastation left by Hurricane Andrew in 1992. He retired with an honourable discharge on 1 April 1995.

In April 1996, Yates rented a house at 2021 East 59th Street, Spokane, although he didn't completely sever his contract with the military because he joined the National Guard in 1997, attaining the rank of Chief Warrant Officer (Grade 4). His fellow guardsmen all respected him; he was the only member in his area capable of flying a Kiowa and he was considered a truly professional soldier.

The following year, he bought his own home at 2220 East 49th Street. This, then, is the family man and respected military veteran who, for reasons known only to himself, led a second, secret and very sordid life involving drugs, prostitutes and multiple murder, becoming one of the most prolific serial killers of recent years.

It is probable that the killing had started way back on Sunday, 13 July 1975, with the murders of 22-year-old Susan P. Savage and Patrick A. Oliver, 21. Savage, a recent graduate of Washington State University, and Oliver, a pre-med student, were swimming and picnicking together along Mill Creek, about 12 miles east of Walla Walla. Both were shot several times. Robert Lee Yates, a prison guard at the time, was still only 23.

And, if that is when it began, it lay dormant until 15 years later, when, around 8.30am on Thursday, 22 February 1990, the homicide division of the Spokane Police Department received a call to go to the 4100 block of East Upriver Drive, where the nude body of a young black woman had been discovered on the embankment of the Spokane River.

Although no spent bullets or shell cases were found, it appeared from the entrance wounds that the girl had been killed with a small-calibre handgun, a .22 or a .25. There was no clothing with the body, only the victim's black wig, two blankets and a towel. One of the blankets looked like a military-issue type, the other was multi-coloured and the towel was white. Detectives had nothing else to go on, despite an extensive search of the area. Given the paucity of evidence, it appeared possible that the girl had been killed elsewhere and transported to the spot where her body was found.

When the details of the discovery were made public, the dead woman was identified as Yolanda Sapp, a 26-year-old prostitute. She had a record of arrests for prostitution and was a known drug user. Friends who knew her said that the last time she was seen alive, in the East Sprague district of Spokane, she had been wearing black jeans, black slip-on flat-soled shoes, black panties, a black T-shirt and a beige rabbit-fur coat. These were all missing, as were nine wrist bracelets, a necklace, two rings and her denim purse.

Another body, bearing the hallmarks of the same killer, was discovered near the Spokane River at around 7.45pm on Tuesday, 15 May 1990. The victim, a white female, was naked. Injuries to her head persuaded the police that she had been hit with a blunt object. Two gunshot wounds were deemed to have been the cause of death, and at autopsy two spent small-calibre bullets were recovered from the body. Around the crime scene, investigators recovered some of the victim's clothing, including her shoes, as well as a plastic bag that bore bloodstains. They also found tyre tracks.

The victim was identified as Kathleen Brisbois, 38, believed to have been a prostitute. An autopsy revealed the presence of morphine and cocaine metabolites in her body. The similarities in

140

the deaths, including the use of a small-calibre gun, convinced the police that they were looking at the work of an emerging serial killer. Nevertheless, with no obvious clue to the murderer's identity, detectives could do nothing but wait.

Almost two years passed without any further killings, during which time it was thought that maybe the killer had moved away, or even changed his methods, throwing investigators off his scent. All went quiet.

However, the silence was breached on Wednesday, 13 May 1992, on Bill Gulch Road, Spokane, when a nude Caucasian female body was found.

A plastic bag covered the victim's head and some of her clothing and her shoes were present at the site. The body was identified as that of Sherry Anne Palmer, at 19 the youngest of the victims so far. Despite her youth, Palmer was a prostitute but had no record of having used drugs. She had last been seen almost a fortnight earlier, on the evening of Friday, 1 May, at Al's Motel in Spokane, a place that was known to be used by prostitutes and their clients. She had left the motel at around 11pm and taken a taxicab to meet her boyfriend. She failed to arrive at the rendezvous.

An autopsy revealed that Sherry Anne Palmer had died from a gunshot wound to the head. There was an absence of blood pooling in the vicinity of the body, which led investigators to believe that the girl had been killed elsewhere and brought by a vehicle to the place where she was dumped and subsequently found. And, it was to be another three years before the next victim of the Spokane Serial Killer turned up, and this time it was near Tacoma, on the other side of Washington State.

The naked body of a 60-year-old woman, Patricia Barnes, was

discovered on Friday, 25 August 1995 in the vicinity of Peacock Hill Road, in Kitsap County. Detective Ron Trogdon of Kitsap County Sheriff's Department went to the scene and noticed that the body was partially covered by cut foliage. The notable fact about this was that the foliage had come from somewhere else. Trogdon also found a number of hair curlers at the scene. There was nothing else. About a mile further up the road, however, investigators found more pieces of the same type of foliage and among it they found a plastic bag containing hair curlers similar to those that were near the body. In the same place there was also some blood, which was found to be that of the dead woman.

Trogdon's enquiries revealed that the dead woman, Barnes, was a woman of the streets, although not a prostitute, and that she had been last seen alive in Seattle on or around 22 August. She was not known to be a drug user but drank alcohol, some of which was found in her system during autopsy. She had been killed by being shot twice with a .22-calibre gun, and the two bullets were found in her. The evidence from the scene of her body's discovery indicated that she had been killed elsewhere and her body had been subsequently transported and then dumped.

Less than a year after the emergence of the remains of Patricia Barnes, the body of another murdered woman was discovered in Spokane. She too had been shot dead and it appeared to be the work of the same killer. The decomposed remains of 39-year-old Shannon R. Zielinski were found near the junction of Mount Spokane Park Drive and Holcomb Road on Friday, 14 June 1996. Unlike Patricia Barnes, this victim was still wearing clothing, a short grey dress, and a towel had been draped across her torso. Her pantyhose, a high black boot and a pair of white socks were found near the body. Other than that, there was no means of identifying the victim and it was left to fingerprint analysis to establish who she had been. A spent shell case was found at the scene. However, the absence of any significant amount of blood at the scene suggested that she too had been killed elsewhere and then transported to the spot where she was found. Detective Marvin R. Hill, later of the Spokane Police Department's Serial Murder Task Force, investigated the dead woman's background and found that she was involved in prostitution and was a drug user. However, by this time, her body was too decomposed for any meaningful analysis in the form of toxicology tests. Hill did find out that she had last been seen by a police officer a little over a fortnight earlier, on 27 May, in the Sprague district of Spokane, drinking with a group of men. Witnesses asserted that she had been wearing the same dress when she had gone out that evening to work as a prostitute and no one remembered seeing her since then.

On that same day, 26 August, another victim was discovered on Forker Road, Spokane. The body was that of a 16-year-old Asian girl, Jennifer Joseph. She had died from multiple gunshot wounds and was identified by means of her fingerprints as there was no form of ID to be found at the scene. A light-blue towel was found with the body and she was wearing black trousers, a blouse minus one of its pearl buttons, panties and shoes. Also found were a used condom and a length of radio antenna. As with the other dead women, it appeared that Jennifer Joseph had been killed elsewhere and then dumped at the spot where her body was found. An autopsy revealed evidence that the girl had probably put up some sort of a struggle with her killer.

Detective Rick Grabenstein of the Spokane Serial Murder Task

Force investigated the murdered girl's movements in the time leading up to her disappearance and found another prostitute who had been working with her in East Sprague on the last occasion on which she was seen alive. This girl said that she had last seen Joseph ten days earlier, on 16 August, at around 11.35pm. She had been travelling in a white Corvette driven by a white male of about 30–40. Although they did not know it at the time, this sighting of the white Corvette turned out to be the first break for the police in identifying the Spokane Serial Killer.

On 29 November 1997, a Spokane County Health District employee who worked with prostitutes reported 34-year-old Linda M. Maybin as missing. Maybin had last been seen on 21 November, by a police officer on East Sprague Avenue. It was four months before she would be seen again but by then she was no longer alive. Her badly decomposed body was found on Wednesday, 1 April 1998, near the spot where, meanwhile, back in December, the bodies of two more victims, Laurel Wason and Shawn McClenahan, had been found: the 4800 block of East 14th Avenue, Spokane. Maybin's body was fully clothed but badly decomposed and had been disturbed by animals. Remnants of plastic bags were found around her head. It was evident that the body had lain there for some time but it was not known for how long. Having found the body in such close proximity to where Wason and McClenahan had been discovered, the police carried out an intensive search of the area, but they found no further bodies.

Investigators learned that Linda Maybin was a user of crack cocaine and that she usually carried a pipe for smoking the drug. She kept the pipe tucked inside her pants but it was not there when she was found. Also missing was a cloth bag, possibly velvet, with a drawstring, that she always carried with her.

'On 12/18/ 97, a female body was discovered in the 11400 block of South Hangman Valley Road, Spokane County, Washington by witness Michael Connors. Crime Scene investigation was done by Detectives Grabenstein, Henderson, Francis and Madsen, as well as Ident Officers Julie Combs and Deb Rowles. No purse, wallet or money found on victim. A vehicle was used to transport victim to the body recovery site. On 12/22/97 an autopsy performed by Dr George Lindholm and P.A. Randy Shaber. At this time the victim was identified as SHAWN L JOHNSON., dob 03/27/61. Two plastic bags covered the victim's head. The cause of death was determined to be two gunshot wounds to the head and both projectiles were recovered. Oral, anal and vaginal swabs were also obtained. Investigation revealed that Johnson was involved in prostitution and illicit drugs.'

The police report makes cold reading. But this is the way it is when a body is found: there is no room for emotion. The discovery on 18 December 1997 of yet another victim of the murderer known as the Spokane Serial Killer was officially, and impersonally, recorded. And so it was for each of his victims.

It was on 26 December 1997 that the bodies of Laurel Wason and Shawn McClenahan were found. They were discovered by Fred Dullanty at 4800 East 14th Avenue, Spokane. Both were Caucasian women and both were clothed but shoeless. Each victim had three plastic bags over her head and had been shot twice in the head. Once again the evidence attached to the bodies indicated that they had both been killed elsewhere before being dumped. On and around the bodies, investigators found samples of several types of plant life which, according to the police report, was 'not indigenous to that specific area'. In addition to the vegetation there were traces of soil, rock, wood, paint and other debris as well as a plant identification tag for a Sweet William. There was also a dyed red feather. The nature of the debris and the efforts made by the killer to conceal the bodies inclined investigators towards the theory that they may have at some time been at the killer's home.

Autopsies were performed on Laurel Wason, 31, and Shawn McClenahan, 39, by Dr George Lindholm. It emerged that both women had been wearing coats but both coats were missing when the bodies were found. McClenahan had been wearing a blue nylon coat and Wason a black trench coat. It crossed the minds of investigators that the coats may have been kept as bizarre trophies by the killer. Both women were involved in prostitution and the use of illicit drugs.

Two months later, on 8 February 1998, another woman's body was found in a ditch on Graham Road, a rural part of Spokane County. This woman had been shot dead and, like Wason and McClenahan, had three plastic bags over her head. Like those two victims, this woman was still fully clothed but without shoes, although these were found near the body. The victim was identified as a prostitute by the name of Sunny Gail Oster. Born on 7 August 1956, she was 41. Oster was a known drug user and had last been seen, working as a prostitute on East Sprague Avenue, on 1 November 1997. At the time she was seen, she was carrying a beige purse, but that was now missing and, investigators believed, may have been kept as a trophy.

It was the summer of 1998 before the next victim of the Spokane Serial Killer was discovered. A witness, Gordon Orlund, found a woman's body at a vacant lot beside 218 North Crestline, Spokane, on Tuesday, 7 July. The naked body was that of 47-year-old Michelyn Derning, a prostitute, who had last been seen alive three days earlier. Derning had grown up in southern California and worked in a variety of odd jobs before moving to Spokane to stay with a friend. As well as the body being naked, the woman's lower denture was missing. Investigators were told that the denture had had her name engraved on it. The body was covered with items of debris from around the site, including two hot-tub covers and a piece of Styrofoam. At autopsy it was established that the dead woman had died from gunshot wounds, and methamphetamine was found in her body.

On Tuesday, 13 October, officers from Pierce County Sheriff's Department in Tacoma went to the 1700 block of 108th Street South, where a man named Bruce Cheshier had found the badly decomposed body of a Caucasian woman. She was Connie L. LaFontaine Ellis, a prostitute and known drug user and she had been killed by a gunshot wound to her head. Three plastic bags had been placed over the woman's head and detectives immediately linked this murder to the Spokane Serial Killer and notified their counterparts in Spokane, even though Tacoma is in the west of the State and Spokane is across in the east, almost on the border with Idaho.

LaFontaine Ellis was known to have carried a 9mm pistol and a 9mm bullet was found at the scene. However, her gun was missing. Investigators believed that she had been shot with her own weapon.

It is important to remember that, when each body was found, the area in which it was recovered and indeed the body itself were subjected to intense examination for clues, no matter how small. In each case, samples of such materials as fibres and hair were retained in sealed bags. This is standard practice. At autopsy, swabs, oral, anal and vaginal were taken from each of the dead women, along with other items recovered from the body such as spent bullets. This evidence was later examined microscopically, analysed and tested as part of the investigation, and some of the information that it revealed was crucial in pinpointing the identity of the killer.

The detectives conducting the investigation into the murders of the prostitutes spent a vast amount of time in those areas where the women most frequently worked, much of it under cover. However, it was a uniformed patrolman who made the first recorded contact with Robert Lee Yates Jr when he stopped him for a minor traffic infringement on Wednesday, 24 September 1997 in the vicinity of Sprague and Ralph. When stopped, Yates was driving a white 1977 Corvette. The Washington licence plate was KIH442. Yates was simply given a ticket and allowed to go. Although the patrolman did not know it, he had just given a ticket to the Spokane Serial Killer and the white Corvette was the car in which Jennifer Joseph had last been seen alive on 16 August that same year. Nor was the connection made straight away by the Task Force because the patrolman had mistakenly described the car as a Camaro when he wrote his report. The error wasn't picked up until later when the Task Force investigators checked the registration of the 'Camaro' and found that it was actually a Corvette. In May 1998, Yates sold the Corvette to Rita Jones.

About a month after the discovery of the murdered body of Connie LaFontaine Ellis, police officers in Spokane, near the corner of 1st and Crestline, an area frequented by prostitutes, observed a silver 1985 Honda Civic, Washington licence plate 918AJH. It was Tuesday, 10 November 1998, at around 1.25am, when the car pulled over and the driver picked up a prostitute by the name of Jennifer Robinson. The officers identified Robert Lee Yates as the driver of the Honda.

Confronted by a police officer, Yates denied that he was picking up Jennifer Robinson for sex. Instead, he told them that he was a friend of Robinson's father, who had asked him to go to the area, collect his daughter and bring her home. The problem for the police was that, in order to save herself from being arrested, Robinson herself corroborated Yates's story, saying she knew him. They could not make an arrest and had to let him go. However, the officer did file a report on the incident and this was passed to detectives of the Task Force.

In early 1999, detectives came across a report that had been filed the previous summer. It proved to be an important step forward. On 1 August 1998, a prostitute named Christine L. Smith reported an assault that had been made on her. The following is an extract from the police officer's report on the incident:

'At about 0327 hours on 08/1/98 I responded to Sacred Heart Hospital in reference to an assault report. Upon arrival, I contacted Christine L. Smith. She told me the following. At about 0100 hours she was working as a prostitute in the area of the mental health building on East Sprague in Spokane WA. She said she was picked up in front of a beauty supply store a couple of blocks away from the mental health building. She described the vehicle as a black colour 70s model van. She noticed some kind of orange colouring on the passenger side of the van but she wasn't sure if it was a sticker or paint. She described the inside of the van as follows. There were dark brown vinyl seats and possibly carpet on the floor. Inside of the van was neatly kept.

'She described the driver as a white male, approximately 50 years of age, 5ft. 10ins, 175lbs. Medium build with sandy blonde hair and blue eyes. His hair was average length, cut above the collar but not buzz cut. She did not note anything odd about his hair. She said, "It just sort of hung there." He had no facial hair and a slightly pockmarked complexion.

'The suspect was wearing shorts, possibly blue in colour, with a belt. He wore a shirt but she is uncertain what kind of shirt it is. She was reasonably certain it was not a t-shirt. She did not notice any tattoos or scars. After she got into the van she made the comment, "You're not the psycho-killer are you?" His response to that was, "There sure are a lot of cops out tonight." She said she was sure he heard her but he never answered her question. She said he did not seem nervous to her at all. She also noted that he was not intoxicated. I asked her if this was something she always noted about her Johns and she said "yes".

'She told the suspect to drive up behind the Rockwood clinic, so he did. During the ride he told her he was a helicopter pilot for the National Guard. He also made the statement well after she asked him that he was not the killer because he said he had 5 kids and wouldn't do that. Their conversation continued and she told him the prices for sexual favours.

'Once they arrived in the area where she directed him to go he moved the van to a darker area. She said they were behind the Rockwood clinic parked on the street by the St Luke's Rehabilitation Center. The suspect asked what the Rehabilitation Center was and she told him that it was part of the clinic. He said, "They probably have security don't they?" She said, "I'm sure they do."

'Once they stopped, the suspect handed her. They went to the back of the van and the suspect pulled his shorts down about halfway and…

'After the 5–7 minute time frame the suspect hit her over the head with something causing her to almost lose consciousness. She fell back and was trying to stay awake and get her wits about her. She remembered looking up at the suspect and he was just sitting there watching her. He never grabbed her or said anything. She was able to stay conscious. The suspect then told her to give him her money.

'She said, "You get it."

'He said, "No. You get it."

'She said the demand for her money seemed like an afterthought. She said it was almost as like he was trying to justify the blow to her head. She didn't think it was his initial intention just by the way he said it. She made her way to the small space between the seats of the van. She was still a little dazed from the blow to the head but she was trying to get into her pocket to get the money. The suspect said: "What was your name again?"

'She said, "Christine."

'He said, "What are we doing here?"

'She said she could feel the blood dripping from her head and she reached up to feel her head with her hand. There was blood on her hand.'

The terrified woman jumped into the front of the van and was able to get out through the passenger door. She ran to St Luke's Rehabilitation Center and tried to get in.

Eventually, by frantically pressing the emergency button in an elevator, she contacted a security guard, who drove her to the Sacred Heart Hospital.

The wound she had sustained was about half an inch long, just behind and above her left ear. It required three stitches. Blood from the wound stained her shirt extensively, round the collar and down the front of her chest.

Although she had no idea exactly what she had been hit with, evidence later came to light indicating strongly that she may have been shot: following an accident in 2000, X-rays showed that she was carrying metal fragments in her head. Moreover, when police examined the van after Yates's arrest, a spent bullet was found in the roof, above the windshield.

From the description of the man who had assaulted Smith, detectives became convinced that it was Yates. What is more, he had now been reported driving both a silver Honda and a white Corvette. In addition, he had mentioned to Smith that he had five children and was a helicopter pilot for the National Guard. In any event, it is certain now that Christine Smith had been very close to becoming another victim of the serial killer.

The white Corvette that Yates had owned until May 1998 had been his pride and joy. It also proved to be his downfall. He had often been seen washing and polishing the car, which he kept in extremely good condition. However, it was this car that finally provided the police with the break they needed to trap the serial killer.

The Corvette was the vehicle in which Jennifer Joseph had last been seen travelling as a passenger. As part of their investigation, detectives had compiled a database of all white Corvette owners in Washington State and neighbouring Idaho. This they then cross-referenced to all people who owned such a car and had been stopped by police in the red-light area. Yates's name appeared on the list. It also came up in connection with the time that he had been stopped on the corner of Ralph and Sprague driving the Honda Civic.

On 15 September 1999, detectives interviewed Yates in Spokane's Public Safety Building. Yates was told that his name had come up during the course of their enquiries, but they did not tell him that he was a suspect. The discussion was informal and he was free to leave whenever he wished. Nor did he have to answer any questions if he chose not to. When asked about the vehicles he owned, he admitted he had owned a white Corvette but said he had sold it. The detectives touched on the incident of 10 November 1998, when he had been suspected of picking up prostitute Jennifer Robinson. Although Yates stuck to his story that he was giving the woman a lift home at the request of her father, he had trouble remembering the name of the woman and her father. The detectives warned him that they thought he was lying but he stuck to his guns. They also asked him for a blood sample but he refused to do so straight away, saying he would think about it.

Yates called the investigators a couple of days later to decline their request for a blood sample. Given that they already knew he had lied to them, this made him an even stronger suspect in their hunt for the killer.

They eventually tracked down the new owner of Yates's white Corvette in January 2000. Records confirmed that Yates had owned the car from 8 September 1994 until 7 May 1998. When questioned by police, the new owner, Rita Jones, said that Yates had told her that he had changed the carpets in the car a year earlier. They took away some fibres for analysis at the Washington State Crime Laboratory. On 5 April, the lab confirmed a very close match with fibres connected with the retrieval of the body of

Jennifer Joseph. Jones allowed the police to tow the car away for a more thorough examination and this yielded evidence that connected Yates firmly to the murder of the teenage prostitute. During the search, as well as carpet fibres that matched those found on Joseph's shoes and traces of her blood that matched with samples provided by her parents, they found the button that had been missing from the 16-year-old victim's blouse. The blood smears had been found on the passenger seatbelt and the car's seats. Interestingly, evidence emerged that the carpets in the car had been changed more than once.

On 14 January 2000, detectives from the Task Force interviewed Yates's previous employer at Pantrol. This man told them that, to his knowledge, while Yates was with that company he had owned several vehicles, including a Ford pickup and a black van. He said Yates had bought the van round about June 1998 but he couldn't recall it well enough to describe it. The investigators assumed that this was the van from which Christine Smith had made her lucky escape. It also prompted the question in the detectives' minds of why Yates had not mentioned either vehicle when he had been interviewed three months earlier.

At 6.30am on Tuesday, 18 April 2000, Yates was driving on Market Street, Spokane, on his way to work at the aluminium smelter, when he was pulled over by police and arrested in connection with the killing of Jennifer Joseph. At the same time his home was cordoned off to allow investigators to begin their painstaking and exhaustive search for evidence.

A spokesman for Spokane County Sheriff's Public Information Office said, 'We are very specifically not saying he is our serial killer. We have evidence that ties him to the homicide of one prostitute.'

Within 24 hours, Robert Lee Yates Jr had been charged with the death of Jennifer Joseph. Several days passed before Sheriff Mark Sterk announced that Yates was the suspect in eight other killings: Darla Scott, Shawn Johnson, Laurel Wason, Shawn McClenahan, Melinda Mercer, Sunny Oster, Linda Maybin and Michelyn Derning.

Two other victims, Melinda L. Mercer and Connie LaFontaine Ellis, had been found across the State in Pierce County, near Tacoma, and would be dealt with separately by the authorities from that area. The two bodies were found near to Camp Murray, the headquarters of the Washington National Guard and the place where Yates conducted his monthly training with the Guard.

Following the arrest, forensic experts found Yates's fingerprints on one of the plastic bags that had been removed from victim Shawn McClenahan's head.

The search at Yates's home yielded much evidence that pointed to his being the killer of Wason, McClenahan and Maybin. Plants in his garden matched the samples found with the bodies, as did other debris. Detectives had also been able to obtain DNA samples from Yates and this matched with DNA profiles from semen found with the victims Scott, Johnson, Wason, McClenahan, Mercer, Oster, Maybin and Derning.

Shortly after the arrest, Christine Smith came forward again. She told detectives that she had seen Yates's picture in the press and believed that he was the man who had attacked her on 1 August 1998. It was at this time that she related how after a car accident she had been X-rayed for injuries and this had shown her to be carrying metal fragments in her head. Doctors had surmised that the scar was in fact an old gunshot wound. While she was not able to say with absolute certainty that Yates had been her attacker, she strongly believed that he was.

In the course of their investigation, detectives rounded up several vehicles that Yates had formerly owned. Among these was a 1979 Ford van, black with an orange or yellow stripe on the passenger side. The van's interior features matched those described by Christine Smith in her statement following her attack. Some stains found in the van tested positively as blood. Investigators found in the van a spent Magtech .25 shell case, the brand and calibre of the ammunition that had been used to kill Johnson, Wason, McClenahan, Oster, Maybin, Ellis and Mercer. They also found a spent bullet above the windshield and this, it is believed, may have been the bullet that was fired at Christine Smith.

In all, Yates stood charged with eight counts of murder in the first degree, although detectives strongly suspected him of up to 18 killings. In addition, he was charged with attempted murder in the first degree and first-degree burglary with regard to the assault on Christine Smith. He pleaded not guilty and was held without bond.

Detectives had suspected Yates of being connected to the disappearance of another woman, Melody Murfin. Forty-three-year-old Murfin was a drug addict who had last been seen alive on 20 May 1998. Because she had disappeared, and in light of her profile, detectives had every reason to believe that she had been murdered and that Yates was the prime suspect in the crime. However, in the absence of a body, investigators could do nothing.

Yates's position was such that he faced a death sentence should he be convicted of the murders. As this outcome looked almost certain, he decided to strike a deal with the prosecuting authorities. On Monday, 16 October 2000, his attorneys announced that he would plead guilty to 13 counts of first-degree murder and one count of attempted first-degree murder in exchange for a life sentence. To add weight to his bargaining position, he agreed to divulge the location of the body of Melody Murfin. He insisted, however, that he would not plead guilty to the charges awaiting him in Pierce County: the killings of Melinda L. Mercer and Connie LaFontaine Ellis.

The prosecution agreed to the deal. Accordingly, Yates sketched out a map showing the location of Melody Murfin's remains. She was buried in his own back yard. The investigation team made their way to Yates's home and began to dig. After about two hours of digging in various spots, they found Melody Murfin, or what remained of her after two years. She lay in a makeshift grave, a bark-covered flower bed, about eight inches below the surface and less than two feet away from what had been Yates's bedroom window.

On 26 October 2000, amid hissing and jeers in the courtroom, Superior Court Judge Richard Schroeder sentenced Robert Lee Yates Jr, the Spokane Serial Killer, to 14 consecutive life terms – 408 years and six months behind bars. The prison terms were the result of the plea agreement that had spared Yates a possible death sentence. The plea deal had been unpopular from the beginning, greeted with contempt and anger by the many who wanted to see Yates executed.

Lewis Kamb of the *Seattle Post* described the hostile scene in court:

'One by one, they stood at a courtroom lectern here yesterday to face the man who murdered their daughters, their mothers, their sisters, their brother. With them, they brought photos, prepared statements, memories. In a simple wooden box, one woman even brought the cremated ashes of her slain sister. And, they brought anger. Anger that seethed and lingered in a hot fourth-floor courtroom filled to capacity, anger that brought tears to the eyes of uniformed lawmen. Anger directed toward Robert Lee Yates Jr, a married father of five, a decorated Army helicopter pilot and an admitted serial killer who shifted in a high-back swivel chair and often averted his eyes from bone-chilling stares. "You need to be turned over to the families of your victims," Ondraya Smith told Yates as she read from the letter of her ex-husband, Ed Oster. Their daughter, Sunny Oster, 41, was Yates's ninth known victim in Spokane. She was dumped in a field with two bullets in her head, which was covered with three plastic bags. "To you, and the people who bargained for your life," Smith said, "may you burn in hell." Throughout the sentencing hearing yesterday, those sentiments were echoed time and again. As were accounts of promising lives cut short, empty seats at holiday dinner tables, family reunions at gravesites.'

Before being sentenced, Yates had made a statement admitting to remorse for his crimes. The futility of that gesture can be measured in the poignant words of Melody Murfin's daughter, Anne, who addressed the killer in a courtroom statement:

'My name is Anne, and I'm also the daughter of Melody Murfin. And I would just like to say that everybody says this is a closure and this is what's going to make us feel better in the end. However, my mother made bad choices but that never made her a bad person. Yates makes bad choices and that makes him a terrible person. And the plea-bargain – I'm grateful that I now know that my mother is never coming back to me. As soon as she doesn't get to be a part of me, I don't think you should be able to get to be a part of, any part of your family. How could you do that to us? How could you take my mother and bury her in your yard? And your family walks around my mother for two and a half years. You stole her soul. I don't think you ever deserve to ever see daylight. Ever see your family. You must be tormented in prison for the rest of your life. Tortured. You're a sick monster. And you will be judged. That's all I have to say.'

Over the following months, the authorities across the State in Tacoma painstakingly put together their case. In 2001 Robert Lee Yates Jr was charged with killing Melinda L. Mercer and Connie LaFontaine Ellis and in October 2002, in Tacoma, at Pierce County Superior Court, he was found guilty on both counts. The jury struggled to find anything that would mitigate his acts and they failed. On Wednesday, 9 October 2002, Judge John McCarthy sentenced the 50-year-old father of five children to die by lethal injection. Yates remained impassive as the sentence was read out but his father and sister wept. His wife and children had stayed away from the court.

During the trial, which lasted a little over five weeks, the prosecutors described Yates's killing as 'his evil hobby'. They said he killed for the thrill of it and because he enjoyed sex with his dead victims.

'He richly deserved the death penalty,' said Chief Criminal Deputy Prosecutor Jerry Costello.

The defence attorney, Roger Hunko, showed the jury photos of Yates as a baby in a tiny suit and drew on the testimony of the killer's father, Robert Lee Yates Sr, who talked about his and his wife's joy at their son's birth. The boy had never given them trouble.

His father did, however, acknowledge that his son had begun to change during adolescence and that he had married his second wife, Linda, before divorcing his first. He said that his son had lost his way. 'He fell away from God. He went to the depths. But he's come back, and I really feel it's sincere.' In tears, the old man said, 'I love him so much, and I've told him a good many times. I abhor what he's done, but I love him just the same.'

Mr Yates told the court that his son had, during the time since his arrest in 2000, returned to his Christian faith and was a changed man. This ultimately had no influence on the jury. They remained unmoved. To those who were to decide his fate, Yates was a monster whose regard for his victims was so callous that he treated them as disposable objects.

Yates himself was allowed to address the jury and made the following statement:

'I prepared this statement so that I might leave nothing in my heart that needs to be said.

'To all my victims' families, to my family and to the people in the community, to the families of Melinda Mercer and Connie LaFontaine Ellis, I know you are suffering great anguish. I find no words to comfort you, to explain, justify or soften all the evil, pain, separation and death that I've caused.

'Some things are inexpressible and inexplicable in terms of human language. The world is a frightening place, and I've made it more so for many. I've caused so much pain and devastation.

'Hundreds of people are hurting and grieving because of my acts. I let sin enter my life. I let it grow and mature until it wrought its direct consequence: death. The wages of sin bring death. Sin and wrongdoing may start small but if left unchecked, they grow into something ugly. I believe that [unintelligible], in and of itself, sin blinds us. It blinded me.

'Within myself I've had no power to defeat this full-blown sinful nature. There were times – long periods – when, in between my horrific crimes, there were periods of relative calm. Nothing evil happened. But that sinful nature, which wrought so much recent violence, never really left.

'Scripture says the heart is deceitful above all things and beyond cure; who can understand? Our hearts can be deceitful beyond our own understanding, and surely mine was. I couldn't rid myself of this sinful nature. Somewhere, through all this devastation, God was knocking on the door of my heart, but I wouldn't let him in. I thought to myself, how could a God love or hear anything that was not clean. I thought I wasn't good enough to even speak to God, and if He wouldn't listen to me, then who would?

'My guilt was like a disease eating away at my soul. I couldn't share that with anyone else. Sin and guilt gnaws at our mind and causes acid to build up in our stomachs. We've all had guilt at some times in our lives. My sin and my guilt was overwhelming. It became hard to live with myself.

'Few men have ever felt the guilt I have from all the horror I've brought into your lives. I tried to cleanse myself from that guilt through denial. That only resulted in making things worse.

'I lived a double life. I stayed in denial – denial of my needs, denial that someone, somewhere could help me. Through my denial, because I couldn't face the truth, I thought I could be self-correcting, that if I kept it all to myself, someday it would all go away. That's denial. By my denial, I blinded myself to the truth – the truth that no one is so alone in this world as a denier of God. But that was me, alone and in denial.

'Even after my arrest in Spokane in April of 2000, for a couple of weeks I persisted. I remained in denial. In May of 2000, as I started to read the word of God for the first time in over 25 years,

I began to understand that someone had seen all the hideous crimes I've committed. Someone else had been there the whole time, watching each of my victims die.

'God had seen it all.

'That realisation was like slamming into a brick wall at 100 miles an hour. It was like standing naked and ugly before the whole world. It was looking at all the ugliness inside me and exposing it for what it really was.

'So the best thing that could ever have happened that April was for me to be arrested and brought to account for my actions. God had seen it all. The public and the families had seen and felt the loss and the death and the hurt caused by my actions. Now it was time for Robert Yates to open his eyes and see all that, too.

'It was impossible to be in denial any longer. It was time to face the truth. When sin has deadened moral perception, the wrongdoer does not discern the defects of his character or realise the enormity of the evil he has committed. For once I listened when God spoke.

'Until God's spirit working through the human agencies of law enforcement and our justice system woke me out of my spiritual blindness, I couldn't see the enormous devastation I had created, the tremendous pain and suffering I had caused. Until I came back to the love of God in Jesus Christ, I could not turn aside from my sinful nature, for the mind of the sinful man – and that was me – brings death. The mind of the man controlled by the Spirit brings life and peace. Someone needed to open my eyes.

'So I turned to God. Until I turned to faith, though before in death, I saw I couldn't face the truth that finally God was bringing me to account. It was me.

'I hadn't felt some of that out in Riverside. God already did it. I had to confess to him so I could admit to myself the enormity of my evil, that I needed to tell someone else who would listen and not condemn. After that I stopped the denial, stopped trying to hide the truth from my attorneys in Spokane. I told them all about my crimes stretching back all the way to 1975. That was the right way – the only way back to God.

'It's been a long road back. One doesn't fall into such a deep morass of evil and climb back out in one day. Hearing the heartbreaking testimonies of all the mothers, wives, sisters, brothers and children of the lost family members I've taken from them burdens me with the incalculable loss of the unending grief and the harm that I've brought to hundreds of people. I'm so very, very sorry.

'If God is the creator of this universe, then there are no unimportant people, and I took the lives of these loving, wonderful, important people from you. I feel your hurt every day and it won't go away. It never will. I've devastated your hopes and dreams. I've left you with only photographs and memories instead of warm family gatherings, cherished hugs and future happiness. The opportunity to say farewell or clear up misunderstandings was not afforded you.

'Please don't squeeze back tears. Tears are part of the adjustments. Tears are jewels of remembrance, painful but glistening with the beauty of your children – children God loved so much. Children that are, as the Bible says, asleep, waiting the day when they will be called forth to be reunited with you. Please trust in that blessed hope. God is not so far from you that he is not touched by your tears. All of heaven shares your sorrow.

'I believe with all my heart that there is a huge battle being waged between good and evil in this world, a spiritual battle that has allowed tragedy in this case, unexplainable evil to step forward.

Why has all this evil been allowed to exist in the world? Someday God will show us. So that's why we have to trust that someday our God, who's absolutely pure, will end this struggle. When He does, the Bible promises that the old order of things will have passed away. There will be no more death or mourning or crying or pain, only the happiness and joy you long for so much this day. That's a promise from God.

'Nothing I have said here today will justify or excuse my wrongs or even make sense of them. My compassion goes out to all I've hurt. There's absolutely no excuse that anyone could ever offer for the depths of pain in this room and in the lives of every person I've touched and all the tragedy I've wrought. There are so many innocent victims in all of this – families, friends and communities, my family, who had nothing to do with any of this. I'm so very, very sorry for what has happened. I and they can offer no justification for any of it. We do offer you all our sympathies and our prayers.

'There are inadequate words for me to express my guilt, my shame and my sorrow for having devastated you in taking away the wonderful people, the wonderful, loving people, the warm human beings you cared for so much. It's my prayer that you will look to God to help fill the hollow I've left in your hearts. My future is in His hands. I share your grief and always will. I'm sorry beyond what words can say. I apologise to all of you, and I thank the court for allowing me to speak.'

Robert Lee Yates Jr, aka the Spokane Serial Killer, is on Death Row in the Washington State Penitentiary at Walla Walla, the prison where he worked for a time in 1975. But, as with the riddle of Jack the Ripper, the story may not have ended. The body count may still be incomplete.

Tierra Capri Gobble

Phoenix Jordan 'Cody' Parrish was four months old when he died on Wednesday, 15 December 2004. Nobody claimed his body, so the people of Dothan, Alabama, the town where he had died, buried him. Hundreds of mourners attended the funeral at Sunset Memorial Park on 23 December, the final chapter in this infant's tragic life.

The journalist Lance Griffin wrote, 'When 4-month-old Phoenix Jordan "Cody" Parrish was murdered, all he had was one pacifier, a few diapers, some clothes and two sippy cups.'

As the little boy's badly broken body was being laid to rest, his mother was in police custody having been charged with his murder.

Born on Monday, 18 April 1983, Tierra Capri Gobble was the mother of Phoenix and his three-year-old sister, Jewell. She and her common-law husband, Samuel David Hunter, the father of the children, lived at Tampa, Florida. Following reports of abuse and neglect, Florida's Department of Children and Families took the children from the parents on a temporary basis. Hillsborough Kids, a Tampa-based agency that handles foster care, then placed them in the care of Edgar J. Parrish, 42, Gobble's great-uncle.

Parrish was instructed not to leave the State or allow any contact between the two children and their mother and father. These instructions he ignored shortly afterwards by both relocating to Alabama and allowing Gobble and Hunter to move in with him. It was revealed at trial that Hunter had a history of violence. The agency workers in charge of the case simply lost contact with the children.

A 911 call was received on the morning of Wednesday, 15 December 2004. The caller reported that Phoenix wasn't breathing properly, and the dispatcher could hear the child gasping for air in the background. Paramedics rushed the baby to Southeast Alabama Medical Center, but he couldn't be saved.

An autopsy showed that Phoenix suffered a fractured skull, five broken ribs, broken wrists and numerous bruises. It was recorded that he died from head trauma consistent with child abuse. 'This four-month-old baby was tortured from the time he was born,' said Sergeant Tracey McCord of the Houston County Sheriff's Office. 'It was the worst killing I had ever seen during my time with the CID. He was all broken up. It looked as if he had been smashed against a wall.'

Tierra Gobble was charged with the murder of her son. At trial, her attorney, Tom Brantley, argued that she was not mentally sound and had endured a harsh childhood 'filled with depression and neglect'.

For the prosecution, Houston County District Attorney Doug Valeska said, 'It's probably the most horrible case I have ever seen.

You had a baby who couldn't defend himself just tortured to death. It's not a case you settle.'

Gobble admitted to hitting Parrish's head on the side of his crib because he wouldn't stop crying. The jury took only 77 minutes to reach a verdict, finding Gobble guilty of capital murder and recommending the death penalty.

Twenty-two-year-old Samuel Hunter, Gobble's common-law husband, was charged with first-degree domestic violence and child abuse. His release date is 25 February 2009. Edgar Parrish was sentenced to ten years for aggravated child abuse and manslaughter.

In the aftermath of the murder, a lawsuit was brought against Hillsborough Kids, the agency contracted by the State to deal with foster care. Two workers involved in the case were fired and another was demoted after an internal investigation found one of the caseworkers had falsified documents showing he visited Phoenix and his sister at their uncle's home in Tampa and had failed to report Phoenix and his sister missing. Alabama attorney Chris Glover, in charge of the lawsuit, said, 'If the caseworkers for Hillsborough Kids had done their duty the child would still be alive today.'

As with many prisoners on Death Row, Gobble makes use of the internet. The following is her description of herself, written from prison and inviting pen pals to correspond with her:

'My name is Tierra, I'm a 23-year-old single female. I'm Spanish and white, 5ft 6in tall, I weigh 160 lbs. I have my curves in the right places. I will also say I'm no Barbie doll but I'm also not a cow. I tend to be very outspoken and impulsive.

'I'm looking for companionship that could possibly turn into more. When it comes to age I like older people, race and religion make no difference to me. I'm also looking for someone who likes children because I have a daughter of my own that I love dearly. My hobbies include reading, writing (letters, poems, etc.), cooking, exercising, and learning to garden. I love spending time with my little girl and that special person in my life. I like the outdoors as well, especially at night. I also love to learn and experience new things. I love new adventures. Though many of these things are not possible while incarcerated, they are all things I love to do. If you'd like to know more, I'm only a letter away. Hope to hear from you soon.'

It is not known whether anyone has taken up Tierra Gobble's disturbing invitation.

William Jay Gollehon

Montana is a big State, the fourth largest, and is also very beautiful. Covering more than 145,000 square miles, it forms part of the USA's border with Canada, adjoining the provinces of British Columbia, Alberta and Saskatchewan. The 'Treasure State' is sparsely populated, having slightly more than 900,000 inhabitants. The largest city is Billings, with a population of some 100,000, and it comes as little surprise to discover that Montana's police officers are seldom called on to investigate a crime as serious as murder.

Statistically, this is a State where the people are, in the main, law-abiding: a fact reflected in the number of those on its Death Row, where there isn't a great demand for condemned cells. Indeed, at the time of writing, only two men are taking up space on Death Row at the State Penitentiary at Deer Lodge.

That isn't to say that there is anything different about the murderers in Montana. They are certainly not more gallant or less violent than in other states as they go about their killing. Taking someone's life is always a terrible crime and Montana's killers can be just as nasty as those anywhere in the USA. There are just fewer of them, which is a good thing, because one of the two condemned murderers, William Jay Gollehon, is a deeply unpleasant and dangerous man.

Billy Gollehon is in his present predicament for having committed the crime of deliberate homicide 14 years ago.

On the morning of Wednesday, 12 January 1994, the body of Donna Meagher was found in a ditch west of the State capital of Helena. Donna had been working the night before at the Jackson Creek Saloon, out on Jackson City Road, off Interstate 15, near Montana City, and she had failed to return home. After her last customer left, sometime after midnight, Donna, working alone, closed the bar. Soon afterwards, she was confronted by two men, Billy Gollehon and Jimmy Lee Amos, who forced her to reopen the bar, where they systematically robbed the cash register and poker machines, pocketing around $3,000.

In an attempt to show that Donna had closed down the bar as usual and left for home, the assailants moved her car from the parking lot to the back of a nearby building and then, with serious malicious aforethought, they drove their victim through Helena to a spot west of town, where they bludgeoned her to death. Her corpse was found the next day.

Donna Meagher's murder generated extensive publicity and a substantial reward was offered to anyone providing information leading to the arrest and conviction of the perpetrators. Police were provided with a lead by one Dan Knipshield and on 31 August

1994 three law-enforcement officers travelled to West Yellowstone to talk with a man called Lawrence, who was locked up in the Park County Jail on an unrelated offence. Lawrence denied any knowledge of the murder, but said Gollehon and Jimmy Lee Amos were responsible. Gollehon and Amos were arrested and charged with the robbery, kidnapping and murder of Donna Meagher. They were convicted on all counts, with Amos being sentenced to life imprisonment and Billy Gollehon sentenced to death.

However, there is much more of a monster in Billy Gollehon than this one murder would imply. This is a man with a history of brutality and violence. In 1993, he had been released from prison having served time after being convicted on two counts of kidnapping, one of burglary and a staggering five counts of deliberate homicide. Nor was he a model prisoner while paying his debt to society.

On the morning of 22 September 1991, Gollehon and eight other Montana State Prison inmates gained access to, and took control of, the prison's maximum security unit. When officers regained control four hours later, five protective custody inmates had died as the result of the riot that Gollehon and others participated in. What follows is taken directly from the official report of the incident.

'The maximum security building is divided into two separate areas. "A Block," "B Block," and "C Block" are located on the west side of the building. "D Block," "E Block," and "F Block" are located on the east side. Control cages are positioned on each side of the building. The west control, No.1260 cage, regulates the power to A, B, and C Blocks, and the east control cage regulates the power to D, E, and F Blocks. Centered between the two units of the building are six separate exercise yards. At the time of the riot, there were ten protective custody inmates housed on D Block, and a total of 68 inmates in the maximum security building. Gollehon was one of the maximum security inmates housed on C Block.

'During the morning of September 22, 1991, thirteen inmates, including Gollehon, were in the exercise yards. While officers were returning some of the inmates from the exercise yards to their cells, Gollehon and eight other inmates broke through the wire fences separating the exercise areas and they eventually gained access to the section of the maximum security building leading to A, B, and C Blocks. Once inside the building, the inmates were able to reach both control cages and ultimately were able to open the doors to all of the blocks in the maximum security unit.

'While the inmates had control of the building, five officers took refuge by locking themselves in a shower facility in C Block. The inmates threatened to burn the officers out of the shower if they did not release keys to other sections of the building. The officers complied, and then heard the inmates say they were going to go to D Block and "get" the protective custody inmates. The officers remained in the shower until they were released by colleagues after the riot.

'Two protective custody inmates who were working outside their cells took evasive action, barricading themselves in the laundry room. The rioters, including Gollehon, tried unsuccessfully to break down the door and to smoke them out of the laundry room by starting a fire. At one point, not expecting to survive the attack, one of the inmates wrote, on the side of the dryer, the names of those who were trying to get at them and Gollehon's name was included. Unable to gain access to the inmates in the laundry room, the rioting convicts entered D Block, opened the cells, and proceeded to kill five of the other protective custody inmates.'

What constitutes 'time off for good behaviour' in Montana appears to be heavily weighted in the prisoners' favour. Those who determine an inmate's release date made a serious error in their judgement of Gollehon's suitability for parole. Quite apart from the murderous crimes that had put him in prison, it is difficult to see how members of the parole board could overlook the gravity of his actions while in prison. However, that is exactly what they did. Just over three years later, this transparently dangerous man was considered to no longer pose a threat to society and he was set free. Back on the streets of Montana, Billy Gollehon brutally murdered Donna Meagher.

Christopher Cornelius Goins

When he stood before a court accused of multiple murder, Christopher Goins was only 21 years old. At his trial his counsel paraded before the jury members of his family who were to depict a misguided but good-hearted young man who was the product of a poor upbringing. This was intended to mitigate his having slain five people and attempted to murder his pregnant girlfriend and her young sister. It did not, however, persuade the jury that Goins deserved leniency and on 1 December 2000 he was executed by lethal injection.

Goins had been convicted of the murders of James Nathaniel Randolph Jr, 35, Daphne Jones, 29, and three of Daphne Jones's four children: Nicole, nine, David, four, and Robert, three. He was sentenced to die for the capital murder of Robert Jones and received four life terms and 73 years for the other crimes.

On the morning of Friday, 14 October 1994, Goins, in a car driven by his friend Barry Scott, arrived at 1008 St James Street,

Apartment C, the home in Richmond, Virginia, of Tamika Jones, where she and six members of her family were passing the time of day. Tamika, just 14 years old, was seven months pregnant with Goins's child, and recently returned from hospital after receiving treatment for complications to the pregnancy.

In the family's apartment, Goins had been sitting talking to Tamika's parents. From the evidence discovered at the crime scene, the conversation was probably on the subject of the supplying of drugs. In her room Tamika had an ultrasound picture of the baby and Barry Scott had taken it from her and shown it to Goins.

According to court records, Goins had said, 'I don't want to see that. Take it back to her. Why are you showing me that…?'

When Scott returned the ultrasound picture to Jones, she admonished him for showing it to Goins and said, 'I didn't want him to see it.'

During the following 30 or 40 minutes, Tamika heard her mother, her father, Scott and Goins talking and laughing in the living room. When the girl went to the bathroom she saw Goins sitting on the sofa. Although she made eye contact with him, they did not speak. She returned to her bedroom and heard more talking and laughing for 15 minutes.

Then she 'started hearing shots'. There were screams and crying, and a set of footsteps coming down the hall. Tamika later testified that she heard more shots and saw 'flashes', before Goins appeared in the doorway of her room and shot her nine times. Goins also shot Tamika's 21-month-old sister, Kenya, whom Tamika tried to shield from the bullets with her body.

When Tamika thought that Goins had left the apartment, she telephoned 911 for emergency assistance. She told the shocked dispatcher that it had been Christopher Goins who had done the shooting, and that other people had been killed too.

At about 9.30am, when the first officers from the City of Richmond Police arrived at the crime scene, they determined that all of the members of the Jones family had been shot. Only Tamika and Kenya had survived. In the kitchen police discovered the body of Tamika's four-year-old brother David Jones, as well as the bodies of her parents, Daphne Jones and James Randolph Jr. In another of the bedrooms they found the bodies of Nicole Jones, Tamika's nine-year-old sister, and Robert Jones, aged three.

Daphne, aged 29, had been shot four times: twice in the head, once in the wrist and once in the right leg. Each head shot was fatal, and autopsy findings proved, through the 'stippling effect' caused by powder burns, that the shots had been 'discharged point-blank'.

James Nathaniel Randolph Jr, aged 35, was, like Tamika, shot no fewer than nine times: in his case, twice in the head, three times in the left arm, once in the leg and once on the chin. Four of these wounds would have been individually lethal. The evidence showed that several of the shots were fired from a distance of less than 'arm's length', and other shots were fired into the man after he had fallen to the floor.

The officers also found three bags of powder and crack cocaine on James Randolph and later learned that Daphne Jones, Tamika's mother, had cocaine in her blood.

Four-year-old David died as the result of a single gunshot to the head, the bullet also having been fired 'execution-style' at point-blank range.

Nicole, aged nine, suffered from two gunshots: one bullet passed through her heart and lung; the other had been fired into her head at close range.

Three-year-old Robert had sustained two lethal gunshot wounds to his head, while little Kenya suffered a wound, measuring around two and a half inches long, through her left wrist.

That Tamika – the principal target of Goins's murderous onslaught – survived is nothing short of a miracle. She was shot three times in the abdomen, three times in her thighs, once in her right hand, once in the neck, and another round tore through her left shoulder. After the attack an obstetrician performed a hysterectomy on her, because multiple bullets had perforated her uterus, her right ovary and fallopian tube. When removed from the uterus, the foetus had sustained a bullet wound to its face and was dead.

Even the most hardened, streetwise cops were sickened to their stomachs. The entire kitchen and bedroom were awash with blood, brain matter and bone.

Crime scene investigators recovered from the kitchen seven .45-calibre cartridge casings, various bullets and bullet-jacket fragments. In the bedroom, where Nicole and Robert were shot, they found two more .45-calibre casings, as well as two spent bullets, a bullet jacket and a fragment of lead. In the bedroom where Tamika and Kenya had been shot, six .45-calibre cartridge casings and two bullets were recovered.

James L. Pickelman, a firearms identification expert at the Commonwealth's Division of Forensic Science, explained that hollow-nose bullets, 'such as those used in the commission of these offences, are designed to explode on impact with the target'. After examining the rifling characteristics on the bullet jackets, he concluded that the jackets had been ejected from a Glock pistol. Shortly afterwards, a firearm found at the home of Goins's girlfriend, Monique Littlejohn, matched 'in every single respect the same extractor marks' and Pickelman determined, along with his colleague Ann D. Jones, that both items had been in the same weapon.

The evidence against Christopher Goins was overwhelming but he had fled Virginia. He remained on the run for about a month after the shootings until he was apprehended in New York with Monique Littlejohn. He had shaved his head to alter his appearance. When he was arrested his first statement to police was: 'I am sorry. I didn't mean to harm them.'

At his trial, it was claimed that Goins had been raised initially by his mother, an inveterate drug user. At an early age he was exposed to the drug culture as she would frequently use drugs in his presence. It was argued that throughout his childhood the boy had been without positive adult role models in his family. Both his mother and aunt were drug abusers and another aunt, also a drug user, had died of AIDS contracted through intravenous drug use. There was also an uncle who served time in prison. Clearly this was an appalling background for a child to grow up in.

At the age of 12, Christopher Goins had been forced to move to New York to live with his grandmother following a period of abuse at the hands of his mother. His aunt, a Ms Dickerson, who provided mitigating evidence at his trial, testified that Goins's mother 'never held, hugged, or nurtured any of her children'. She told the court that Goins had been devastated when his grandmother had died, because she was the only person who had shown him any love. Other members of Goins's family provided testimony to the court regarding the life of abuse Christopher suffered when a child. One cousin described Goins as 'a kind man who liked to play with his six-year-old cousin Phillip'.

However, the Christopher Goins that his family attempted to portray was markedly different in character from the young man who was described to the court by Tamika Jones. She testified that he frequently went to her home to visit her mother, Daphne, with whom he would often stay overnight. The family were aware too that Goins was a drug dealer, but that doesn't seem to have been a handicap in his forging a friendship with either of the parents. Apparently, Tamika had at one time wanted to go to live with an aunt because of all the drug dealing that was going on at home.

Despite his deep involvement with the drug trade, however, three years after meeting Goins, Tamika began a sexual relationship with him, although she was only 12 at the time. She admitted that on one occasion she had even looked after $2,400 for him, proceeds from drug dealing. In March 1994, aged just 14, she became pregnant by Goins. She later learned that Goins had made another girl, Monique Littlejohn, pregnant, but Littlejohn had lost the baby in June of the same year, 1994.

After the trial, Tamika Jones moved to California. Shortly before Goins's execution, she told the *Richmond Times-Dispatch*: 'I just want him off this Earth. I just want him away from here so he can go to God and let God deal with it.'

On the day of the execution, as Goins was brought into the death chamber, he said, 'Look, we've got an audience.' After he was strapped to the gurney his last words were: 'There's no God but Allah.' Seven minutes later, at 9.04pm, he was pronounced dead.

Among those who witnessed the execution was Richmond Commonwealth's Attorney David Hicks, who prosecuted Goins and said afterwards that he 'died showing no remorse'.

For her complicity in the crime, Monique Littlejohn received prison sentences totalling 188 years.

Andrew Sasser

According to court records, Andrew Sasser joined the ranks of Dead Men Walking in Arkansas 'for causing the death of Ms Jo Ann Kennedy, on or about 12 July 1993, in the course of or in immediate flight from his commission or attempt to commit the victim's rape or kidnapping under circumstances manifesting extreme indifference to the value of human life'.

While that in itself sounds brutal enough, fleshing out that bald description and discovering what actually happened to Jo Ann Kennedy on the night she was murdered reveals the story of a repulsive crime.

Twenty-nine-year-old Sasser had been driving aimlessly around Garland City in his brother's pickup truck and during the course of his wanderings he had stopped at an E-Z Mart two or three times to buy potato chips and use the telephone between 3pm on Sunday, 11 July 1993 and approximately 12am the following day.

Jo Ann Kennedy was the store clerk on duty that night and was working alone, and as a result of Sasser's final visit to the store she died of multiple stab wounds and head injuries. When found, she was nude from the waist down and her slacks and panties were found in the E-Z Mart's men's bathroom.

Sasser was quickly apprehended for the crime and taken to the Lafayette County Sheriff's Office, in nearby Lewisville, where he was interrogated by Arkansas State Police Investigator Robert Neal and Miller County Sheriff H.L. Phillips.

According to his tape-recorded statement, Sasser claimed that he had driven up to the window at the Garland City E-Z Mart and ordered nachos from the victim. He described the victim as a 'lady who had an attitude', and she was angry because someone else had ordered nachos but had then failed to pick up the order. He stated that the woman tried to sell him two orders of nachos, but he declined. He went on to say that they argued and the woman slammed the drive-through window on his hand. Sasser stated that he then jerked the window open, whereupon the woman cut him with 'a knife-like object with a blade'. Sasser grabbed the woman but she jerked him through the drive-through window.

According to his account of the episode, they scuffled, moving from the drive-through window area, down the counter area, out into the store's interior, back to the store office at the rear of the store, and up to the potato-chip rack at the front of the store. Sasser stated that Jo Ann Kennedy opened the store's front door, they exited the store and she followed him to his pickup truck, the pair still fighting. Sasser claimed that he got into the vehicle and left.

Sasser told his interrogators that he did not recall going into E-Z Mart's restrooms but that he 'had to go back there'. He stated the victim had hit him repeatedly with her fists while they scuffled. During the scuffle he wrested the victim's knife-like object from her and used it to hit her, before finally dropping the object near the pickup. Sasser stated he did not know why the victim's clothes were removed. When asked whether he did not remove the victim's clothes or did not remember doing so, he replied, 'No sir.' He insisted that he did not try to rape the victim or to rob her.

At his trial the State of Arkansas introduced a witness whose account of the murder differed from the story told by the killer. Jeanice Pree testified that she and her mother, Gloria Jean Williams, lived across the street from the Garland City E-Z Mart. She testified that she had an unobstructed view of the store. Pree also worked at the E-Z Mart and believed its front door was locked at midnight so that after this time customers were required to use a drive-through window. According to Pree's testimony, she was sitting on her couch watching television when she looked out of her window. She saw the victim and a man behind the store counter and assumed he was a friend of the victim. Pree testified that shortly afterwards she looked back and saw the victim and the man coming to the store's front door. She said that she could tell the victim was being forced to come out 'because it looked like her hands were behind her back'. This was very much at odds with Sasser's statement that his victim had followed him fighting all the way.

Pree was greatly concerned at what she was witnessing and telephoned 911. The police dispatcher testified he received her 911 telephone call at approximately 12.46am on 12 July, and that she stated 'there was a woman that she believed was being killed at the E-Z Mart, being drug through the window'.

Gloria Williams testified that she watched the E-Z Mart from the window in her house while her daughter, Jeanice, telephoned 911. Williams told the court she saw a truck leave the store and then the victim 'came around from the side of the E-Z Mart. She reached for the door and she just collapsed, right there.'

Miller County Sheriff's Deputy Jim Nicholas testified that Jo Ann Kennedy was found lying just outside the E-Z Mart door on the sidewalk and appeared to be dead. He said that the woman was nude from the waist down and what appeared to be her panties and pants were located in the men's restroom of the store. Nicholas told the court that one of the victim's shoes was in the front aisle and one behind the counter, and a large wad of hair was found behind the cash register near the drive-through window. He further testified that blood spatters were observed at the drive-through window, on the store's 'outside aisles' counter and on the men's bathroom wall. The Deputy told the court that the drive-through window was open.

Numerous items of physical evidence and photographs were introduced into evidence through the testimony of Nicholas and Miller County Sheriff's Department Investigator Toby Giles, including a photograph of the drive-through window and cash-register area showing two plastic containers of nachos.

The autopsy report showed that the victim died of multiple stab and cutting wounds and blunt-force head injuries, and that no anal or vaginal injury or any spermatozoa were present.

For Sasser, this was not a once-in-a-lifetime aberration. He had a record of a similar attack on a woman, only on this occasion his victim had survived his brutality. The State's final witness at the Jo Ann Kennedy murder trial was Jackie Carter, who testified that

Sasser had attacked and raped her on 22 April 1988. The assault had taken place at the E-Z Mart store in Lewisville.

Jackie Carter told the court that she was the only employee on duty when Sasser entered the store at approximately 1am. He purchased cigarettes, before returning 15 minutes later to purchase a soft drink. Five minutes later he was back at the store. This time he asked to use the telephone and said he had had an accident on his motorcycle. She testified that he then stood in the store after saying that he was waiting for his wife to pick him up. At approximately 1.35am, a truck drove up and Sasser went outside to talk to its occupants. During this time, not suspecting she was in any danger, Jackie Carter moved from behind the cash register and began putting up items in the freezer. It was while she was doing this that Sasser approached her from behind and hit her on the back of the head with a soft-drink bottle. The woman said that she struggled with her attacker but he continued to hit her and forced her to a utility room/bathroom at the back of the store.

At this point, another man approached in a car and Sasser decided to take his victim outside. He forced her out of the store, picked up his bicycle and then pushed both Jackie Carter and the bicycle into an alley. Once the other man had driven by, the brutal Sasser forced her across the street and told her to pull down her clothes. He then pulled down his own clothes and raped her. Carter said that Sasser then told her he should not have done it and that he really should kill her. Terrified and in a state of shock, she begged him not to and eventually agreed to say that a truck had dropped her off and Sasser had found her. Satisfied with this idea, Sasser forced her back to the store, where the police were by now waiting. Jackie Carter later identified Sasser as her attacker.

Dead Men Walking

The Varner Unit, a high-security State Prison, is situated in Lincoln County, Arkansas, and it is here that Andrew Sasser lives out the remainder of his days, awaiting the lethal injection that will end his life.

John Martin Scripps

'They won't hang me. I'm British,' said John Scripps four days before he was hanged at Changi Prison, Singapore, on 19 April 1996.

During his career Chris Berry-Dee has met and interviewed many of the most notorious serial killers and, with one exception, they all have been American. The exception was an Englishman, John Scripps, who was hanged in Singapore in 1996. In the months leading up to the execution, Chris became close to Scripps's family and was given sole access not only to personal material but also to the killer himself, flying to Singapore and attending the trial. Just four days before he was hanged Scripps gave an exclusive interview to Chris in the infamous Changi Prison and this account is based upon Chris's extensive coverage of the case and his conversation with Scripps during that interview.

Described by the media as 'The Tourist from Hell', Scripps

became the first Westerner to be hanged in Singapore for murder, and only the second for any offence. (Dutch citizen Johannes van Damme was executed by the Singapore authorities for drug trafficking in 1994. Arrested on Wednesday, 27 September 1989 and found to be carrying four kilograms of heroin, he was sentenced to death on 26 April 1993.) Scripps also earns the dubious distinction of being the last British murderer to be hanged since the abolishment of capital punishment in 1964.

John Martin Scripps was born in Hertford, the county town of Hertfordshire, on 9 December 1959. The family moved to London when he was a small boy and he remembered a happy childhood during which he was close to his sister Janet. When he was nine years old he experienced the loss of his father, who committed suicide after he learned that his wife was leaving him for another man. John found his father at home with his head in the gas oven. At about the same time his mother was diagnosed as having throat cancer and, although she recovered, John's world fell apart.

John became increasingly introverted. He cut himself off from his friends and found it impossible to concentrate on learning to read and write. He acquired these skills later on, in prison, although his handwriting always remained very childish.

At 14, he disappeared while at a training camp in France organised by the Finchley, north London, unit of the Army Cadet Force. A year later he was in juvenile court for burglary and theft.

His first adult conviction was for indecent assault in 1978, when he was fined £40 at Hendon Magistrates Court. There followed a grim catalogue of offences, including burglaries in London and then jail in Israel for stealing from a fellow kibbutz worker.

In 1982, Scripps was jailed again for burglary and assault in Surrey.

He managed to abscond from the prison system and embarked on a crime journey throughout South-East Asia and America. In Mexico he met and married 16-year-old Maria Arellanos, but by 1985 he was back in Britain and once again facing a prison sentence for burglary. Prison could not hold him and he absconded yet again to return to his drug-smuggling activities in South-East Asia and America. Justice caught up with him in 1987, when he was jailed for seven years in London for heroin offences. The following year, his young Mexican wife divorced him. While on home leave from prison in June 1990, he disappeared for the third time and flew to Bangkok.

When later interviewed by Customs and Excise officers, Scripps said that he had flown to Bangkok to meet a girl he had been writing to. On arrival in the Thai capital he booked into the Liberty Hotel for three days, taking a cheap room costing about £10 a night. Accompanied by his girlfriend, he frequented a few bars and visited the local tourist attractions, including the historic former capital Ayuthaya, where they stayed for two days. The couple then moved on to Pattaya, known as 'Sin City', and from there to Phuket, where they lived at Nilly's Marina Inn at Patong Beach. Scripps spent ten days in Thailand before deciding to fly back to London. He had spent £1,000 during his sojourn in the East, including £270 on clothes and just over £100 buying 48 phoney watches. He also bought a quantity of heroin.

On Wednesday, 29 August, at 1.20pm local time, Scripps boarded Gulf Air Flight GF 153. His destination was Muscat in the Sultanate of Oman, where he arrived in the transit area of Seeb International Airport to await his connecting flight to Heathrow, London. He was travelling on a UK passport issued in the name of Jesse Robert Bolah. This travel document, number 348572V, had been stolen.

While killing time in an airport bar, he met Christopher Davis and the two men conversed as they waited for their flight. As Scripps prepared to board Flight GF 011 to London, he was subjected to a routine security check which included a body frisk. Police Corporal Saeed Mubarak of the Royal Oman Police found two packages wrapped in red tape in his pockets. Thinking the packages might contain explosives, he summoned assistance from Inspector Saeed Sobait. The two police officers went through Scripps's hand baggage, where they discovered a larger packet containing white powder. The dilemma for the authorities was that the white powder could not be tested without detaining the passenger. It was therefore decided to give one of the packets – which later turned out to contain 50 grams of diamorphine – and the passport to the captain. Scripps was then allowed to proceed to London, effectively under detention and the responsibility of the Gulf Air flight crew.

Scripps nervously boarded the Tri-Star and settled into seat 39H. Midway through the flight, schoolteacher Gareth Russell, sitting in 39K, noticed his fellow passenger drop something on the floor and kick it under the seat.

As soon as the aircraft entered British airspace, the pilot contacted HM Customs & Excise and, moments after the plane taxied to a stop, a rummage team headed by David Clark boarded the aircraft. The packet which Scripps had kicked under his seat was found. After a field test for opiates had proved positive, he was charged under Section 3(1) of the Misuse of Drugs Act 1971, contrary to Section 170(2) of the Customs & Excise Management Act 1979.

Scripps was held in custody that night to allow Customs and police officers to search 6 Gordon Road, Farnborough, Hampshire, where he stayed with his uncle, Ronald White. A folder of documents was found containing a West German passport in the name of Robert

Alfred Wagner and a Belgian identity card in the name of Benjamin George Edmond Stanislas Balthier and bearing Scripps's photograph. The men named in these documents had been reported missing many years previously and there has been no trace of them since.

Later that day, Scripps was interviewed again and asked how he earned his money, how he could afford to travel all over the world and how he could afford a very expensive Samsonite suitcase. He cockily replied, 'It may be very expensive to you, but it isn't to me. If you can't afford a suitcase like this, it's because you're working as minor subservients of the State for a standard wage, and you're not willing to go out and work all hours.'

At 10pm on 31 August, Scripps was released in the name of John Martin, and instructed to answer bail on 29 October 1990. He failed to report and on 28 November he was arrested by Detective Constable Malone, at his mother's home at 11 Grove Road, Sandown, Isle of Wight. Police found more drugs and he was charged with possession of 50 grams of diamorphine of 80 per cent purity. The street value of this amount was estimated at around £9,500, while the remaining 191.5 grams of heroin he had tried to smuggle through the airport was valued at £38,550. Aware that Scripps possessed drugs valued at over £48,000, the police now understood how he could afford his well-travelled lifestyle.

Because Scripps had previously absconded from a seven-year custodial sentence for drugs offences, he was held on remand in Winchester Prison until his trial. He instructed his solicitors that he would plead not guilty. His defence was simple enough. His case would stand or fall by his claim that he had found the red-taped package containing heroin on the ground at Muscat Airport and had handed it in to the police. He categorically denied that any drugs were found on his person at Muscat. Further, he argued that the traces of heroin found in the pockets of the jeans he was wearing at the time resulted directly from his being asked to open the package he had found containing drugs. He denied any knowledge whatsoever of the traces alleged to have been found in the pocket of a shirt. But, although he managed to wriggle out of that, he was still not completely out of the woods, for the police had found heroin on him when he was arrested in Sandown and his wallet was stuffed with £2,000 in cash. The implication was that he intended peddling drugs on the Isle of Wight, yet another claim that he denied.

Prisoner V48468 Scripps was given legal aid and case number T 910602 was heard at Winchester Crown Court on 6 January 1991. Represented by Bruce Maddick QC, Scripps suddenly changed his plea to guilty in an effort to gain leniency. Despite this ploy, he was sentenced to 13 years' imprisonment. Amazingly he spent just three years and ten months in jail before contriving to abscond once again.

Scripps started his prison term at Albany Prison on the Isle of Wight and during a six-week period in March and April 1993 was instructed in butchery by Prison Officer James Quigley. 'He was shown how to bone out forequarters and hindquarters of beef, sides of bacon, carcasses of pork, and how to portion chicken,' said Quigley, adding, 'He was a quick learner, and very fast on picking up on how to slaughter, dismember, and debone animals.'

What the authorities could never have guessed was that, while they were training an inmate in butchery skills, they were also equipping him to slaughter and dismember humans, the gruesome calling to which he subsequently turned his hand.

Scripps's ultimate odyssey began on 28 October 1994 when he failed to return to the Mount Prison in Bovington, Hertfordshire, after four days' leave. During the week before he walked out of the open prison gate, he had been openly selling his possessions to finance his escape. He had even bragged to fellow inmates that he was going on the run. This was picked up by the prison staff, but they failed to act on it. When he did not return, the Governor, Margaret Donnelly, said, 'He was no longer considered a risk. He had no history of violence. He was quiet and reserved.' What, it appears, the Governor did not know was that Scripps had absconded from every home leave he had ever been granted. And, far from being quiet, reserved and no longer a risk, the smooth-talking drug dealer was about to become a vicious serial killer.

After absconding, Scripps went on a globetrotting, three-nation murder rampage. His first port of call before the killing started was the Netherlands, where he met a former drugs dealer whom he had previously encountered while on remand in Winchester Prison. He travelled next to Belgium and Spain and in late November reached Mexico, where he attempted a reconciliation with Maria Arellanos. He told her that he had been released from prison on a technicality and that he was returning to Thailand to buy silk clothes and wanted them to set up a boutique together in Cancun. He told her that he was now a deeply religious man and, to convince her, became a devotee of the Virgin of Guadeloupe, Mexico's patron saint.

To finance this venture, Scripps befriended Timothy McDowell, a British backpacker who was holidaying in Belize and had travelled to Mexico in 1994. It is believed that he beat to death the 28-year-old Cambridge graduate and management consultant, dismembered his body and dumped it in an alligator-infested river. Shortly after the murder the victim's bank account was milked dry to the tune of £21,000, the money being transferred to Scripps's account in London.

This sum of money was later moved to another account in the United States under the name of Simon Davis, one of Scripps's many aliases.

Thirty-three-year-old Gerard George Lowe arrived at Singapore's Changi Airport on the morning of 8 March 1995. Dressed casually in khaki Bermuda shorts and an orange T-shirt, he was indistinguishable from all other international travellers as they stumbled wearily off the plane and on to the moving walkway. He was just another tourist, and that was the point. Travelling alone in a strange country, Lowe was looking for a friendly face. And, as people do in airports when they are trying to establish their bearings, he found himself talking to a complete stranger. The tall, soft-spoken Englishman in his thirties politely introduced himself as Simon Davis. As they chatted, Lowe explained that he was a South African brewery design engineer who was on a shopping trip to Singapore to take advantage of the low cost of video recorders and cameras. When Scripps caught sight of Lowe's gold credit card, he knew he had found another victim.

It was apparent to Scripps that his new acquaintance was thrifty, so he suggested they share a hotel room. Scripps recommended the River View Hotel. This is a middle-class businessman's stopover, with a greying marble reception area and a tacky boutique selling plastic orchids and Hong Kong Girl perfume. The hotel was full and the two men had to wait several hours for a room. 'They seemed very normal,' the hotel's manager, Roberto Pregarz, later testified at Scripps's trial. 'They were smiling and laughing together. There was nothing strange.'

Within minutes of booking in, the two men made their way to Room 1511. After they had unpacked their cases, Lowe settled down at a small, round table, from which he could admire the panoramic view of Singapore and, picking up a pen, started to compile his shopping list.

Scripps chose this moment to steal up behind Lowe and bring down a three-pound camping hammer on his victim's head in a single crushing blow. And this is what Scripps said in Changi Prison when he recalled the murder; it makes for disturbing reading:

'I think he [Lowe] was a bit surprised when I hit him. At first he thought I was mucking about. That made me mad with him because I thought that he was a homosexual. I threw him against the wall and he started to fall down. He was shaking and then he pissed himself. I knocked him about a bit, and got him to tell me his bank card PIN number. When he was in the bathroom he was conscious. There was water dribbling from his mouth. He gurgled, or something like that.'

Without a trace of emotion, Scripps added, 'Well, I cut his throat an' let him bleed to death like a pig.'

The following exchange between John Scripps and Chris Berry-Dee took place when he was in prison and under sentence of death:

CB-D: So, let's get this right, John. You smash this innocent man against the wall of the room, then beat him half senseless, or something like that. Then you drag him into the bathroom, lift him into the bath, forcing his head down to his knees. You turn on the taps, and cut through the back of his neck to paralyse him. Then you stab him in the neck, or whatever, and let him bleed to death. Did he know what was going on, John?

JS: Do you want the fucking truth?

CB-D: Yes.

JS: Yes.

CB-D: Yes, what?

JS: Do you want blood out of a fuckin' stone?

CB-D: Did Mr Lowe know what was going on?

JS: Yes! He pissed and shit himself. It made a stink. He was shitting himself. Yeah. Right. Oh, fuck it. Yeah. Really, I can't say about it. It wasn't good and I spewed up. He really shit himself, but he couldn't do much about it, could he?

CB-D: I suppose not, John. What did you do after you'd killed him?

JS: I cut him into parts so's I could dump the body.

CB-D: Is it true that you used the little saw that went with your Swiss Army knife?

JS: That's bollocks. I have a knife like that for camping. But anyone will tell you you can't use a little saw like that for cutting carcasses.

CB-D: OK. What did you use?

JS: A six-inch boning knife. I was taught how to look after knives, you know.

CB-D: Now, I know you're telling the truth. Go on.

JS: Well, after the blood had been washed away, I took his head off. Just like a pig. It's almost the same. You cut through the throat and twist the knife through the back of the neck. There ain't much mess if you do it properly... I cut off his arms at the elbows. Then, I cut off his upper arms at the shoulders. You just cut through the ball and socket joints. You don't saw anything.

CB-D: And?

JS: Well, the legs. Um, on a pig you have the legs, and you have to use a saw to make ... I think it's called a 'square cut'. But, honest ... I just stuck the knife in and twisted and cut until the legs came away at the hip joint, I suppose. When I got to the knees, I just cut through and they snapped back so's I could fold them up. Fuckin' heavy stuff, right?

After packaging the body parts in the black bin bags Gerald Lowe had brought with him to wrap up his duty-free purchases, Scripps deposited the bundles in the room's only wardrobe. He liberally sprayed Lynx deodorant around the room in an attempt to mask the smell of his own vomit but it proved inadequate to the task, for a couple who stayed in Room 1511 in the days that followed reported a strange, fishy odour lingering around the room.

Finally, Scripps washed his hands and cleaned up the bathroom. Again he was not absolutely thorough and missed a few tiny spots on the shower curtain, door and toilet bowl. These were to provide crucial evidence when he was eventually brought to court to answer the charge of murder.

Murder committed in this meticulous fashion can rarely be a crime of passion. It is an eminently practical business, carried out with the studied objectivity of a professional. It requires thought, planning and an ability to attend to every detail with cold-blooded efficiency. Scripps may have left traces of his butchery in the bathroom, but he demonstrated a clinical, unhurried persistence after the event. He started by forging his victim's signature practising on tracing paper.

His next move was to visit a computer shop, where he told the sales assistant he was Gerald Lowe and he wanted to buy some laptop computers. By 9pm he was back in the hotel's River Garden Restaurant, sitting down to a plate of fillet steak and a bottle of white wine. It was a balmy evening. The string of multi-coloured lights around the patio reflected in the waters of the nearby Singapore River. John Scripps was at peace with the world.

The next morning Scripps informed the hotel receptionist that his companion had checked out and that he would settle the bill when he left. He then went on a spending spree in Singapore's glittering shopping malls, threading his way from one air-conditioned shop to another using Lowe's gold credit card again and again. His first purchase was a pair of Aiwa loudspeakers, and then came a pair of Nike shoes and socks, as well as a video recorder, which he arranged to be sent to his sister in England.

On the morning of 9 March, Scripps used the credit card for another shopping bonanza. He also drew S$8,400 in cash from a local bank and made a telegraphic transfer of US$11,000 to one of his accounts in San Francisco in the name of John Martin. He used the gold card to buy a S$30 ticket to attend a concert of Brahms and Tchaikovsky played by the Singapore Symphony Orchestra. Finally, in an extraordinarily whimsical but callous bid to maximise his gains, he bought five Big Sweep lottery tickets.

Later that night, he packed the dismembered body parts of Gerald Lowe into a suitcase and caught a taxi to Singapore harbour, where, under the cover of darkness, he dumped the gruesome contents into the waters swirling around Clifford Pier. The next day, flush with cash, he flew to Bangkok.

Sheila Damude, a 49-year-old school administrator from Victoria, British Columbia, had flown into Bangkok for a two-week stay with her son, Darin, who was on a 'gap year' tour of the world. The 22-year-old had broken his leg while travelling with friends and she wanted to give him some motherly attention. The two had decided to take a tourist trip to Thailand's 'Paradise Island' of Phuket.

On 15 March, mother and son arrived at Phuket Airport and were collecting their thoughts in the usual arrival turmoil when Scripps sidled up to them. 'I was on the same plane as you. Do you have a problem?' he enquired. Within minutes Scripps had gleaned the information that Sheila and her son wanted to get to Patong Beach but were not sure how much to pay for a taxi.

With his marauding instincts fully attuned, Scripps, ever the experienced traveller, told them about Nilly's Marina Inn, where a room would cost them about US$18 a night. The small luxury hotel lay on the quiet, southern end of Patong Beach, one of the most popular beaches on the island. Scripps suggested that the three of them share a taxi to save money. Mother and son exchanged glances and nodded their agreement. They were clearly very impressed by this helpful young man and soon they were on their way along the dusty roads to Patong Beach.

At Nilly's Marina Inn Scripps signed himself in as Simon Davis, a shopkeeper from London. No one noticed, in a revealing slip of the pen, that he had inadvertently signed his name 'J. Davis'. The consummate traveller, he had stayed there before, always drawing admiring looks from the pretty female staff, who referred to him as 'Mr John'.

The Damudes caught the lift to the second floor and were shown into a spacious, deluxe suite overlooking the bay, a 'Miami Vice' view with jet skis and speedboats, sparkling sea and white sands. Scripps took a nearby room just across the corridor which overlooked scrubland at the back of the hotel.

The Damudes had two king-size beds, a well-appointed mini-bar, IDD telephone, colour television, air conditioning and a kitchen area. There was a separate bathroom and shower and even a safe for storing their valuables.

If the room was quite luxurious, especially at the low cost, the view from their window was priceless. Situated across from a long, sandy beach and a narrow road was the crystal-clear waters of the Andaman Sea. From their balcony they could see two tall palm trees, below which two local girls were breaking open coconuts. When the girls looked up and saw the handsome young Darin they broke into giggles. At that moment the Damudes thought they had found Heaven, but before long they would be pitched into Hell.

Meanwhile, after a short walk to Patong's exciting nightlife quarter, the Damudes spent the evening exploring the shops for silk garments. Scripps hired a high-powered 450cc Honda motorcycle and ended up on the seafront at the Banana Bar. Throbbing with music, the place was full of good-time girls selling their young bodies for less than the price of a meal. Scripps danced the early hours away and had sex with a young woman on the beach before retiring for the night. The Tourist Police admired his yellow and green motorcycle parked on the double-yellow lines outside the hotel and decided it was not good policy to issue a parking ticket to a holidaymaker.

The following morning, Sheila and Darin came down for breakfast, which they ate in the sunshine. Afterwards they searched the rather dismal fish tank for signs of life, and Sheila flicked through the postcard rack for something suitable to send to her husband back home. This was the last time they were seen alive. It is believed that they returned to their room to make plans for the day.

Around 11am, people wandering about outside of the small hotel next door noted a large flood of red-coloured water flushing down an open drain that led from Nilly's Marina Inn to the sewer under the road.

Because John Scripps has never been charged with the murders of Sheila and Darin Damude, he refused to discuss the case with

Chris Berry-Dee. Nevertheless, using the known evidence, it is possible to reconstruct what happened when the Damudes returned to their room at Nilly's Marina Inn.

Scripps knocked on the door and entered their room on some pretext and, within seconds, he had zapped them with a stun gun. Such a weapon was found in his possession when he was arrested. With his victims immobilised, he took out his hammer and beat them to death – swabs from his hammer matched bloodstains on the carpet in the room occupied by the Damudes – after which he dismembered their bodies using the butchery skills he had learned so adroitly at Albany Prison.

After stealing his victims' travel documents, passports and credit cards, he went on yet another shopping spree. The skulls, torsos and several limbs belonging to the Damudes were found between 19 and 27 March, scattered about the local countryside. Also during this time, a Thai woman out walking her dog in the area found other gruesome remains partially tipped into a shaft of a disused tin mine. The identity of the victims was later confirmed using dental records.

The Western world has become hardened to this kind of cold-blooded multiple murder. The gruesome details of the killings perpetrated by, for example, Kenneth McDuff, Harvey Carignan and Peter Sutcliffe have become all too familiar. When the latest sensational murder case features in the headlines we have the feeling that we have read it all before. Dismembered corpses, anonymous victims, apparently motiveless crime and strange acts of violence have become common currency.

But this is not so in Singapore, where violent crime and murder are unusual. In this draconically ordered city-state, where even the pavements seem to have been scrubbed clean and the glass of the skyscrapers sparkles spotless in the sun, crime comes in rather more sanitised forms.

Famously harsh punishment awaits those who dare drop litter or chewing gum. Taxis are fitted with a warning bell which rings automatically if the driver exceeds the 50mph speed limit. It is not that Singaporeans have not encountered murder before. They have their share of domestic homicide, averaging fewer than 50 murders a year in a population of two and a half million. Murders committed in the heat of the moment always seem to be more understandable.

It fell to Acting Superintended Gerald Lim to lead the investigation into the crimes committed by John Scripps. At the time of Gerard Lowe's murder, he was the senior investigating officer with the CID's Special Investigation Section, and his work began on 13 March 1995 in Singapore harbour with the discovery of a pair of feet poking out of a black bin bag and tied up with a pair of large blue Woolworth's underpants.

A boatman made the next discovery. Bobbing among the pleasure boats off Clifford Pier were two thighs – white, hairy and bound with strips of orange fabric. Finally, on 16 March, a plump male torso was retrieved from the water. These items all belonged to the same male Caucasian body but the head and arms have never been recovered.

Lim had dealt with fatal fights between immigrant building workers and he had come across domestic murder. But this was something completely and horrifyingly different. He examined the green-tinged, rotting flesh and wondered at the person who could be responsible for such cold and calculating destruction of another human being. And this body was not just headless and armless, it was nameless.

As most visitors to Singapore were registered as hotel guests, the detective's first stop was the centralised hotel registration computer. Within hours a fax had been sent to every hotel in Singapore asking if any guests were missing or had left without paying their bill. The Riverview Hotel responded immediately. Two guests, Gerard Lowe and Simon Davis, had checked out of Room 1511 without paying. But there was something else, the manager said. His duty reception staff recalled that the Englishman had been seen lugging a heavy suitcase through the foyer the night before he and his companion disappeared. It was also noted that when he returned to the hotel several hours later he was empty-handed.

On 14 March, the police in Johannesburg, South Africa, received a report from a distressed Mrs Vanessa Lowe that her husband was missing. He had not called her from Singapore to say that all was well, which, she explained, was totally out of character. Her concern soon reached Gerald Lim, who invited her to fly to Singapore to view the disarticulated body and a few items of wet clothing. Before Vanessa Lowe arrived, Lim had determined that 'Simon Davis' had been using his victim's gold credit card. 'Davis' was now the prime suspect and a warrant was issued for his arrest. Police now believed he had murdered Lowe for his money.

When the distraught woman arrived, Superintendent Lim met her at the airport and, as delicately as he could, asked her to identify the corpse. Bravely she pointed out various marks on her late husband's body. She recognised the appendectomy scar on the abdomen, the freckles on the back and the bony lump just below the right knee. She also identified the underpants, used by Scripps to tie up his victim's thighs, and the orange strips were from her husband's T-shirt.

For some inexplicable reason, Scripps returned on 19 March to

Singapore, where, after a short struggle at Immigration Control, he was arrested and taken into custody. When officers opened the backpack of the man calling himself Simon Davis, which had been seized during his arrest, they were amazed at what they found. There, along with an 'Enjoy Coca-Cola' beach towel, a Pink Floyd cassette, a bottle of Paul Mitchell shampoo and some Featherlite condoms, was what they came to describe as a 'murder kit'.

Scripps was carrying a 10,000-volt Z-Force III stun gun, a 1.5-kilogram hammer, a can of Mace, two sets of handcuffs, some thumb cuffs, two serrated knives and two Swiss Army knives. But this was not all. Another of his bags was filled with clothes suitable for a middle-aged woman, consisting of skirts, dresses and even some pearl earrings. Hidden among them were passports in the names of two Canadian citizens, Sheila and Darin Damude, each of them containing crudely pasted-in photographs of Scripps. He was also found to be carrying more than US$40,000 in cash and traveller's cheques, together with the passports, credit cards and other belongings of Lowe and the Damudes.

In the Singapore equivalent of committal proceedings, the preliminary enquiry received written statements from as many as 77 witnesses for the prosecution in support of the murder charge and 11 other charges ranging from forgery, vandalism and cheating to possession of weapons and small quantities of controlled drugs. Douglas Herda, representing the Royal Canadian Mounted Police, also wanted to question Scripps about the murders of Sheila and Darin Damude in Phuket. The Singaporean authorities refused his request.

The trial of John Martin Scripps started on 2 October 1995 in Singapore's new high-tech court. Security was heavy throughout the session, with the defendant sitting between two armed uniformed officers in a glass and metal cage. His legs were shackled to a metal bar. He had entered no plea but 'claimed trial', which, under Singapore law, means he was contesting the charges. Singapore does not have trial by jury: a judge alone hears the evidence.

The first witness was James Quigley, who testified that he had taught Scripps butchery in Albany Prison, back in the UK. Chao Tzee Cheng, a government pathologist, said that the manner in which Lowe's body was cut up indicated that only a doctor, a veterinarian or a butcher could have dismembered it. 'I told the police, "Look, you are dealing with a serial killer,"' he said in his evidence.

The prosecution alleged that Scripps, using a false name, had checked into the same hotel room as Gerard Lowe and killed him.

In what amounted to a confession, Scripps told the court he met Lowe at Changi Airport on 8 March and they had agreed to share a hotel room. He admitted killing him in the room after he was awakened by a half-naked Lowe, who was smiling and touching his buttocks.

'I am not a homosexual,' claimed Scripps, 'and at that time it appeared to me Mr Lowe was a homosexual. I freaked out; I kicked out and started swearing. I had experience of such things in the past and I was very frightened.'

Scripps said he used the hammer 'to hit Lowe several times on the head until he collapsed on to the carpeted floor. My right hand was covered with blood. Everything happened so quickly.'

After realising Lowe was dead, Scripps testified, he sought the help of a British friend, whom he refused to name. The friend disposed of the body without telling him how. He denied that he cut up the body.

The defence, led by Joseph Theseira, tried to show that Scripps had not intended to kill Lowe and the murder was an act of manslaughter, which carried a maximum penalty of life in prison.

The prosecution claimed that he committed premeditated murder with the intention of robbing the dead man.

On the fourth day of the trial, the prosecutor, Jennifer Marie, said that Scripps had practised forging Lowe's signature, suggesting that the murder was premeditated. She showed the court items seized from his luggage, including a notebook and tracing paper with practised signatures of Lowe's name.

In a nitpicking exercise, the defence questioned two police officers, trying to show that they conducted an inadequate search for blood traces next to the hotel-room bed where Scripps claimed Lowe fell and bled to death. Both officers said there were no traces of blood on the carpet, only in the small bathroom. The prosecution argued that this evidence supported their contention that the killing was premeditated. Clearly on a losing wicket, defence lawyer Edmond Pereira implied that, if the police found no blood traces on the carpet, it could have been because they did not conduct sufficiently thorough tests, and not in the exact spot where Lowe fell.

During the court proceedings on 24 October, Scripps said that while in police custody after being arrested he had tried to commit suicide by slitting his wrists with a small, sharp piece of glass to escape being hanged. 'I believed I was going to be hung,' the 35-year-old said on his fifth day in the witness box. 'I kept thinking about Lowe and the Filipino lady that got hanged.' He was referring to the Filipino maid Flor Contemplacion, who was hanged on 17 March 1995 after she confessed to two murders.

Now digging his own grave, Scripps agreed with the suggestion by Judge T.S. Sinnathuray that it would take about five minutes for a skilled butcher to dismember an animal. Then the prosecutor jumped in. 'Could your skills be used to dismember a human?'

'The bones look similar,' Scripps replied.

Cutting to the chase, Jennifer Marie asked again, 'Did you dismember Mr Lowe?'

Scripps looked down at his shackled legs and replied unconvincingly, 'No, I don't have all the skills you mentioned.'

On his sixth day on the witness stand, Scripps was asked by the prosecutor why he did not report killing Lowe to the police. 'Because this man died at my hands,' he said, 'and under Singapore law that is an automatic death sentence. That's what I understood at the time.'

'So who is the mystery man who dismembered Mr Lowe?' asked the prosecutor.

'He is a British friend staying at a hotel on Sentosa. While he was doing it I fled,' Scripps answered. He said he had known this 'friend' for eight to ten years, and remembered that he had once worked at an abattoir. 'He's a very dangerous man,' he said meekly. 'I fear for the safety of my family.'

The judge then cautioned Scripps that his reluctance to give even basic information on his friend could harm his defence. 'Here you are facing a murder charge,' he said, 'which carries the death sentence in this country. I have to ask myself, at the end of the day, this question. "Did the accused, John Scripps, go to a hotel on Sentosa?"'

Sitting back in his seat, the judge sighed as Scripps still declined even to describe the hotel, a refusal which drew a sharp accusation from the prosecutor that the defendant was lying and that the activities of his friend were all a 'complete fabrication'. Discrepancies between his earlier statements to the police on 29

April and his testimony in court were also highlighted. 'You made no mention of attempted homosexual assaults while in prison in 1978 and the alleged 1994 assault by Mr Lowe, did you? I am suggesting that this 1994 incident never occurred,' said Marie. 'It's yet another fabrication of yours.'

With Scripps now firmly on the hook, the prosecutor started to reel him in. Pressed about his movements between 8 and 11 March, Scripps said that his memory was hopeless.

'You have got a good memory?' Marie asked.

'I haven't,' he replied nervously. 'I'm dyslexic. I get things mixed up.'

On 6 November, Jennifer Marie told the court in her closing arguments, 'The conduct of the accused after the killing suggests that he was cold, callous and calculating, a far cry from the confused, dazed, forgetful man walking in a dream world, the picture he gives himself. He is a man very much in control of his faculties. When he embarked on the shopping spree using Lowe's credit card, buying a fancy pair of running shoes, a videocassette recorder, and a ticket to a symphony orchestra concert, he becomes a man who has no qualms about lying continuously, consistently, and even on the stand.' She added, with a rare touch of venom, 'This man's excuse that he killed Mr Lowe because of a homosexual advance is just one of a string of lies to mask a premeditated murder by a greedy serial killer who preyed on tourists. And, Mrs Lowe has stated on oath, a decent loving wife has come here to say that her husband had come here on a shopping holiday. He most certainly was not a homosexual. The accused has not only murdered and dismembered her husband; he now rubbishes his good name.'

In his closing statement for the defence, Edmond Pereira said, 'We urge this court to come to a finding that the accused is not guilty of murder, but is guilty of culpable homicide not amounting to murder. The killing occurred in a sudden fight in the heat of passion upon a sudden quarrel,' adding, 'He is not a man prone to violence.'

Pereira also urged Judge Sinnathuray to ignore the information from Thailand. 'There is no evidence to suggest that the accused is responsible for the deaths of the two Canadians,' he said, calling the Thai information 'nothing more than circumstantial and prejudicial'.

On 7 November 1995, Scripps, dressed in khaki with a prison-style crew-cut and standing in the courtroom's glass cage, was said to be laughing and joking with his guards before the verdict. 'Karma is karma. It's in God's hands now,' he said, but his attitude changed within minutes.

The judge told the packed court, 'I am satisfied beyond a reasonable doubt that Scripps had intentionally killed Lowe. After that, he disarticulated Lowe's body into separate parts, and it was he who subsequently disposed of the body parts by throwing them into the river behind the hotel.' Having announced the guilty verdict, Judge T.S. Sinnathuray sentenced Scripps to death by hanging. The condemned man was less glib as he was taken away to a place of lawful execution.

After the verdict, defence counsel Edmond Pereira told reporters, 'Scripps has a right to an appeal, which he can exercise within 14 days, and he shall be advised of that right.'

Privately in an interview for the research for this book, the judge said that he was convinced that Scripps had killed the Damudes, but added that he decided Scripps's guilt independently of the Thai evidence. 'On the evidence, I had no difficulty to find that it was Scripps who was concerned with the deaths of Sheila and Darin, and for the disposal of their body parts found in different sites in Phuket. The disarticulation of the body parts of Lowe, Sheila and Darin have all the hallmark signs of having been done by the same person. The Thai evidence was materially relevant because it rebutted Scripps's defence that he killed Lowe unintentionally during a sudden fight.'

On hearing the news at her home in Sandown, Isle of Wight, Scripps's mother, 58-year-old Jean Scripps, said, 'I brought John into this world. I am the only person who has the right to take him out. I cannot believe how my boy could have changed from a kind human being into the monster described in court.'

On 4 January 1996, John Martin Scripps virtually signed his death warrant when he wrote to the prison authorities to withdraw his appeal which was scheduled to be heard on 8 January, but confirmed he would file for a clemency plea. This was the only sensible avenue open to him, and he had a brief six- to eight-week window of opportunity to complete the paperwork.

The death penalty was in use during the colonial period in Singapore, and was retained after the city-state became an independent republic in August 1965. Today death sentences may be imposed for various offences under the Penal Code; the Internal Security Act, 1960; the Misuse of Drugs Act, 1973 as amended in 1975; and the Arms Offences Act. Capital offences include: murder, treason, hurting or imprisoning the President, offences relating to the unlawful possession of firearms and explosives, and perjury resulting in the execution of a person indicted on a capital charge. The 1975 amendment to the Misuse of Drugs Act made the death penalty mandatory for possession of over 15 grams of heroin, or fixed amounts of other drugs.

Capital offences are tried before the High Court. The defendant has the right of appeal against conviction to the Court of Criminal Appeal and the law guarantees legal counsel. On dismissal of appeal, prisoners may seek permission to appeal to the Judicial Committee of the Privy Council in England, which serves as the final court of appeal for Singapore. If the Privy Council upholds a sentence, prisoners may submit a clemency petition to the President of Singapore.

On 14 February 1996, a spokesperson from the British High Commission in Singapore visited Scripps in prison. Afterwards, she told reporters, 'He won't be putting in an appeal. He's eager to get it over and done with. He's just waiting for the day.'

This loose comment surprised Edmond Pereira, who was moved to say, 'There are some instructions Scripps has given to me, but I'm not at liberty at this stage to make any comment because the matter has not been finalised,' adding, 'But, even if a prisoner refused to petition for clemency, the matter still has to go before the President; however, if he does not request clemency, they won't exercise clemency.'

While he was being held in solitary confinement at Changi, Scripps spent most of his time watching television and reading. A priest visited him weekly, and once a fortnight a consular representative went to check on his welfare and pass on messages from his family.

Singapore's *Sunday Times* reported on 10 March that Scripps had declined to seek a pardon from President Ong Teng Cheong. 'It was his wish to let the law take its course,' the story concluded.

It was announced that John Scripps was to die at dawn on Friday, 19 April. He had turned down a request by Scotland Yard detectives to interview him about the murder of British backpacker

Timothy McDowell in Mexico in 1994. He spent his last two days in his cell writing garbled love poems to his former Mexican wife, Maria, described as the one true love of his life. He was confined in a windowless cubicle measuring eight foot by six, lit constantly and kept under continuous camera surveillance. There was a hole-in-the ground lavatory and a straw roll-mat to sleep on.

Scripps's sister Janet and mother Jean said their farewells to him in his cell 12 hours before his execution. They had turned down an offer to be present at his death. Janet said in an interview with the author, 'How do you say goodbye to your own brother like that? We didn't actually say the word. I just couldn't.'

In a semi-literate scrawl on a scrap of paper, Scripps wrote that he had given himself to God who had betrayed him. 'You may take my life for what it's worth, but grant thows I love, pease and happiness.'

For his last meal he asked for a pizza and a cup of hot chocolate. He then requested another scrap of paper and left a final, rambling note: 'One day poor. One day reach. Money filds the pane of hunger but what will the emteness inside? I know that love is beyond me. So do I give myself to god. The god that has betrad me. You may take my life for what it is worth but grant those I love peace and happiness. Can I be a person again. Only time will tell me. What really upset me was when you are told every day that you are not a member of the uman rase.'

In accordance with the execution procedure, hangings in Changi Prison are carried out in private on a large gallows which can accommodate up to seven prisoners at a time. Hangings are carried out with a black hood covering the head and the use of the 'long drop' method.

The recommended drop is based on the need to produce a force of

1,260 pounds on the neck and upper-spine region of the condemned person as he plunges through the trap. This figure, divided by the prisoner's weight in pounds, gives the length of drop in feet. Therefore, to kill instantaneously, it is crucial to get these calculations correct.

It is also normal practice in Singapore to hang several prisoners simultaneously, although no specific details of the executions are released to the news media. The 'official' version, which is issued on the occasion of every execution as a matter of policy, stated: 'John Scripps was woken by guards at about 3.30am, and escorted to a waiting room where he, and two other prisoners, two Singaporean drug traffickers, were prepared. He spoke to a priest and a prison chaplain before his time came when he walked bravely to his death.'

The relatives of Scripps's partners on the gallows received identical letters with only the names being changed.

The impression of an apparently smooth procedure was later emphatically dispelled when the priest who had attended the execution unexpectedly resigned. As part of his clerical duties he had witnessed most of the executions at Changi during the previous ten years, but he was so horrified by the death of John Scripps that he resigned immediately afterwards. And, far from walking bravely to his death, Scripps put up a fight to the bitter end.

The guards did indeed come for Scripps at 3.30am. He was ordered to step out of his prison-issue shorts to avoid soiling them with urine and excrement, and told to dress in his civilian clothes. When he refused, his prison garb was torn from him.

He should have been weighed to calculate the drop, but he had told Chris Berry-Dee that he would give his jailers an execution to remember, for he hated these men who daily reminded him that he was not a member of the 'uman rase'. Crucially, he refused to be weighed for the drop, with all the consequences that might have for the efficiency and humaneness of his execution.

Too long a drop and he could be decapitated; too short a drop and he could strangle to death at the end of the rope. In the event, it took 12 guards 20 minutes to drag him to the holding cell next to the gallows. During this struggle he sustained a broken nose, cheekbone and jaw, two black eyes and multiple bruising.

As the appointed time drew near, Scripps was heard to be sobbing. The two other doomed men were already pinioned and hooded on the trap when he was prepared. Again he lashed out before being bound with leather straps. Now 'neutralised', naked and tightly buckled, he lost control of his bodily functions. Quickly a rubber bung was forced between his teeth. Then came the hood, followed by the rope, which was snapped tight under his left ear, then, with a pull on a lever, John Scripps plunged into eternity.

For half an hour his body swung silently in the pit before being taken down. The consequences of the failure to calculate a proper drop were only too obvious, for his head had almost been ripped from his body.

At 10.30am, Scripps left prison for the last time. Wrapped in a white sheet and placed in a cardboard coffin, his body joined the other two corpses in an old green, tarpaulin-covered truck, and he was taken to a funeral parlour in Sin Ming Drive. The two Singaporeans were dropped off en route for cremation. When Jean Scripps and her daughter viewed the body, she almost fainted. With the press pack beating on the funeral-parlour door, they finally made good their escape and Scripps was cremated later that afternoon, at the Republic's expense.

In a final irony, John Scripps spent that night at the Riverview

Hotel. The urn containing his ashes was in the charge of one of the representatives of the Scripps family, lots having been drawn to decide who should have this responsibility. Back in England, at a private service attended only by relatives and close friends, the ashes were scattered at a secret location.

John Martin Scripps had followed the tourist trail to Thailand and Phang-Na, popularly known as 'James Bond Island', which was one of the film locations for *The Man with the Golden Gun*. While there he had had his photograph taken and printed on a souvenir plate. 'I can't believe he killed them,' said Nipa Eamsom-Ang, the receptionist at Nilly's Marina Inn at Patong Beach. 'He was not crazy. I liked him very much,' she added. 'He was always smiling, smiling, smiling.' Locals say she has become nervous about ghosts since Scripps was convicted, though she seemed nonplussed when asked whether hotel business had suffered in the aftermath of the murder.

Everyone who knew Scripps agrees he seemed 'a really nice guy'. During his trial, he looked sensible, decent even, and chatted politely to his guards about the weather. Once, when the judge sneezed, he turned around and said quietly, 'Bless you.'

The Roman Catholic priest whom John called 'Father Frank' said, 'I try to imagine how his face would have looked when he was chopping up the bodies,' concluding, 'It's impossible. I can only see him as he was with me – young, handsome, soft-spoken and gentle.'

This is an all-too-familiar perception. When people meet serial killers they often think they are shy, quiet, nice people who are not easily upset. The reality is that of the over-controlled personality, which in certain situations may well lead to occasional outbursts of rage.

So what was Scripps's motive? Was it the lure of money that drove him to kill? Strangely, in view of his actions, many observers think this unlikely. He robbed his victims, but there was more to it than that; as Brian Williams, liaison officer for the Royal Canadian Mounted Police in Bangkok, said, 'You can rob without killing, and you can kill without cutting up the body into bits. This man went to such an extreme and I can only think that he relished what he was doing.'

Brian Williams may well be correct in his commonsense appraisal, but ultimately it comes down to a common enough motive and this, the authors believe, is financial gain.

Scripps was a cold, calculating killer, who had planned his *modus operandi* almost to perfection. His butchery skills merely added to the clinically efficient way he disposed of the bodies. Whether he 'relished' the dismemberment is open to debate.

John Scripps was neither insane nor mad in the medical or legal sense. When he killed Gerard Lowe in their hotel room in Singapore, he was deluding himself if he believed that the island republic's system of justice would not hand down a death sentence to an Englishmen. As an experienced traveller in South-East Asia, he must have known that some countries in the region have an unequivocal attitude to murder and drug smuggling, crimes which there carry a mandatory death sentence.

For their part, the Singapore authorities are tough on criminals. The Deputy Superintendent of Police, Chin Fook Leon, told Chris Berry-Dee during an interview, 'We impose the maximum sentence of death without concern for race, colour or creed. Break the penal code in Singapore and suffer the consequences.'

The deterrent value of the death sentence in Singapore is there for all to consider if there is an intention to break the law. It is even printed on red and white notices prominently posted around the city. Singaporeans argue that it is effectively the individual's own choice. Go against the law of the country and suffer the consequences, and this uncompromising attitude is always applied.

Five Thai men who entered Singapore illegally as labourers and were held as 'guests' of the Republic took it upon themselves to abuse their hosts by robbing construction sites between November 1991 and January 1993. In committing their crimes they murdered one Myanmar and two Indian nationals.

Panya Marmontree (22), Prawit Yaoabutr (22), Manit Wangjaisuk (31), Panya Amphawa (29) and Prasong Bunsom (32) were sentenced to death on 16 January 1995. Their appeals against execution were dismissed on 10 July and they were duly hanged at Changi Prison on Friday, 16 March 1996.

The Thai Ambassador, Mr Adisak Panupong, told Chris, 'My countrymen were aware of the laws and punishments of Singapore and, in breaking them, they also knew what the consequences might be. The decision was theirs to make.'

John Scripps had made visits to the Far East before he killed Gerard Lowe, so he must have known and understood the law very well. He was aware of the risks of committing serious crime in both Singapore and Thailand, and of the consequences of being arrested and found guilty of drugs smuggling and committing murder. When he killed Lowe, he did so for financial profit and the Singapore authorities took the view that, by committing this murder on their soil, he merely validated his own execution. It is consistent with this outlook that he demonstrated, by his unlawful behaviour, that murder was permissible. As far as the Singapore authorities were concerned, those were *his* standards, and he was treated accordingly.

Consideration of punishment, whether it meant life in prison or execution, was also determined by Scripps's own actions. It was not his victim, nor the police, the Singapore judicial system, the department of prisons or the executioner, who initiated the sequence of events that led to his death by the judicial process. It was down to John Scripps himself. And, if he had escaped the noose in Singapore, what would have been his fate in Thailand? It would have been execution by machine gun.

Legislation in Thailand had now been extended to include imposition of the death penalty for offences other than murder. The Royal Act on Habit-Forming Drugs, 1979, introduced an optional death penalty for the possession of more than 100 grams of heroin, while maintaining a mandatory death sentence for its production, import or export. Although Thailand is reluctant to implement the death penalty in respect of convicted Europeans, who usually receive commutations by royal pardon, the number of people under sentence of death and the number of executions carried out on Europeans have both been rising steadily.

Therefore, John Scripps was playing a lethal game in which his own life was also at stake. Not only did he risk the death sentence for international drug trafficking, he had committed two counts of aggravated homicide, which carries the mandatory death sentence in Thailand. A final dimension to his recklessness was provided by Singapore Drugs Squad Officers who discovered a substantial amount of heroin in a safety deposit box he had rented in the city. This was his stash, which alone would have been enough to send him to prison for the rest of his life. It seems that he was doomed in any event.

Socorro 'Cora' Caro

The bald facts of this story are that Socorro 'Cora' Caro was sentenced to death in California on 5 April 2002 for shooting dead her three children. Caro, born on Tuesday, 27 May 1957, committed the murders and then turned the gun on herself but failed to take her own life. But there is much more to this case. It is the story of a marriage that had reached the end of the road and it resembles a classical Greek tragedy in the inevitability with which events unfolded.

Socorro and her husband, Dr Xavier Caro, 52, had been married since 5 July 1986. Dr Caro, a rheumatologist, was a staff physician at Northridge Hospital Medical Center in the San Fernando Valley, where his wife worked as his office manager. The couple had four children, all boys. The three eldest were Joseph, Michael and Christopher, aged eleven, eight and five respectively at the time of the killing. All three were shot dead by their mother at the family's Santa Rosa Valley mansion on Saturday, 23 November 1999. The youngest boy, Gabriel, was only 13 months old. He alone of the children survived and was unharmed.

In August 1999, the couple's marriage was coming to an end. Xavier Caro discovered that Cora had been mismanaging the finances. The rent was in arrears, creditors were not being paid and the practice was $44,000 in debt. He also discovered that his wife had given her parents, Greg and Juanita Leon, $105,000 during the past year. Faced with a financial crisis, he fired her and took away her chequebook and credit cards.

Money wasn't the only threat to the marriage. Xavier had begun an affair with a woman who worked at the practice and he had seen a divorce lawyer. During his talk with the lawyer he had taken some notes which his wife found later. These concerned the way the couple's assets would be split in the event of a divorce. Around this time Cora had confided in a friend that she was deeply unhappy and wanted to kill herself. Despite all of this, the Caros managed to work through their many difficulties and were still together in November. In fact, by October there were indications that things had begun to improve. But it was a false dawn.

On the day of the killings, 22 November, the family ate their evening meal together. Joseph had made a sarcastic comment about his parents' drinking and an argument began between the two adults. It ended when Dr Caro left the house and drove to his office in order to allow things to cool down.

At about 11.20pm, a 911 call was received from a man who thought his wife had slit her wrists. The man making the call was Dr Xavier Caro. His voice sounded concerned but controlled. He asked the dispatcher to send an ambulance and explained that his wife was unconscious on the floor. Moments later, his voice changed. It rose and his speech quickened. He had turned his wife over and found a gunshot wound to her head and a gun next to her body. He assumed she had shot herself.

The dispatcher asked if there were any children in the house. The man put the phone on speaker and went off to check on his four sons. According to a report, the next time the man spoke, the dispatcher heard a voice that was almost not human, 'the guttural savage shrieks of a man who had just found three of his children dead'. The dispatcher recorded that the man had screamed, 'Why did you do this? My son was going to be somebody! Oh God! Oh Jesus!'

A report in the *Ventura Star* details Xavier Caro's testimony, in which he described finding the carnage at his home:

'With his demeanor on the witness stand oscillating almost instantly from a distraught, heartbroken father to a systematic, concerned doctor, Xavier Caro described first seeing his wife on the floor of their bedroom with blood-soaked froth spewing from her mouth, then discovering her .38-caliber Smith & Wesson revolver underneath her and shell casings near her body.

'"I just became very confused," he said before a courtroom filled with his and her families. "It just didn't compute. I was puzzled, perplexed, bewildered. I kept asking myself, 'What is going on here?' I remember thinking, 'Perhaps she was playing Russian roulette.'"'

At 11.21pm, he called 911 and the operator eventually asked him if any children were in the house. So he went to his first-born son's room to see whether his 11-year-old son Joey was OK.

'I saw Joey,' he moaned, exhaling deeply. 'I saw my Joey.' The boy lay face up, his eyes and mouth open, Caro said. 'He was so pale. It was so bad. There was so much blood. He looked like a starfish. It was horrible. It was just terrible.'

During the 911 call, Caro was heard screaming repeatedly. Then, as the emotion disappeared from his voice, he said that he had checked Joey for a pulse but found none. He couldn't bring himself to examine the body further.

Caro then walked through the 'Jack & Jill bedroom' – two bedrooms with an adjoining bathroom between them – his three sons shared and into Michael and Christopher's bedroom, where they slept together on the bottom of a bunk bed.

'I saw my babies,' he told the packed courtroom. Now in tears, he continued, 'Oh, man. Oh, Golly. It's so bad,' as he looked at the bloody crime-scene photos of Michael and Christopher. 'They weren't moving or anything,' he said. 'They were really pale. They were just as still as could be.'

'What were you thinking?' asked Deputy District Attorney Cheryl Temple, to which Caro replied, 'I thought Cora had done just a terrible thing.'

Caro then testified that he returned to the master bedroom, where his wife remained on the floor, and kicked her once. He then said he thought of his fourth son, 13-month-old Gabriel, who slept in an alcove in their bedroom. As he approached his crib, he braced himself for 'another mess', adding, 'I thought he would be shot, too. He started to move and I knew he was alive.'

With his fourth son unharmed, he said he became 'inspired' to try to save his other children despite their deathly appearance. Returning to Joey's room, he looked at the son he called his best friend. 'There was so much blood,' he cried. 'You have no idea.' Then he returned to the younger boys' room, and heard something that gave him hope – a gasp from Michael.

Caro gave the boys two breaths of cardiopulmonary

resuscitation, but received no response. So he put his hand on the back of Michael's head to prop him up and a piece of the boy's skull fell off. 'My baby's skull was in my hands,' he said through tears.

Within minutes, three sheriff's deputies and three firefighters arrived at the house at 12404 Presilla Road. The three boys were determined dead, and a helicopter airlifted Cora to hospital.

Socorro 'Cora' Caro was charged with the murders and pleaded not guilty by reason of insanity. She accused her husband of the killings and the defence team argued that Dr Caro had tried to frame his wife. However, the evidence against her was overwhelming, and included two of her bloody handprints on the door of the boys' bedroom. According to witnesses, she had attacked her husband on several occasions and had caused him several injuries, including serious eye damage that required surgery.

The jury deliberated for five days before arriving at a guilty verdict. On Friday, 5 April 2002, Ventura County Superior Court Judge Donald Coleman sentenced Cora Caro to death. He said the killings had been 'wilful, premeditated and committed with malice aforethought'. Calling the slayings the 'mass murder of innocent children', the judge added, 'The weight of this factor is quite simply enormous. The brutal murder of these three children occurred in the sanctity of their homes ... [they had become] sacrificial symbolic pawns of a failed marital relationship.'

Socorro 'Cora' Caro is currently held on California's Death Row for females at the California Institution for Women, Corona.

John Albert Boltz

The City of Shawnee, Pottawatomie County, Oklahoma, is the birthplace of Brad Pitt and the resting place, in a grave on Harrison Street, of Brewster Higley, the composer of the song 'Home on the Range'. All very nice so far, but Shawnee has another, much less savoury, distinction. In 1984 John Albert Boltz committed a murder in the city that resulted 22 years later in his becoming, at 74, the oldest man to have been executed by the State of Oklahoma. How he came to earn this celebrity is a horrifying story.

After work on the evening of Tuesday, 18 April 1984, Patricia Kirby, who was married to John Boltz at the time, had gone to nearby Stroud to meet a close friend, her former boss Duane Morrison. Boltz suspected his wife of having an affair and had followed her.

At this stage there was something slightly comical about the actions of the suspicious husband: he was dressed in combat fatigues and wearing dark glasses. When he saw that his wife was meeting Morrison, however, the comic aspect evaporated and the situation assumed a very serious, sanguinary complexion. Boltz flew into a rage. He swore at Morrison and threatened to cut off his head. Almost in meltdown, Boltz claimed that he had killed men, women and children during the Korean War and killing 'didn't faze him'. He added that that he had cut off people's heads in the war for less serious matters.

Her evening in ruins, Pat went to the trailer home that she shared with her husband. She wrote a note telling him that their marriage was over. Having done that, she packed some clothes and telephoned her 22-year-old son Douglas Kirby, asking him for help with moving some of her things into his home. She then left and went to her mother's home.

In the meantime, Boltz had been drinking at the Veterans of Foreign Wars hall. When he returned home to the trailer, he found the note from his wife. Assuming she had gone to her mother's home, he drove there to see her. On arriving at his mother-in-law's home, he forced his way into the house and began yelling a tirade of abuse and accusations at his wife. Shaken by the ferocity of her husband's behaviour, Pat called the Shawnee Police Department and asked them to remove him from the premises. In the circumstances, the incident was classed as a low priority and the police dispatcher told the caller that they were busy but they would try to deal with the problem later. It is always easy to say these things with hindsight, but the delay in responding eventually cost a life. The call was made at about 9.30pm and shortly afterwards Boltz had left of his own accord.

Some time later, Pat telephoned the police again to ask if her husband had been arrested. She was told that he had not been taken into custody, because the police were busy. Pat left her mother and made her way to the home of her son Doug, where she intended to stay until she could find somewhere of her own.

Doug, a bachelor, had bought a small, two-bedroom house because he wanted a home to accommodate visits from his small son, Nathan. John Boltz had returned to his trailer home and made three phone calls to his stepson Doug's house. Doug answered the first call and they spoke for a few minutes. Minutes later the phone rang for a second time. Again it was Boltz and again Doug answered it. This conversation was shorter and, when he had put the phone down, Doug told his mother that he was going over to Boltz's trailer to talk with him. He didn't appear to be upset or angry and he left almost immediately. This was a mistake that was to prove fatal.

After Doug left, 15 or 20 minutes passed until the third call came. Pat picked up the phone to hear her husband spitting vitriol. 'I am gonna cut your loving little boy's head off,' he ranted. 'I am also gonna kill you.' He promised her she would be dead within the hour.

Pat was terrified. Immediately she dialled 911 and reported the threats. The phone call was recorded and played to the jury during the subsequent trial. At one point Pat said to the dispatcher: 'Cheryl, this is Pat again. I hate … I hate to keep calling, but John just now called and said he was going to cut my son's head off, and my son is over there in the trailer park, and John is over there at the trailer. That was Lot 119.'

For those of us who have never been in such a situation, it isn't possible to imagine the mounting panic that Pat felt as she spoke. This woman knew her husband better than anyone. He was drunk and he was enraged and she was only too aware that her son was in great danger. She ended the call by saying that she was going over to see Boltz. Then she set off.

Tense with dread, she drove to the trailer park and went straight to Lot 119. There, in her headlights, she was confronted by her worst nightmare imaginable. Her son's blood-drenched body was lying on the ground outside his car, the victim of a crazed, knife-wielding madman. John Boltz had virtually fulfilled his threat to cut off her son's head.

The young man had suffered eight stab wounds to the neck, chest and abdomen, and his neck had been cut three times. His neck was injured so severely that both carotid arteries had been severed, the voice box and oesophagus were cut and the spinal column was damaged. One of the stab wounds pierced his back. Bloodstains were discovered leading from the front porch to the driver's door of Mr Kirby's car as well as inside the vehicle. A .22-calibre revolver was recovered from the passenger seat; the gun had no blood on it, but the seat was spattered with blood.

After the killing Boltz drove to the American Legion in Midwest City, where he told some friends that he had killed his stepson and that he had 'probably cut his head off'. The police were called and Boltz was arrested without incident. Although he admitted to the killing, he did not elaborate on the circumstances leading up to it and he was charged with first-degree murder.

Refusing to plead guilty to voluntary manslaughter, Boltz went to trial. At trial the killer did not dispute the State's contention that he stabbed Douglas Kirby to death. Rather, his strategy was to present a self-defence theory. Boltz testified that Kirby had called him that evening and threatened to kill him. He claimed that when Kirby arrived at his trailer he kicked in the front door and as he went for a gun Boltz stabbed him twice, but he did not remember anything after that point.

A Ms Witt, who lived next door to Boltz, testified that during that evening she heard the screeching of brakes, a car door slam and loud, angry noises. Hearing a sound like 'someone getting the wind knocked out of him', she looked out of the window and saw Boltz standing over Doug Kirby, who was lying on his back on the ground and not moving. Boltz, she said, was standing over the helpless man screaming obscenities and beating him. She told the court that she told her own son to call the police and she observed Boltz pull something 'shiny' from his belt and point the object at Doug. When Boltz looked up and saw her watching, she turned away out of fear.

Dr Fred Jordan, who performed the autopsy on Doug Kirby, testified that he had died from a total of eleven wounds, including eight stab wounds to the neck, chest and abdomen and three cutting wounds to the neck, one of which was so deep that it had cut into the spinal column. He told the court, 'The carotid arteries on both sides of the neck were cut in half and the major arteries in the heart were also cut.'

As John Boltz's execution drew close, he tucked into what appears to be the standard meal provided by the Oklahoma Department of Corrections. Selecting from a Kentucky Fried Chicken menu, he chose fried chicken, potato wedges, baked beans, coleslaw, an apple turnover and a dinner roll.

Blond-haired, blue-eyed John Albert Boltz, standing six feet two inches tall and weighing 200 pounds, expressed no remorse when he was strapped to the gurney at 7.15pm on Thursday, 1 June 2006. He did not apologise to family members and he did not acknowledge two of his friends who attended the execution. Instead, he blamed members of Doug Kirby's family for his execution, which was delayed more than an hour because staff had trouble finding a vein in which to inject the lethal cocktail.

'Shrouded with a white sheet with two pillows supporting his head, he looked more like a grandfather taking a nap,' claimed a police officer who witnessed what would become Boltz's longest sleep.

'This is a time for gladness for me, and a time of sadness because I think of all the people involved who got me here and what's in store for them,' said Boltz into the microphone above his head. Without reciting the verses, he referred to a passage in the Old Testament book of Deuteronomy. 'They need to read this portion of the Bible and see what's down the road for them,' he said. 'I've seen so much pain for all these years. And now it's come down to this.'

The condemned man took a few heavy breaths after his statement and then a deep sigh as he closed his eyes. His rosy face turned ashen, then purple, as the drugs paralysed him and then stopped his heart seven minutes later.

Boltz's passing was witnessed by the victim's brother, Jim Kirby, who said that the execution was 'long overdue … it was a horrific crime and it deserved the punishment that was given. We are all relieved that it's all over with.' Jim Kirby said Doug was working at an industrial plant in Shawnee before his death, but aspired to be a businessman. Doug was a member of the Shawnee Jaycees, a chapter that instituted an outstanding community service award in his remembrance.

In a letter to the State Pardon and Parole Board, Nathan Kirby, 26, said he only knows his father through photos and stories. 'Not only have I missed out on having a father, but my father has missed out on having a son,' he said. 'John Boltz dying will bring us all some peace, but it will never bring Doug back to us.'

Jim Kirby said, 'I think about that every time I look at a family Christmas picture and he's missing.'

It is true to say that John Boltz brought about his own death sentence, not through his murderous act but through his strange stubbornness. Initially the prosecutor offered him the option of pleading guilty to the lesser charge of voluntary manslaughter. Boltz refused this. In fact, at the appeal stage he argued that he should have been declared incompetent after refusing to accept the prosecutor's plea bargain. Had he accepted the offer, it is possible that he would have been a free man by 2006, the year in which he was executed. However, the court turned down his appeal on the grounds that his refusal to plead guilty to manslaughter did not indicate incompetence, just a failure by the former used-car salesman to recognise a good deal.

Former Pottawatomie County Assistant District Attorney John Canavan revealed that the offer had been extended to Boltz in order to spare Pat Kirby from having to testify. She had told prosecutors she was close to a nervous breakdown and was worried about the effect that the stress of a trial would exert on her fragile mental state. In the end, however, it was Pat Kirby's testimony that swayed the jury to opt for the death sentence. 'We were all sort of shocked,' Canavan said, 'because juries rarely give the death penalty in domestic killings. This one was just so mean. A total innocent was killed just to get back at her.'

The passage from Deuteronomy to which John Boltz made reference is Chapter 19, verses 18–21:

'And the judges shall make diligent inquisition: and, behold, if the witness be a false witness, and hath testified falsely against his brother;

'Then shall ye do unto him, as he had thought to have done unto his brother: so shalt thou put the evil away from among you.

'And those which remain shall hear, and fear, and shall henceforth commit no more any such evil among you.

'And thine eye shall not pity; but life shall go for life, eye for eye, tooth for tooth, hand for hand, foot for foot.'

Precisely what John Boltz wished to convey by quoting this passage has never been made entirely clear. However, one thing is transparently certain and that is that when he was executed his life was the price that was to be paid for that of his victim, Douglas Kirby.

James Delano Winkles

'I regret that he can only die one time.
Every day since Sept. 9, 1980 I wish he could die
that many days. You have no idea the torture he
put the families through. It's something that
never goes away, like a thorn in your foot for
20-some years. I would say, "May God have mercy
on his soul, but he has no soul."'

Gary Muchmore, boyfriend of murder victim Elizabeth Graham

When, as sometimes happens, police detectives are presented
with a confession from someone who claims to have carried
out many murders, they are obliged to investigate each and every
case without exception. There are no short cuts and the work can
be laborious and time-consuming. In the majority of such instances
the confessor will turn out to be an attention-seeker, but this
cannot be left to chance. No policeman wants to be responsible for

having ignored someone they considered a time-waster only to find subsequently that he or she was nothing of the sort, but instead a dangerous serial killer.

James Delano Winkles is one of these disturbing individuals who court notoriety of the most repugnant sort and are prepared to pay the highest of prices for their strange obsession. At one stage Winkles claimed to have kidnapped and murdered 26 people between 1967 and 1982. However, investigators had difficulty separating fact from fiction and they found actual evidence of only two murders that they could treat as authentic. When it comes to murder, two is more than enough. There is always a danger that, when a man like Winkles appears, giving the impression of being something of a Walter Mitty character, his wildly exaggerated claims will attract a level of ridicule and draw attention away from the gravity of the crimes that have actually been committed. That would be a mistake. The murders that Winkles carried out were ghastly and cruel, involving the kidnapping and rape of two women.

Winkles lived in Pinellas Park, Florida, where he worked as a mechanic and ran a lawn-maintenance operation. It began on Wednesday, 6 January 1982, when Winkles called at the office of Zigler Realty in Seminole County, Florida. Eighteen-year-old Donna Maltby, a married woman, was the salesperson who dealt with him. He identified himself as David Longstreet and asked to view several remote properties. The woman did precisely as she was asked. However, Winkles wanted something more remote, so a meeting to view some other properties was arranged for the next day.

The next day, Thursday, Donna Maltby received a phone call from 'David Longstreet'. He told her that his car had a flat battery and asked if she could come to his motel to help him get the car started. When she arrived at the motel, Donna was surprised to find that 'Longstreet's' engine was running. He asked her if she would drive with him to look at a property he had located just down the street. She agreed and they set off. When they had driven out of town, he suddenly stopped the car. After pulling out a knife, he stuck it in her left side, cutting her hand. He began to threaten the panic-stricken woman, saying that he wanted money and that if she did not give him some cash from her office he would rape then kill her. Terrified, the girl agreed, staying as calm as she could in the circumstances. En route to the office, 'Longstreet' stopped to buy gas and while he was talking to the attendant Donna managed to make a break for freedom.

Police arrested 'Longstreet' nearby. In the boot of his car was what can only be described as an abduction kit: drugs, handcuffs, rope and duct tape. Bizarrely, in an overnight case, was an assortment of women's undergarments. These he carried so that his victims would have something sexy to wear.

For his attack on Donna Maltby, Winkles/Longstreet was charged with kidnapping, aggravated assault and armed robbery. During their investigation of him detectives learned that, under the alias of Jimmy Delano Hawk, Winkles had a 1963 conviction for assault with intent to commit robbery. Further enquiries also led them to discover that more recently he had been charged with land fraud involving the very same land on which the headless body of a woman named Margo Delimon had been found in October 1981. Winkles's common-law wife, Mary Thomas, was questioned and she told investigators that she and Winkles had once camped on that land. She also revealed that he had been in possession of some jewellery that she didn't recognise and a driving licence which carried Margo Delimon's photo. These things connected James Winkles to the dead woman but nothing more.

There was no evidence to charge him with Delimon's murder, but for the offences against Donna Maltby he was sentenced to life imprisonment and was housed at the Hardy Correctional Institute, where he remained silent until 1998. He had been in prison ever since 1982 and was not due to be considered eligible for parole until 2013.

Late in 1997, the Pinellas County Sheriff's Office had received a telephone call from the Superintendent at the Hardy Correctional Institute. James Winkles had something he wanted to get off his chest, but he insisted that he wanted to be granted immunity from the death sentence if he made a confession. Detectives visited him but explained that they weren't able to make such a deal, and the matter was left at that.

A few months later, however, Winkles had a change of heart. Again he asked to speak to the police, this time attaching no conditions to his admission. The police agreed and arranged to interview the prisoner.

On 27 March 1998, Winkles told detectives that he had been suffering remorse for many years over the murder of a woman called Elizabeth Graham. His account of the murder came as a surprise to his interrogators but the biggest surprise was that she was not his originally intended victim.

'The actual abduction was supposed to be somebody I'd seen a couple of weeks before and really took a shine to,' Winkles said. 'But she got sick or something the day I was supposed to get her and Graham showed up. Graham was actually a victim of circumstance.'

Nineteen-year-old Elizabeth Graham was working as a dog

groomer for the Pampered Poodle dog-grooming company in St Petersburg, Florida, This job entailed going to customers' homes. On the day she disappeared, 9 September 1980, Winkles had made an appointment by phone. He arranged for a dog-groomer, a woman he had met earlier, to go to a vacant house for sale on Bedford Drive, in the High Point area of Pinellas County, as he had a dog that needed attention. When Elizabeth arrived, Winkles decided that she was as good as the other woman, his intended victim. As she opened the doors of her van he put a gun to her head, pushed her down, handcuffed and gagged her before putting her into the back of his station wagon. Her company van was later found parked in the driveway with a flat tyre that had been caused by a knife puncture between the treads. Now that his victim was trussed up, he drove her in his station wagon to the home he shared with his grandmother at 14896 63rd Street North, Clearwater.

'When I went in I took her straight to my bedroom and told her stay there and remain quiet and I went in there and told my grandmother and my aunt who was there at the time that I had a guest,' Winkles explained to the police. He said he later fired his gun, a .22-calibre automatic, twice inside the house to show Graham he was serious. Using two pairs of handcuffs he shackled her legs. He told her that there would be no problems if she did what she was told and had sex with him.

Despite the fact that his grandmother and an aunt were there in the house all the time – not suspecting a thing – Winkles kept his victim captive for four days and nights, forcing her to dress up in various different types of women's outfits he kept at the house. Although the violent sexual predator repeatedly raped her, he claimed that he had frequently assured her that she would not be killed. His assurances, however, amounted to nothing.

On the third day of her captivity, Winkles saw Elizabeth reading his grandmother's address on her magazines. He realised then that she would be able to identify him if he released her, so he decided to kill her. The next day he sent the two elderly women out to buy groceries. While they were gone he drugged Elizabeth with four Flexeril muscle-relaxant pills. Then, when she was asleep, he put an umbrella over her head to stop the blood spattering the room and shot her three times in the head. He cut off her clothes and burned them along with the bed sheets.

The killer buried the girl's body in woods near the Pinellas County landfill and Gandy Boulevard. Later he returned to the grave and removed her head, taking it to Lafayette County in the Florida Panhandle. There, he says, he dumped the head in a river. Divers found it a year later.

In 2002, Winkles took a team of forensic experts to where he claimed to have buried a metal box containing pictures of some of his victims. They dug and found nothing. Elizabeth Graham's body has never been recovered, but her toothless skull was found in the Steinhatchee River, near US 19, on 3 July 1981. The skull was identified by DNA analysis in the late 1990s.

A year after the disappearance of Elizabeth Graham, Clearwater real-estate saleswoman Margo Delimon vanished. Winkles later became a suspect in the case. But there was no direct evidence at the time, and no charges were filed. However, 17 years later, at Pinellas County Jail, the killer provided detectives with the details that would at last allow them to close the case.

After he had recounted the story of the Elizabeth Graham

killing, the murderous sexual deviant went on to relate how he had abducted and killed Margo Delimon. The 39-year-old married woman worked for Oben Realty in Pinellas Park selling log cabins. Margo disappeared while working on Saturday, 3 October 1981. Her abandoned car was found at the company's model-home location near US 19. A little more than a fortnight later, on 21 October 1981, her headless corpse was discovered near the Withlacoochee River in Citrus County. It was more than six months before her toothless skull was found in Hernando County on 23 May 1982.

The detectives listened grimly as Winkles recounted the story of how he abducted and murdered the real-estate saleswoman and provided them with the details that had eluded their predecessors all those years before. He told them how, back in the late summer of 1981, he and his wife had visited a log-cabin model home being constructed near US 19. Several weeks later, they returned to see the cabin in its completed state. They had been shown around the place by Margo Delimon and Winkles had found her very attractive. After a further few weeks, she was still on his mind and he phoned her to ask if she would have a drink with him, an invitation that she declined.

The next morning, 3 October, he went to the cabin at about 8.15 and persuaded her to have breakfast with him. He drove her to some woods off 49th Street and, as he had done with Elizabeth Graham, pulled a gun on her. He told her he was 'really attracted' to her and that she was being kidnapped. Then he handcuffed her and drove her to his cousin's house, next door to where his grandmother lived. The house was for sale and was vacant.

Over the next four days, while the missing woman's family

frantically searched for her, she was being subjected to frequently repeated rape at the hands of the appalling monster Winkles. It is not possible to imagine the level of fear that was experienced by both Elizabeth Graham and Margo Delimon during the days that each of them endured as captives of this evil rapist. Although not a tall man at five feet eight inches, he was solidly built, weighing well over 200 pounds, and neither woman had the slightest chance against him. And while they would both have desperately nursed the hope, however forlorn, that the horror would end and they would eventually be rescued or set free, they must also have faced up to the chilling reality of their predicament and the numbing acknowledgement that they were never going to emerge from the nightmare alive. Those cold, stark days filled with terror, shock, pain and humiliation were a tunnel at the end of which there was no light to be seen, only death.

For Margo Delimon, death came in the shape of a heavy dose of sleeping tablets. In his account of the woman's death, Winkles didn't say that he killed her. Instead, he hid from the brutality of his crime behind another word, 'terminated', as if to distance himself in some way from the act of murder.

'I terminated her, obviously, because we had been all over the damn place and she knew exactly where that safe house was at. I overdosed her with sleeping pills and it took her a long time to die,' he told the detectives.

At first he buried her body in woods near Clearwater Airport, St Petersburg. A fortnight later he returned, dug up the body and moved it to Citrus County, where he buried it on the bank of the Withlacoochee River. A few days after that he returned, recovered the skull, pulled out the teeth, then tossed her head out of his car window as he drove along US 19. His victim's watch and earrings he gave to his aunt; her wedding ring he pawned for $400.

A couple who were fishing found parts of the body about a week later. It was another two years before the remains were identified as those of Margo Delimon.

In some ways Winkles resembles the attention-seeking maniac Jack Harrison Trawick. He courts notoriety. During interviews with the press, Winkles has insisted that he abducted dozens of women in the Tampa Bay area for his sexual pleasure and that he killed some of them.

This strange, unhinged killer is quoted as saying: 'I got away with stuff for so long. Things I've done make Ted Bundy look like a choirboy. Ninety-nine per cent of these incidents were not planned. When the urge hit, they were targets of opportunity.'

Whether or not Winkles is speaking the truth is a matter of some conjecture. Detectives remain to be convinced. They say that most of his claims about other victims have not been substantiated despite thorough investigation. They acknowledge that he provided details about the Graham and Delimon murders that only their killer could have known, but no other murder case has been confirmed. Sheriff's Sergeant Mike Ring said, 'The investigation is still open, but so far we have only verified two murders. We believe he's done others, but not as many as he claims.'

Whatever the truth may be regarding his many other claims, James Delano Winkles pleaded guilty to the murders of Elizabeth Graham and Margo Delimon on 3 April 2002. A year later, on 14 April 2003, he was sentenced to death.

Born on 18 December 1940, Winkles is now in the foothills of old age and has frequently expressed doubts that he will survive ill-health long enough to be executed. Whether he 'cheats the hangman' remains to be seen, but there will be some disappointed people if he does. In the days before the killer went on trial for the two murders, State Prosecutor Fred Schaub said, 'If you think of what he did to these women, he deserves the death penalty. Being kept alive for a week, almost like a slave, knowing he's going to kill you – mentally, it would just play on somebody's mind.'

This white-haired, florid-faced serial killer, inmate # 009547 Winkles, is currently on Death Row, Union Correctional Institution, Raiford, Florida.

Sean Richard Sellers

'There are books I still want to write. There are people I still want to guide, people I think need me. And I know as long as the world is in a state where there are people who actually need what a Death Row inmate has to say to them, then that's one heart at a time, I can bring light to some darkness, mend some wound, strengthen some unsteady hand.

'I don't know. Maybe I'm a hedonist, because doing it really makes me feel good. People might say, "What the hell does some murderer have to offer that's worth a damn to anyone?" I've heard those exact words more than once. Sometimes from my own soul. But I think I have an answer. I don't think many people realise this. It doesn't take a lot to make a difference in someone's life. I only have two things of worth to offer anyone. A little bit of wisdom from past mistakes and a sincere effort to help. So, with every kid who writes me, every young person who tells me I was the only one to ever listen to and really care for them, I go to God and ask WHERE is everyone? Have you all become so busy climbing the mountain that you've forgotten to see all those stranded on the cliffs around you? The world should be ashamed at every teenager who has written me, because it's one they have missed. I've often thought about that. I know the contempt a Death Row inmate has in our society. I've seen barbeques and firecrackers and cheers outside the prison walls when one of us is executed. So what point does a kid have to be at before he actually picks up a pen and writes to a Death Row inmate for help? How many times has he reached out elsewhere, how many times have the people around him failed, walked past him, ignored him, forgotten him? All it would have taken was some sincere effort to be what he needed at that moment. So do I want to live? Yes. If for no other reason than this. I know as long as I do live I will TRY to make a difference for good in this world. I will really, purposefully try. And I know for so many the trying is all it takes. I'm just not done yet. That's why, no matter how hard it gets to take the next breath, to face the next day, I keep hoping for more. I haven't yet done all I set out to do.

'But God willing, I will.'

Those words were written by Sean Richard Sellers on 25 November 1998. His wish, to be able to continue to help people, was not granted and he was executed at the Oklahoma State Penitentiary McAlester, by lethal injection shortly before midnight on Thursday, 4 February 1999.

The words themselves were taken from a journal that Sellers wrote during the weeks leading to his execution. From the pages of his journal there speaks a deeply spiritual person, one who is a committed Christian. His writing is that of an intelligent, rational and unselfish man who is reconciled with the course that his life has taken. But it was not always so. The story of Sean Sellers is a tragedy of the highest order. He ended his young life on Death Row, having been convicted of committing the cold-blooded murders of three people. His first victim was Robert Paul Bower, a supermarket night-clerk who was shot to death on 8 September 1985.

The other two victims were Sellers's own mother and stepfather, Vonda and Paul Bellofatto, who were murdered while they slept. Chillingly, the cold-blooded killer was only 16 years old.

What gave the story of Sean Sellers its great notoriety was his attachment to Satanic worship and the lurid headlines that this attracts. The dark side of the occult will always draw to it the lost and the lonely. With its promise of attaining the otherwise unattainable, its glamour seems irresistible to those who view their lives through a badly distorted lens. History is littered with examples of those who sought elements missing from their lives and yet failed to find what it was they pursued. Their misguided fervour leads them almost always to disillusion and often to misery. And so it was for Sean Sellers.

Sean Richard Sellers was born in California on Sunday, 18 May 1969. His parents, a mother who was only 16 years old when he was born and a father who was described as an unstable alcoholic, divorced when Sean was three or four. The mother, Vonda, then married an ex-serviceman and veteran of the Vietnam War, Paul 'Lee' Bellofatto. The former Green Beret had become a truck driver, and Vonda would frequently accompany him when he travelled the country in a truck. This meant that from the age of five Sean was frequently left to live with relatives, usually his grandparents, Jim and Geneva Blackwell, in Oklahoma. When the opportunity arose for the couple to settle in a place for a time, Sean would go to live with them. He was eight when they moved to Los Angeles and lived in his stepfather's aunt's apartment. Children weren't allowed in the apartment block, so Sean had to keep quiet.

At his school Sean was bullied and he generally hated his time in LA. He was glad when he had to move back to Oklahoma but the itinerant life was not good for his development: By the time he was 16 he had moved home some 30 times.

Sean claimed that around the age of six or seven he began to hear voices in his head. The voices weren't always friendly and often criticised him. At the time he didn't consider this to be anything other than normal and thought that all people heard such voices. For most of his adolescent years, he displayed extremely unusual behaviour. He has described how he would fix threads to doors and brush the nap of the rug in one direction before he would leave his bedroom. He did this in order to see if anyone had entered his room during his absence. Moreover, the young Sean experienced extreme mood swings, sometimes becoming euphoric, other times suicidally depressed.

He also suffered problems in his family life, being beaten by his mother and his grandfather. His mother was particularly volatile and would hit him hard in the mouth or over the head with whatever came to hand. Worse still was his treatment at the hands of an uncle who would make him go around in nappies when aged 12 and 13 because he sometimes wet the bed. If he wet the bed two nights in a row, the uncle would make him wear a soiled nappy on his head all day. During his time in Los Angeles he was also sexually abused by a male relative.

It is fair to say that the Sellers family endorsed a culture of violence. Both Sean's mother and stepfather carried guns when they travelled. One of the boy's uncles used to take him hunting and exposed him to its more savage side, for instance teaching him to put his foot on an animal's head and pull its legs to kill it. Sean later recalled to a psychiatrist how he saw his uncle put an axe on a wounded racoon's head and pull on its legs until the head tore off. When he showed reluctance to take part in these acts, he would be called a wimp by his uncle and chastised by his stepfather.

Surprisingly, given his early upbringing, Sean Sellers was an intelligent boy who performed well at school. He was happiest in his early teens, particularly so when he was 15 and the family lived in Colorado. It was in those early adolescent years that he developed a fervid interest in the game of Dungeons and Dragons and also in martial arts. He joined the Civil Air Patrol (CAP) as a cadet and attended special training schools, becoming a NEAT (National Emergency Assistance Training) qualified Ranger and graduating with outstanding cadet merit. After a few months, he became the squadron's cadet commander.

There is no doubt that Sean Sellers had a good intellect and an aptitude for learning. A natural leader, mature for his age and capable of self-discipline, he had a leaning towards the spiritual philosophy and meditation practices that underlie the culture of martial arts. In his own words, 'I began to ask myself, "Do I really know what Ninjutsu is all about?" I began to study. I learned about the spiritual focusing of Zen meditation and began disciplining my mind even more. At night, I prepared to organise my CAP squadron, worked out punching out candle flames, and meditated.'

This disciplined attitude was something that Sean applied to the serious way he approached his Dungeons and Dragons role-playing games and it was as he was developing this that he encountered the world of Satanism. In an open letter that he wrote and which was published on the internet, he described the origins of the Satanic beliefs that would eventually lead him to murder and the destruction of his own life:

'At a common trip to the library, I researched the origins and legends of dragons. The people I played D & D with were getting too cocky. Their characters needed to learn humility, I had decided. So I planned to bring to life in the game a powerful dragon from mythology that could only be defeated with a riddle. Zen had taught me that battles were won in the mind first and didn't always have to be fought physically. I wanted to teach that to those I played with. The research on dragons led me to the Time/Life series of books on the occult. I began reading about wizards and witches, and remembering an episode when I was younger in which a baby-sitter had checked out some books on witchcraft and Satanism for me, I turned my study toward that. All day I looked through the library card catalog and shelves. I looked up demons, witches, Salem, witchcraft, evil, Satan, Satanism, Voodoo, and whatever I could find. There was something that mysteriously connected all this with my study of Ninjutsu, and I resolved myself to find it. There was power in the supernatural world, and I wanted to learn how to harness and use it.'

This, on the face of it, does not make for very disturbing reading. It resembles the fanciful ramblings of most adolescents who flit from one fad to another. However, it assumes a different complexion when one realises that the writer is a youth who is not just impressionable in the way that most teenagers are: despite his being an intelligent young man, Sean had no one among the adults in his family to whom he could go with questions or for advice. In this respect, he was very much on his own and it was this absence of guidance that allowed him to develop his Satanic beliefs unchecked.

Sean's writings reveal just how emotionally vulnerable he was in his early to mid-teens and how close to tragedy he came:

'It was then when I became angry with God and began to hate Him. I had met a girl and fallen in love, regardless of everyone telling me I was too young to know what love is. During a phone call one night while my parents were gone for a few days, she told me to get out of her life and leave her alone. I had met the girl a year before in church. She was my first real kiss. And now I felt dead inside. I decided to kill myself. I went to my bedroom, got my shotgun, and placed it in the middle of the living room floor. With my cleaning kit, I began to take it apart and oil it. As I did so, I began to think about how everyone would feel with my being gone. I began to miss me. And as I placed the number four shell into the newly oiled chamber and pulled the bolt back, placing the gun barrel to my chin, I said out loud, "What, am I freaking crazy? What the hell am I doing?" I put the gun down, called a friend, and asked him to come over. When he walked in, he saw the gun, and after hearing the story decided to stay the night. We got drunk. I had prayed to God that this girl would love me as I loved her. God had failed me. He didn't love me. I hated Him. I wanted nothing to do with God any more. It was my friends, not God, not my family, who were there when I needed them. I could depend on my friends, no one else … except myself.'

The time living in Colorado came to an end when the family moved again, back to Oklahoma. There Sean met his old friends and journeyed further into the dark world of Satanism. This was to be the final chapter of his life in the world outside of prison:

'We moved again. Returning to Oklahoma, I was reunited with old friends, but l had changed. I left, a short-haired football player who wore Wranglers. I returned with long hair, wearing my NEAT Ranger beret, a Levi jacket and 501s, carrying a double-edged boot knife tucked in my pants at the small of my back, and NIKE high tops. When I left, I had been in a few fights and shown I could fight. Now, I carried an air of being downright dangerous. I was cool. Time heals wounds, and in time, I met a new girl. This one, knowing I was interested in witchcraft, introduced me to a witch. Her name was Glasheeon. Some of her first words to me were, "You can go white magic or black magic. White magic is sort of hypocritical. If you want real power, go black magic." "Let's go black magic," I replied. She said the first step was praying to Satan and gave me a special incantation to call forth the powers of evil. Now I was mad at God, but it still took me a day to get up the nerve to pray to the Devil. That night was a turning point.'

It was indeed a turning point. Sean Sellers, aged just 16, stepped from the role-playing world of Dungeons and Dragons and his adolescent fantasies of Ninja warriors into the darkness and the unknown dangers of Satanic worship, allowing its powerful, unfettered influence to flood into his mind and take control. Where occult issues are involved, opinions are sharply divided between believers and unbelievers. Regardless of that, there are undoubtedly those who behave in ways that suggest they are governed by some external or supernatural force that cannot be explained in a rational way by science. Whatever that force may have been, to Sean Sellers it was real and he believed it to be the presence of Satan in his life. That night Sean performed his first Satanic ritual and he described the moment later:

'By Glasheeon's instructions, I stripped naked and laid down. "Satan, I call you forth to serve you," I prayed aloud and recited Glasheeon's incantation. I felt the room grow cold and experienced the unmistakable presence of utter evil enter. My blood pressure went up. The veins on my arms were bulged. I got an erection and began to feel a lifting sensation. Then something touched me. My eyes flew open but saw only spots, as they had been closed so tightly. Again I felt something touch me, and I shut my eyes terrified and thrilled. It felt like ice-cold claws began to rake my body caressingly, and I shook in an erotic pleasure as they explored every inch of my body. I heard an audible voice speak three words in a whisper, "I love you." I continued to pray, telling Satan I accepted and would serve him. One by one the invisible clawed hands touching me disappeared, and my blood pressure fell. I was alone. I sat up exhausted, hooked, unbelieving. I hadn't been on drugs. I'd never smoked a joint. It had been incredible, and I knew it was real. I had found what I was looking for or so I thought. I had to know more. I questioned Glasheeon crazily, learning what was myth and what was real. I went to the school library and researched biographies of prominent witches and Satanists. I searched bookstores for occult related books, often stealing those I found. I studied. I learned. And then I got my friend involved.'

The friend to whom Sean referred was Richard Howard. Richard was Sean's best friend and closest confidant. Once he had begun to share Sean's beliefs, they would discuss and plan evil acts involving rape, violence and robbery. They contemplated robbing Richard's boss when she went to deposit the takings at the bank's night safe and they entertained the idea of sex crimes. While at this stage they were only fantasising about such things and had no real intention of carrying out their plans, the details of what they envisaged are disturbing: 'We talked about torture for a friend's ex-girlfriend. We would tie her down, slice her breasts, cut her throat, but only after we would rape her for a few days.' They also began using drugs, mainly amphetamines and marijuana. Alarmingly, Sean was also drinking blood, his own, which he carried in phials.

Sean's commitment to his new doctrine was total. He made a pact with Satan which involved writing in his own blood: 'I renounce God, I renounce Christ. I will serve only Satan. To my friends love, to my enemies, death … hail Satan.' Then he signed his name.

'I hated the hypocritical Christian community and was determined to eliminate them from society. We began performing rituals, but something seemed to be wrong. There was a barrier put up between us and the power we needed to invoke. We brought forth demons, but we wanted more. It was time to prove our allegiance to Satan.'

The fantasy was over for the two young Satanists. They began breaking the Ten Commandments until there remained only one to be transgressed: 'Thou shalt not kill.' To the teenagers this was the act by which their commitment would be judged. 'We talked about things such as waiting at a stop sign in the middle of nowhere and blowing away the first person who was fool enough to obey the law.'

For Sean at least, they had reached the point of no return. He was going to kill someone. Richard too was enthusiastic about the idea and came up with the names of two intended victims, Al

Hawks and Robert Paul Bower. Hawks was the father of Richard's girlfriend, Tracy, and he had apparently hit his daughter, giving her a black eye. To Richard this seemed a good enough motive for his murder. Robert Bower, the second of the intended victims, worked at a Circle K store outside town and had recently refused to sell beer to Richard because he was under age. For this relatively trivial reason, Richard selected Bower as a murder victim.

On the night of 8 September 1985, following a Satanic ritual, the two decided to embark on their mission to kill. The plan appears to have been that they would each kill one of the two targets: Richard would kill Al Hawks while Sean would kill Robert Bower. Richard obtained the guns for the job. He got his brother's .22 rifle and his grandfather's .357 revolver, the latter loaded with five hollow-point shells.

They made their way to the store and for about an hour chatted to Robert Bower about a variety of subjects, including the security of the store and the lack of CCTV surveillance. The boys bought drinks and then, when Bower was sipping a cup of coffee, Richard held up an item and asked how much it was. Sean fired the revolver at Bower's head. He missed and the terrified victim ran, almost colliding with Richard in his panic. Again Sean fired, wounding the man, and on his third attempt he hit Robert Bower in the head, killing him.

'It was after a lust ritual with my second priest that Satan took over our actions. In a game-like surreal euphoria, we drove to a convenience store where a man worked who had insulted my friend's girlfriend and refused to sell him beer. In my hand I held a cold steel killing tool, a .357 Magnum loaded with hollow points. After much conversation with the man who thought we were friends, my friend distracted him and I raised the gun from beneath the counter, pointed it at his head, and squeezed the trigger. It missed. I fired again. My friend cut him off from getting away. The second shot had only injured him. I caught him. His terror-stricken eyes searched mine for mercy behind the smoking barrel. I squeezed the trigger and he collapsed, knocked back from the impact – dead. Blood covered the rear wall and ran on to the floor. And two teenagers walked out, taking no money, no merchandise. Only the life of an innocent man for Satan.'

From the Circle K store the two accomplices drove off, laughing over their senseless crime. Fortunately for Al Hawks, they decided not to go ahead with his execution. Instead, they returned Richard's grandfather's gun after burying the bullets and spent shell cases in the ground outside the grandfather's house.

The mystery surrounding the murder of Robert Bowers went unsolved and Sean and Richard continued their lives as if it had never happened. However, Sean's perpetual strife with his mother continued. He had met a girl by the name of Angel. Only 15, she smoked and dressed outlandishly. It may have been that she reminded Vonda a little too much of herself when she was 15 and had become pregnant. In any event, she constantly fought with her son over his choice of girlfriend, calling Angel a bitch and a little tramp, while doing whatever she could to prevent Sean from seeing her.

'After punching holes in the bathroom wall of a teen club called Skully's, I got a job there as a bouncer. Friday and Saturday nights were spent drinking, getting high and partying with the Rockies – the people who attended *The Rocky Horror Picture Show* – who frequented Skully's after the movie. With live teenage bands rocking out the sound of "Breaking the Chains", I would sit wearing black tank top, camouflage fatigues, high tops, bandanas, and eye liner, drinking beer from plastic cups, and smoking cigarettes while my new girlfriend, Angel, would eye me from across the table wearing a black and red spandex unitard, black knee-high boots, my white vest and black hat, and a choke collar and dog leash from her neck. We danced, borrowed back seats from our friends before I got my pickup, and slept together. We would get high, talk about life, and remain the center of attention at Skully's.

'Satanism had become our lifestyle. It was no longer something bragged about, or showed off. It was serious to us and the center of our lives. I continued to study and perform nightly rituals taking more and more speed to keep going. The Elimination had disbanded, leaving me to pursue my own, more mature, practices, including a worship of the dead, again in combination with Ninjutsu, as I searched for true enlightenment. And here I was. I wasn't happy. The blood, drugs, sex, hate, all of it had become boring. But I knew no other way. I had searched everywhere and come up empty. My life stunk. I was angry with my parents. I continually thought about suicide. I just wanted out.'

It was a time of sharp deterioration for Sean. Despite the cushion of his rituals and Satanic beliefs, the killing must certainly have affected his frame of mind during the months following Robert Bower's murder. And it was in this time, with his home life now just one continuous battle with his mother, that his thinking degenerated to the extent that he was being drawn inexorably to the moment when he would commit the act that would put him on Death Row.

Shortly before midnight on Tuesday, 4 March 1986, the 16-year-old snuffed out two candles – one black, one white – in his bedroom and crept along the hallway. Barefoot and stripped to his underpants to move as quietly as possible, he held a .44 Smith & Wesson pistol belonging to his stepfather.

He opened the door of the master bedroom, where Vonda and Paul Bellofatto, his mother and stepfather, were asleep. Pausing just long enough beside their bed to ensure they were sleeping soundly, he calmly raised the gun and fired a shot into Paul's head.

Vonda Sellers Bellofatto woke in confusion from the noise and was reaching out to her husband when Sean turned the gun on her and fired again. Unlike her husband, she did not die instantly. The first bullet passed through the side of her mouth and she flailed on the bed in a hazy panic, trying to identify the killer in the dark. At the second shot blood spurted from the side of her head and she slumped motionless on her pillow.

Sean showered and dressed, then returned to the master bedroom and ransacked it. After removing a security bar he opened the patio door to give the impression of a break-in. Then he drove ten miles to the home of his friend Richard Howard, where he hid the pistol. The two teenagers talked all night about what Sean had felt when he shot his mother. At 8.30 the next morning, Sean walked in the door of the pizza restaurant where she worked and asked to see her. He said he was late for school, having stayed with a friend overnight, and needed her to write a note for him. But she was not due in until 9am, so he left, saying he would catch up with her at home.

Sean returned home. Thirty minutes later, neighbours in the quiet suburb of Summit Place saw him running up and down the street, screaming something about blood. It took a few minutes before anyone could calm him enough to get any sense out of him. He asked for an ambulance.

Later that morning he was interviewed by Oklahoma City PD Detective Ron Mitchell. Meeting the officer's questions with candid blue eyes and a clear, polite voice, the youth could account for all of his movements during the time in question. He consented to be fingerprinted and gave permission for the house to be searched.

With the property showing signs of a bungled burglary, there was nothing at first to support Detective Mitchell's hunch that Sean was not as innocent as he seemed. But victims of botched burglaries are not usually asleep when they are attacked and closer inspection revealed that the patio door had been opened from the inside.

Mitchell's breakthrough came later that day in a phone call from the principal of Sean's school, Putnam City North High, at 11800 North Rockwell, Oklahoma City. The previous day Sean had handed in a frightening essay which began with a quotation from the Californian cult manual *The Satanic Bible*. 'Behold the Crucifix,' it ran, 'what does it symbolise? Pallid incompetence hanging from a tree!' Sean had then described his own conversion to Satanism: 'Satanism taught me to be a better person for myself rather than for the benefit of others… Why should I not have sex or worship other gods? I treat others not as I would have them treat me, but as they treat me.' He had given sinister hints about the fruits of his new faith: 'I am free. I can kill without remorse. I have seen and experienced horrors and joys indescribable on paper.'

When Detective Mitchell heard this, he immediately recalled the recent unsolved murder of a night-clerk at a local supermarket. Robert Paul Bower was an ex-hippie who had taken the job and was 38 when he was shot. Mitchell also knew that he could stop looking elsewhere for the killer of Paul Bellofatto and Vonda.

The school had also told Sean's mother about the essay, on the last day of her life. Realising that she had neglected her son, she sat down to write him a long supportive letter. 'I'll always love you,' she wrote. 'If you'll let me in, I'll help you. I'll always be here when you need me, no matter what, until the day I die.' She left the letter in Sean's room and was already asleep when he came home that night. He didn't bother to read it.

It was childish bragging that finally gave Sean Sellers away. As police attention focused on Putnam City North High School, they found several students who had heard him say he knew how it felt to kill.

But it was Richard Howard who provided the crucial information. He told police how Sean had come to his home after killing his parents and he led officers to the murder weapon. He had also been at the Circle K supermarket on 8 September 1985, when he had seen Sean shoot Bower. On Thursday, 6 March 1986, Sean Sellers was charged with three counts of first-degree murder.

When friends had asked him what he would do if caught, Sean had coolly replied, 'I'll plead insanity.' When State Prosecutors were informed of this statement, they were unable to use it against Sellers. But a psychologist did diagnose Sean as a sociopath, which meant he was sane but incapable of feeling any remorse.

The trial began on 24 September 1986 at Oklahoma County Courthouse, Judge Charles Owens presiding. Sellers pleaded not guilty. For the rest of the trial the blond, blue-eyed boy killer sat mute, perhaps observing the Satanic Code of Silence.

The prosecution strategy, led by District Attorney Robert Macy, was to demonstrate a rational motive for the crimes. As Sean's school friends one by one took the stand, Macy focused on the defendant's attitude to his mother. Sellers had often told people that his mother disapproved of his girlfriends and that it would be better if she were out of the way. Complaining about the way she was 'pushing him around', he told one girl, called Angel, 'I've killed people for less than that.' He was referring to the murder described to the court in eyewitness detail by Richard Howard. Macy described this as a 'cold-blooded trial run' for Sean's attack on his parents.

In reply, Sean's lawyer, assistant public defender Bob Ravitz, claimed that his client was the victim of Satanic possession. A Californian detective named Curtis Jackson who specialised in occult homicides had been on hand during the investigation, but local police had paid little attention to him. Ravitz now seized on Jackson's theory that Sean had murdered his mother and stepfather in a ritual blood sacrifice. And he set out to show how Sean could have slipped helplessly into a demonic state of mind.

He prepared his ground by having Vonda's final letter read out, to discredit Macy's theory that mother and son were at odds. When he heard her supportive message to him, Sean broke down for the only time in the trial. Ravitz then produced expert witnesses on Satanic cults and on Dungeons and Dragons, which is often the means by which, he claimed, children discover the occult. Most of these 'experts' were in fact parents who had lost a child in sinister circumstances. Their testimonies were emotional and effective. Finally, Ravitz established that the murders of which Sean was accused all took place on or near festivals requiring blood sacrifices in the Satanic Calendar. His arguments reinforced a sense that Sellers was 'possessed', although the Satanic Calendar calls for no rituals to be performed on the murder dates in question. But it was a good try anyway.

After deliberating for 24 hours, the jury found Sean Sellers guilty on all three charges. Media interest in the 'possession' defence had backfired, making Ravitz seem like a cynical manipulator of public sympathy. Macy had asked for the death penalty in his summing-up, and on 14 October 1986 Sellers became the youngest inmate on Oklahoma's Death Row. On Thursday, 4 February 1999, he was executed, having spent his entire adult life on Death Row.

Convenience-store Killers on the Green Mile

I n all US states where the death penalty is the ultimate penalty, the deciding factor which ensures lodgings on Death Row is one of capital, or first-degree, murder. Anyone who kills a public official, say a law-enforcement officer, or commits homicide in the furtherance of a crime, or kills in an effort to avoid arrest commits capital murder. The robbery of a convenience store, linked to homicide, is therefore classified as the ultimate offence.

Recent studies carried out by Secretary of Labor Alexis M. Herman of the Occupational Safety and Health Administration (OSHA) revealed that nearly 28 per cent of all Death Row inmates in the United States have been involved in convenience-store robberies, abductions and murders. So, apart from that of a police officer, by far the most dangerous occupation in the United States has, for many years, been reserved for convenience-store employees – and often their customers – working the 'graveyard shift' at night.

And, to highlight the perils of citizens serving the public throughout the dark hours, the authors have provided examples, all shocking in the style of Stephen King, and in many cases so dreadful that they are beyond the comprehension of the sane.

However, what makes them stand out from the other Green Mile residents in this book is that convenience-store killers murder for a few bucks. Most of these angry, mindless individuals are hooked on booze and drugs and need money to feed their habit. For a few dollars they deprive innocent people of their lives, bringing decades of heartache to the victims' next of kin. They kill with as much compassion as one swats a fly.

Thomas Warren Whisenhant
On Friday, 21 November 1975, while on federal parole, 28-year-old Thomas Warren Whisenhant shot and killed Patricia Hitt at a Compact Food store in Mobile County, Alabama. Six months later, he raped, mutilated and murdered Venora Hyatt after kidnapping her from a 7-Eleven food store. Seven months later, this monster raped and killed a third convenience-store clerk, Cheryl Gazzier Payton. Whisenhant is currently on Death Row.

Roosevelt Green and Carzell Moore
During the evening of Sunday, 12 December 1976, 18-year-old nursing student Teresa Carol Allen was working in a convenience store at Cochran, Georgia. She needed the extra cash to help her through college. Roosevelt Green and Carzell Moore robbed the cash register of $466. Teresa's body was found two days later. She had been raped, shot in the head and left to die. Both men were executed by electrocution on 9 January 1985.

Robert Anthony Preston

On the afternoon of Monday, 9 January 1978, the nude and mutilated body of 46-year-old Earline Walker was discovered by police in a field in Seminole County, Florida. Multiple stab wounds and lacerations on the body were so severe that they resulted in near-decapitation.

Earline had been employed as a clerk at a convenience store. An officer of the Altamonte Springs Police Department on routine patrol discovered her missing from the store at approximately 3.30am. He also found that $574.41 was missing from the store.

Robert Preston was arrested the following day on an unrelated charge. While he was in custody, a deputy recovered a pubic hair from Preston's belt buckle. The day after the arrest, police searched Preston's mother's home, where he lived. In his bedroom they found a jacket belonging to Preston and several detached food stamp coupons. An analysis confirmed the coupons had been used at the convenience store to purchase items several days before the murder. Blood samples from the victim and Preston were compared with bloodstains found on Preston's jacket. The stains were of the same blood type and enzyme group as those of Earline Walker. Analysis revealed that the hair recovered from Preston's belt and another discovered on his jacket originated from the victim.

Six-feet-six, 224-pound Preston is currently on Death Row in Florida.

William Quentin Jones

Shortly before midnight on Saturday, 7 March 1987, several employees and customers in a Fast Fare store on North Person Street, Raleigh, North Carolina, found themselves thrown into a nightmare of shocking reality when in walked 18-year-old William Quentin Jones.

Wearing a ski mask, drunk on beer, high on cocaine and stoned from smoking marijuana, Jones opened the door and immediately sprayed a burst from an Uzi 9mm semi-automatic machine pistol. Two bullets struck customer Orlando Watson, who, after surgery, survived his wounds. 'This is a stickup,' Jones shouted, before turning and firing twice at 32-year-old Edward Peebles, a plasterer who had called in for a cup of coffee. The Parabellum bullets ruptured Peebles's aorta and a large vein, causing massive haemorrhaging and untimely death.

Jones then ordered the clerk, Charles Taylor, to open the cash register. Shaking with fear, Taylor was unable to comply with the robber's demands, at which point Jones grabbed the machine and pulled it by the electrical cord out of the front door and around a fence to the side of the building, leaving a trail of scratches and gouges on the sidewalk as he went.

In total, ten shots were discharged, with the entire incident being recorded on a security camera, and it was his brief cinematic career that went a long way to putting Jones on Death Row.

The first police officer to arrive on the scene was Tony Wisniewski. Racing into the store, he radioed for assistance, transmitting a description of the gunman given to him by Charles Taylor. Within minutes, more police officers arrived on the scene and Sergeant Inman was cautiously edging his way behind a low wall when he saw the silhouette of someone's head. The officer chambered a round into his shotgun and ordered the man to 'Freeze!' Jones took to his heels, and after a short chase he was arrested at a ball park several blocks away.

With the gunman now safely locked into a cage car, police found the ski mask, a red NC sweatshirt, the cash register, upon which were the robber's dabs, and the Uzi. In police parlance Jones was caught 'bang to rights'.

Mr Jones, it seems, was a frequent visitor to Fast Fare outlets: he had previously robbed at least six of their stores. It also transpired that, on Friday, 20 February 1987, Jones and two accomplices had broken into Cary Jewellery & Pawn and stole seven firearms including the Uzi.

However, and if there is any mitigation whatsoever, to be fair to William Jones, one must acknowledge that he was born on the wrong side of the tracks, spending most of his childhood and adolescence in poverty and devoting much of his time in search of food for himself and his brothers and sisters. His mother, who struggled with heroin addiction, was unable to care for the family, and his father was a paranoid schizophrenic who was no stranger to a mental institution: he had been admitted to Dorothea Dix Hospital, Raleigh, 15 times since 1973.

On 3 November 1987, William Quentin Jones was sentenced to death in Wake County Superior Court for the capital murder of Ed Peebles. He also received consecutive sentences of 40 years for robbery with a dangerous weapon and 20 years for assault with a deadly weapon with intent to kill inflicting serious injury.

Jones was to spend the final 16 years of his life at Raleigh's Central Prison. He was to join more than one thousand who have been sent to North Carolina's Green Mile since 1910. Housed in the cell block of Unit III, he had in his cell a bed, a lavatory commode and a wall-mounted writing table. He could watch TV in the adjacent dayroom between 7am and 11pm.

After several unsuccessful appeals, on 17 August 2003, Jones, with all of his possessions, was moved to one of the four Death Watch cells adjacent to the execution chamber, where he was watched 24 hours a day by a sergeant and a correctional officer.

At 5.30pm on Friday, 22 August 2003, Jones ate his last meal – tossed salad with shredded carrots and cheese, thousand island dressing and a soda – and waited to learn whether State Governor Mike Easley would stop his execution. The reprieve never came.

Thirty-four-year-old Jones was taken into the execution chamber at 2am and secured to the gurney by lined ankle and wrist restraints. Cardiac monitor leads and a stethoscope were attached and he was covered with a white sheet.

He seemed animated and began trying to get messages to both his family members and the next of kin of his victim who were present. 'I'm sorry,' he said. Then he mouthed the words 'I love you' to his attorney. His last statement, a plea for mercy, was made in English and Arabic.

As the lethal drugs started to poison him, he said, 'I'm sorry. I'm gone. I love you.'

At 2.16am, the EKG monitor flat-lined. Five minutes later Jones was pronounced dead.

Ronald Woomer and Eugene Skaar

During a bloody crime spree on Thursday, 22 February 1979, ex-cons Ronald Woomer and Eugene Skaar robbed a South Carolina mini-mall, then abducted two female employees. Della Louis Sellers was shot dead; Wanda Summers was shot and disfigured for life.

Skaar committed suicide before he was arrested. However, on Friday, 27 April 1990, Woomer earned the distinction of becoming the last person to be executed by electrocution held at the Central Columbia Correctional Institute. The old fortress prison, on the banks of the Congaree River, has since been demolished.

Wilbur May and Van Roosevelt Solomon

It was Sunday, 17 June 1979. Roger Dennis Tackett was the manager of a Cobb County, Georgia, Tenneco self-service gas station, and two of his employees, Linda Rosenfield and Carol Menfee, suddenly realised that they didn't have the keys to lock up the premises when it closed at midnight. They telephoned Roger at home and at 11.20pm he turned up with the keys.

After the station closed, Roger stayed behind to catch up on paperwork, enabling him to clear his desk so he could spend quality time with his family the next day, Father's Day.

Around 1am, Linda Rosenfield drove past the gas station, noticing that her boss's car was still parked outside. At 1.50am, Officer Kendle of the Cobb County Police Department drove up and spotted a green Dodge car with its driver's door wide open. He peered inside and saw a loaf of bread on the seat. His suspicions were immediately aroused – something was very wrong.

As Kendle took a look around inside the premises, he saw a black male open the storeroom door. It was Wilbur May, who spotted the officer and slammed the door shut. Then there were several shots. Moments later May and Van Roosevelt Solomon were under arrest. Close by was the body of Roger Tackett, who had been beaten and tortured to reveal the keys to the cashbox, then shot five times with a Colt .38 short revolver.

Both felons were sentenced to death. Solomon, a former Baptist minister, was executed on 20 February 1985. His last words were:

'Blessings to everyone who seeked to save my life, and I'd like to curse everyone who seeked to take my life.'

At the time of writing, the disposition of Wilbur May, aka Brandon Astor Jones, is unknown.

Warren Eugene Bridge and Robert Joseph Costa

Nineteen-year-old former cashier and restaurant worker Warren Bridge and his 20-year-old sidekick Robert Costa were short of folding money. On Sunday, 10 February 1980, in an effort to relieve their pecuniary plight, the duo robbed the Stop-N-Go store at 710 Fourth Street, Galveston, in the process fatally shooting the clerk, 62-year-old Walter Rose, four times with a .38-calibre pistol.

For their deadly enterprise, Bridge and Costa netted the princely sum of $24. The two killers were arrested on 20 February. Walter Rose died of his wounds four days later.

Bridge, a hazel-eyed, brown-haired native of Fauquier County, Virginia, had previously been awarded a 15-year prison sentence for burglary in Georgia in 1978, only to be released on probation a year later. And while on the Green Mile in Texas he was implicated in the September 1984 bombing of another inmate's cell.

In March 1985, Bridge all but fatally stabbed another Green Mile associate and was given a ten-year sentence for aggravated assault.

Warren Bridge was executed by lethal injection at Huntsville Prison on Tuesday, 22 November 1994; his last words: 'I'll see you.'

Robert Costa got off lightly: sentenced to 13 years for aggravated robbery, he was released on mandatory supervision five years later. By all accounts he has not been in trouble since.

Jesse James Gillies and Michael David Logan

The 29th of January 1981 was a chilly Thursday, and 23-year-old Suzanne Rossetti, who had a steady boyfriend and was living a healthy backpacking life, had locked herself out of her car parked at a Phoenix convenience store. She was upset because her mother and father had driven down from Saugus, Massachusetts, to meet her at the Rodeway Inn, near 24th and Van Buren Streets.

'I was standing in front of the Rodeway Inn lobby,' Louise Rossetti later told police, '…and looked out on Van Buren and saw what I thought must be Suzanne's car parked up … saw her backpacking bumper sticker … saw she was sitting between two men. I hesitated, wondered if it was Suzanne, then started walking toward the car. And it rolled away … if only I'd run to that car.'

The two men were Jesse James Gillies, 20, and Michael David Logan, 27. Both had violent criminal records.

A happy, outgoing young woman, Suzanne was only too pleased to thank the men who had assisted her. She bought them a beer, even going so far as to offer them a ride to nearby stables, where they claimed to work. But, once in the car, Gillies took the wheel.

Gillies and Logan drove their victim to a secluded area where the two men raped her. Then they tied her up, put her in the back of the car and took her to their Scottsdale apartment. Again they raped her, then drove her to the Superstition Mountains. Eight hours after the horror began, the men led Suzanne to the edge of a cliff and told her to jump. She refused. Gillies punched her, then Logan kicked her over the edge.

Hoping Suzanne was dead, the two monsters scrambled down, only to find the young woman still clinging on to life. She pleaded for mercy, telling her tormentors, 'Leave me alone, I'm going to die anyway.'

They didn't. At least one of them – each man later blamed the other – beat her repeatedly over the head with a rock. Then they interred her beneath a heap of rocks and dirt. At autopsy, it was determined that Suzanne had been buried alive.

Within days, loose-mouthed Gillies started to boast about the murder. He was soon arrested by homicide detective Jack Hackworth, who told Gillies that he could face execution. 'All that for killing a fuckin' slut bitch,' Gillies replied.

Gillies, a true monster of the Green Mile, was executed on Wednesday, 13 January 1999. For his part, Logan pleaded guilty and was given a life sentence.

Richard Boyde Jr

In 1981, after committing robbery and grabbing US$33, Boyde kidnapped California store clerk and part-time wrestling coach Dickie Lee Gibson and shot him three times in a nearby orange grove. Boyde is currently on Death Row, San Quentin State Prison, California.

Johnny Watkins Jr

In 1983, Betty Jean Barker was shot to death during a convenience-store robbery in Danville, Virginia. She suffered four gunshot wounds and her killer escaped with $89.89. Eleven days later Watkins used the same gun to kill Carl Douglas Buchanan during another convenience-store robbery, which earned him $34.74. Watkins was executed on Thursday, 3 March 1994.

Marion **Albert** 'Mad Dog' Pruett

In 1979, Pruett was released from a 23-year federal penitentiary sentence for bank robbery, in exchange for his testimony against an underworld figure with whom he was serving time. Pruett was given $800 and the new name of Charles 'Sonny' Pearson, and placed in the Federal Witness Protection Program in New Mexico, where he lived with his wife, Pamela Sue Carnuteson, also known as Pamela Sue Barker or Michelle Lynn Pearson.

Carnuteson was found murdered in April 1981, her body beaten with a ball-peen hammer and burned with petrol. Before authorities could gather enough evidence against him, Pruett fled and embarked on a cross-country spree of armed robberies, abductions and murders.

Among Pruett's more brutal offences were the murder of Peggy Lowe, a savings and loan officer whom he abducted during a robbery in Jackson, Mississippi, and later shot in the back of the head, and the murders of James R. Balderson and Anthony Taitt, two store clerks whom he shot during separate robberies on the same day in two Colorado cities.

On 11 October 1981, 'Mad Dog' arrived in Fort Smith, Arkansas, and began scouting the city for a place to commit yet another robbery. He looked for a bank or a store, but since it was Sunday and most establishments were closed he decided to park his car in a secluded, wooded area known as Horseshoes Bend. There he injected himself with cocaine and drank whiskey for several hours. Sometime after midnight he drove to a nearby Convenience Corner grocery store that he had noted when he arrived in town. Through the window he could see that Bobbie Jean Robertson, the young woman who worked the 11pm to 7am shift, was alone.

In his later confession he said, 'I pulled in and was going to get gas and I seen that there was a girl working there by herself, and I said, "Well, hey, I think I'll just rob her and kill her," and that's what I done.'

Pruett entered the store armed with a .38-calibre revolver and ordered the clerk to place the $165 from the cash register into a bag. He told her to get her pocketbook, then he marched her to his car.

As he drove back to Horseshoe Bend, he assured Bobbie that if she cooperated she would be released. But when they stopped she started walking away, then turned and asked if she had left her purse in the car. Pruett raised his gun and fired. The first bullet struck the woman on the upper thigh, fracturing the femur. She struggled and tried to run away when another round struck her in the right shoulder. She fell to the ground. Pruett climbed out of the car, walked over to her and fired a fatal shot into Bobbie's left temple.

The next day, police discovered Bobbie Robertson's body in a thicket of weeds and small brush, just a few feet from the dirt road where she had been murdered.

Five days later, Pruett was stopped for speeding in Texas. The officer saw the holster containing Pruett's revolver protruding from beneath the front seat, and arrested him.

During his time on the Green Mile, Pruett asked a local newspaper to pay him $20,000 to disclose the location of Bobbie Robertson's ring. It refused.

Aged 49, Mad Dog was executed by lethal injection at 9pm on Monday, 12 April 1999 in the Cummins Unit, Arkansas Department of Corrections. His last words were: 'I would also like to ask all the people that I ever hurt, and their family members, to forgive me for all the pain. And I forgive everybody for what's about to happen to me.' He asked God for forgiveness, then closed his eyes as he was injected.

But Pruett left behind a dreadful legacy. He had also admitted the murders of Kenneth Staton and his daughter Suzanne, whom he shot dead during a 1980 robbery at their store. Eugene Wallace Perry was convicted of the crime and protested his innocence. The courts, however, rejected Pruett's confession and refused to overturn Perry's conviction. On Wednesday, 6 August, 1997, Perry was executed. His last words were: 'I am innocent of this crime. I take refuge in the Buddha.'

Shep Wilson Jr

On Monday, 27 January 1986, 44-year-old Shep Wilson kidnapped a 20-year-old convenience-store clerk in Sylacauga, Alabama. Monica Denise Cook was raped and beaten before Wilson, who had an extensive criminal record dating back to 1975 and was on parole for rape, strangled her to death. After the murder he told a female friend, Sonya Gardens, that he had 'shot the redhead bitch because she made me mad'. He is currently on the Green Mile in Alabama.

Edward Bennett and Joe Beeson

A particularly heinous murderer, 19-year-old Edward Bennett pulled out a .45-calibre handgun and shot a Las Vegas convenience-store clerk between the eyes in what prosecutors called a 'thrill kill'. Michelle Moore, 21, died instantly at the Stop-N-Go Market at 1201 East Sahara Avenue on Monday, 8 February 1988. Bennett then lifted Moore's head and marvelled in detached wonderment that he could see the floor through the bullet hole. A customer, 17-year-old Derrick Franklin, was shot and wounded.

Bennett is currently on Death Row. Joe Beeson, who accompanied him, was later murdered in prison while serving a natural-life term for his part in the crime.

Clinton Lee Spencer

It was Friday, 19 May 1989 when Clinton Spencer met up with Shandora Johnson-Marrow and Stacy Moore at a Circle K store in Mesa, Arizona. After luring her away from her colleague, Spencer sexually assaulted Shandora, stabbed her twice and tried to set her body ablaze using a liquid accelerant. With a criminal history as long as his arm, 31-year-old Spencer currently resides on Arizona's Death Row.

Eric John King

The face smiling into the camera of Arizona Death Row inmate # 046581 may soon lose that grin, for in the not too distant future he will be strapped to a gurney and sent to perdition with burning drugs flooding his heart and veins.

Wednesday, 27 December 1989 saw Eric King and an accomplice, believed to be Michael Page Jones, shoot dead Phoenix Short Stop clerk Ron Barman and security guard Richard Butts. Witnesses spotted King returning to the crime scene to wipe off the holster of Butts's .357-calibre revolver, which he had used to kill both men. The two criminals shared the $72 haul between them.

Pete Carl Rogovich

On Sunday, 15 March 1992, Pete Rogovich robbed a Phoenix,

Arizona, Super Stop Food Mart and shot the clerk, Tekeberhan Meskal Manna.

Shortly afterwards, he went to the Palo Verde Trailer Park and shot dead Phyllis Mancuso. Moments later he broke into the home of Marie Pendergast and shot her too. In what the judge later described as a 'homicidal rampage', this 26-year-old maniac went on to shoot down Rebecca Carreon in her driveway.

But the day was not quite over for Rogovich, who fled the trailer park on foot to a local restaurant, where at gunpoint he took a vehicle from one of the employees. After driving to a Circle K store, he robbed that as well. He was arrested after a pursuit by local police.

Now awaiting execution, he uses the internet to search for pen friends. No one should give him the time of day.

Kenneth Allen McDuff

On Monday, 1 March 1992, serial killer Kenneth McDuff was seen pushing a Ford Thunderbird a short distance from the Quick-Pak No. 8 convenience store in the 4200 block of La Salle Avenue, off Interstate 35, south of Waco, Texas. Richard Bannister said he noticed the incident at about 3.45pm.

A little later that afternoon, 22-year-old Melissa Northrup went missing from the Quick-Pak store, where she worked. Described as four feet eleven inches tall and weighing 110 pounds, with shoulder-length brown hair and blue eyes, Melissa was two and a half months pregnant. She lived with her accountant husband, Aaron, at 3014 Pioneer Circle, Waco. The diminutive young woman would have proved no match for a man of McDuff's size: he stood over six feet tall and weighed 245 pounds.

At around 4.15am, a local man who knew Melissa saw her car heading north on Interstate 35. She was in the front passenger seat and looked frightened.

When she did not return home, Aaron phoned her, and after receiving no reply he drove to the store, which was closed. The cash register was open and the contents were missing. 'A customer was in the store,' Aaron later told police, 'and when he saw me he got real scared and threw his hands up in the air. I threw him the bathroom keys, and told him to please go look for my wife.' Then Aaron dialled 911.

Police soon determined that $250 had been stolen from the cash register and, despite the fact that several people were sleeping in their cars close to the store, there were no witnesses to Melissa's abduction, although McDuff's Thunderbird was found nearby.

A fisherman discovered Melissa's corpse floating in a water-filled gravel pit in south-east Dallas County, at 6pm on Sunday, 26 April. The body was partially dressed, in a purple suit and a dark jacket. Part of the lower torso was missing. The victim's car, a burnt-orange 1977 Buick Regal with a white vinyl top, licence plate number TX LP287 XHV, was found parked just a mile away. After forensic tests had been completed, human hairs, identical in every respect to those taken from McDuff, were found on the car's upholstery.

Kenneth McDuff was executed in Huntsville, Texas, on 17 November 1998. His final words were: 'I'm ready to be released. Release me.'

Note: The full and shocking story of Kenneth McDuff – a man who had formerly escaped execution for the murder of three schoolchildren, only to be released from prison to kill again and again – is included in *Talking with Serial*

Killers by Christopher Berry-Dee, who interviewed McDuff on Death Row for a TV documentary in 1995.

Chad Alan Lee

It seems that Arizona's Green Mile is better stocked with convenience-store killers then most US states, and Chad Lee is yet another example.

On Monday, 6 April 1992, Lee, 20, and his 14-year-old accomplice David Hunt kidnapped Pizza Hut delivery girl Linda Reynolds from a vacant house. The pair forced her to strip in the backyard, then drove her to a desert area near Camelback Road and 115th Avenue, where they sexually assaulted and robbed her.

But Linda's night of terror had only just started. Having raped her, the men drove her to the First Interstate Bank at 83rd Avenue and Indian School Road, where they forced her to withdraw $20 from the ATM. After taking the terrified woman back to the desert, Lee tried to execute her with two shots to the head. Still hanging on to life, she groaned. Lee pulled out a knife and stabbed her twice in the chest, perforating her heart and lung.

Nine days later, on 15 April, Lee and Hunt robbed and murdered Metro Taxi driver David Lacey with four shots fired at point-blank range. Later the same day, Lee walked into the AM-PM Minimarket on 19th Avenue, Phoenix. He repeatedly shot the clerk, Harold Dury, then dismantled his revolver and threw it into a dumpster across the street.

David Hunt is currently serving a natural-life sentence. Chad Lee was convicted on 24 March 1994 and sentenced to death a few months later. While on the Green Mile, he has 'expressed remorse'.

Samuel Lee Ivery

Though not on Death Row – he might have been had he not been diagnosed as schizophrenic – on Saturday, 15 August 1992, Ivery, a drifter, drifted into a Mobile, Alabama, gas station and robbed it of $320. Then, almost as an afterthought, he hacked off the head of the sales assistant, 27-year-old Debra Lewis, a single mother.

Ivery had been recently released from a California mental facility after – wait for this – being locked up for committing two identical slayings in Louise, Illinois, just a month earlier. He claimed that God had ordered him to commit the murders.

Richard Eugene Hamilton and Anthony Floyd Wainwright

After meeting as prisoners at the Carteret Correctional Center in Newport, North Carolina, Richard Hamilton and Anthony Wainwright planned an escape, which took place on Sunday, 24 April 1994. They stole a green Cadillac and the following morning they broke into a house and found money and firearms including a Winchester 30-30, a shotgun and a Remington single-shot .22 rifle.

The men worked their way south to Daytona Beach, where they spent the night in the car behind a church. Next they headed west until the Cadillac started to overheat in Lake City. There they pulled into a grocery store parking lot to look for another vehicle. What they found was 23-year-old nursing student and mother of two Carmen Gayheart loading groceries into her Ford Bronco.

Carmen had been attending the Lake City Community College. After morning class on 27 April she met up with her friend Jennifer Smithhart and they ran a few errands around lunchtime before returning to the campus at 12.15 because Carmen needed to collect her two children from the day-care centre at 12.30.

Before picking up her kids, Carman drove her Bronco to a nearby Winn Dixie store to buy a few grocery items. It was here that she was accosted by Hamilton and Wainwright, who bundled her into her car at gunpoint. Hamilton drove off with Carmen while Wainwright followed in the Cadillac, which was soon dumped.

Now, with all their weapons in the Bronco, the men drove north on Interstate 75, with Carmen crying hysterically on the floor next to the driver's seat. Hamilton slapped her several times, then the car was stopped and she was dragged on to the rear seat and repeatedly raped.

One cannot begin to imagine the humiliation, the pain, suffering and terror Carmen was subjected to. And then Wainwright tried to strangle her. When that failed, Hamilton shot her twice in the back of the head with the .22-calibre rifle, reloading after the first round had been fired. The two men dragged their victim's body 70 feet and drove off, discarding her clothing, jewellery and purse en route so that none of her personal effects would be found when the corpse was discovered.

The next day, Mississippi State Trooper Leggett saw a blue Bronco with tinted windows exceeding the speed limit. When the officer ran the tag through his dispatcher, he was told the vehicle was stolen. He gave chase and as he closed with the suspect car Hamilton rolled down a window and started shooting at him. The chase ended when Wainwright swerved, lost control of the car and hit a tree. A short gunfight ensured before both men were arrested.

Hamilton, 44, and Wainwright, 37, are currently on Death Row in Florida.

Billy Don **Alverson**, **Michael L. Wilson** and Darwin Brown

This duo are among the 88 condemned men residing on Death Row at the Oklahoma State Penitentiary, McAlester.

Michael L. Wilson and 30-year-old Richard Yost were employees at the QuikTrip store at 215 North Garnett Road, Tulsa. At 11pm on Sunday, 26 February 1995, Wilson finished his shift and Yost took over. Then, in the early hours, Wilson, 20, Alverson, 24, and two accomplices, Richard Harjo and Darwin Brown, returned.

The store's surveillance tape makes for shocking viewing.

Yost was cleaning the windows on the coolers with Wilson and the other men surrounding him. As Yost was walking along a passageway, all four men attacked him and dragged him into the back room, where they handcuffed him and tied his legs with duct tape. Alverson came out, picked up a few items that had been knocked off the shelves and kept watch for customers. A few moments later, Alverson and Harjo walked out of the front door of the premises, and Yost can be heard screaming for help.

Alverson and Harjo returned, Harjo carrying a black aluminium baseball bat. The camera picked up the sounds of the bat striking Yost. At autopsy, it was determined that the bat struck the handcuffs on Yost's wrists, which he was holding above his head to ward off the blows.

As the beating continued, Wilson walked from the back room, checked his hands, put on a QuikTrip jacket, went behind the counter and tried to move the safe. Then several customers came in. Wilson greeted them in a friendly manner, then said, 'Thank you, come again, and have a nice day.'

Wilson pulled the safe from under the counter, emptied the till and pulled money out of the currency exchange machine. He removed the video from the recorder and the four men wheeled the safe, containing $30,000, out of the store on a dolly and loaded it into Wilson's car.

At 6am, Yost's body, lying in a pool of blood, milk and beer, was discovered by a customer, Larry Wiseman. Part of a broken set of handcuffs was found near his right hip. During the post-mortem examination, a pin from the cuffs was found embedded in the victim's skull.

It didn't take long for detectives to learn that Wilson had been at the store between 4 and 6am. When he failed to show up for work at 3pm, Officer Allen set up surveillance on Wilson's home and around 4pm he spotted Wilson, Alverson, Harjo and Brown in a grey car. The vehicle was stopped and the men taken into custody. With the exception of Wilson, each was carrying a large amount of money.

During a search of Alverson's apartment, the stolen safe and the video were found, along with other damaging evidence. The baseball bat, the victim's bloodstained QuikTrip jacket, the other cuff from the set of broken handcuffs, and Wilson's Nike jacket, which matched the one he wore on the surveillance tape, were discovered in Wilson's home.

Harjo received a life sentence. His three accomplices are working their way through the appeal process while on Death Row.

Douglas Alan Roberts

When ordering his last meal, Douglas Roberts didn't hold back: three Southern fried chicken breasts, two bacon, lettuce and tomato sandwiches, three enchiladas, ground beef, two grilled pork chops, six corn tortillas, four devilled eggs, 12 green olives with Italian ketchup, butter beans and cabbage seasoned with hambone, broccoli with cheese sauce, fried onion rings, French fries, picante sauce, onions and jalapenos, all washed down with Diet Pepsi. And he was certainly upbeat and animated when he was executed by lethal injection in Texas, at 6.21pm on 20 April 2005:

'Yes, thanks Warden. I've been hanging around this popsicle stand way too long,' he said. 'I want to tell you all, when I die, bury me deep, lay two speakers at my feet, put some headphones on my head and rock 'n' roll me when I'm dead. I'll see you in heaven some day.' Then, as the lethal cocktail of drugs was administered, he looked at the witnesses and smiled, mouthing during his last breath: 'I love you all… I've got to go.' He gasped and spluttered and moments later he was dead.

On 18 May 1996, 34-year-old Roberts, high on cocaine, stole a car from a woman at knifepoint at a San Antonio convenience store. Fearing that the vehicle had been reported stolen, he later drove into the parking lot of an apartment complex and abducted 40-year-old Jerry Velez in his own car. Roberts robbed the man of his cash and ordered him to drive along Interstate 46 to a rural area in Kendall County. There he ordered Velez out of his car, but Velez charged at his abductor and landed on his large Bowie knife. Roberts stabbed the man repeatedly, then drove over him in his own car.

Following the killing, Roberts drove to Austin. When the effects of the cocaine wore off, he became full of remorse and called 911, telling the dispatcher that he had kidnapped and killed Velez.

An autopsy determined that Velez was stabbed five times and that his ribs were fractured or broken and his right lung was punctured. He had also suffered 'blunt trauma' to his brain.

At his trial, Roberts instructed his attorney to call no defence witnesses and to pick a jury that favoured the death penalty. His only prior conviction as an adult was for credit-card fraud in 1993, but he had a juvenile conviction for aggravated robbery.

In an interview from Death Row, Roberts said, 'I was stoned out of my mind. I was lost in an unfamiliar place and saw Velez and thought, "This guy is gonna take me out of the city." So, I kidnapped him and his vehicle. I guess he decided at the last minute he didn't want to be stranded, or thought he could overpower me. So I killed him.'

As his execution date approached, Roberts asked his lawyers not to file any last-minute appeals on his behalf. He told a reported that he had no desire to die but saw his execution as a way to end the loneliness and isolation of the Green Mile, which he described as: '23-hours-a-day in a cement box. I killed the guy they said I killed. There's no question about that... So if you've got to spend the rest of your life like this, and if you're like me and know the Lord, today's a good day to go.'

Ernest Eugene Phillips

On 19 July 1996, after yelling racial slurs at a group of black people in a convenience store in Durant, Oklahoma, four-time convicted felon and prison escapee six-foot-four-inch Ernest Phillips, 26, stabbed and killed 17-year-old Roderick Jason McFail. Witnesses to the senseless act heard Phillips shout, 'You niggers need to get your asses the hell out of town. Now run, niggers, run.'

When McFail lifted his shirt, blood pumped from his chest with every heartbeat. He collapsed, crying. Phillips sneered, 'That's right, nigger, how do you like that, you fuckin' nigger ... feels good, don't it?' Phillips was arrested outside his brother's house the next day. He denied any involvement in the murder.

Gangland UK

Christopher Berry-Dee

It was the most brutal killing crusade Nottingham has ever seen. Two cruel brothers and their henchmen synonymous with robbery, torture, bribery and corruption, presided over a murderous reign so brutal that Nottingham was pushed up to fourth position in the UK's gun crime league. David and Colin Gunn were the modern-day Krays, with an evil multimillion-pound crime empire founded on fear and corruption. Their shocking story is among a dozen others of thugs and mobsters explored in this chilling book.

Renowned crime expert Christopher Berry-Dee turns his attention to the machinations of the gangster's mind, looking at the unique reality of their lives and documenting the extent of heir brutishness and cruelty.

From Tam McGraw – one of Scotland's most wealthy and infamous gangsters – to 'Public Enemy Number 1' Kenny Noye, Britain's ultimate crime boss; from the ruthless, money laundering Adams Family to Manchester's Desmond Noona and his feared brothers, the individuals in this book are a mixed breed. All of them, however, are united in their depravity: all are hardened crooks, oft-times violent, psychopathic individuals; self-serving people without regard for lawful morality, undeserving of sympathy, whose circumstances and personalities have set them on the path to destruction.

A must have for any fan of true crime writing, *Gangland UK* is the startling and fascinating portrait of day-to-day life in Britain for thousands of people you would rather – but won't be able to – forget.

ISBN 978-184454-613-8

John Blake Publishing Ltd

Coming Soon

Prime Suspect

Christopher Berry-Dee and Robin Odell

The true story of John Cannan, the only man police want to investigate for the murder of Suzy Lamplugh.

Before being sentenced to three life terms for the murder of Bristol newlywed Shirley Banks in April 1989, John Cannan boasted of over a hundred one-night stands. He was charming, he was handsome and he wooed his conquests – among them professional women – with flowers and champagne.

When Suzy Lamplugh disappeared in July 1986 following her meeting with 'Mr Kipper', Cannan had only been out of prison for three days following an eight-year sentence for rape. After Cannan was convicted for the murder of Shirley Banks, the Lamplugh case was closed. To this day, Cannan denies his involvement in the Lamplugh case and protests his innocence in the murder of Shirley Banks. His appeal had been dismissed.

Drawing on the latest psychological profiling knowledge developed in America by the FBI and, most importantly, an intense three-year correspondence with Cannan, Christopher Berry-Dee provides a chillingly personal, comprehensive portrait of a complex, intelligent but disturbed man.

ISBN 978-1-84454-612-1

John Blake Publishing Ltd

Coming Soon